Lecture Notes in Artificial Intelligence 1715

Subseries of Lecture Notes in Computer Science
Edited by J. G. Carbonell and J. Siekmann

Lecture Notes in Computer Science

Edited by G. Goos, J. Hartmanis and J. van Leeuwen

T0223227

Springer

Berlin
Heidelberg
New York
Barcelona
Hong Kong
London
Milan
Paris
Singapore
Tokyo

Petra Perner   Maria Petrou (Eds.)

Machine Learning and Data Mining in Pattern Recognition

First International Workshop, MLDM'99
Leipzig, Germany, September 16-18, 1999
Proceedings

Springer

Series Editors

Jaime G. Carbonell, Carnegie Mellon University, Pittsburgh, PA, USA
Jörg Siekmann, University of Saarland, Saarbrücken, Germany

Volume Editors

Petra Perner
Institut für Bildverarbeitung und angewandte Informatik
Arno-Nitzsche-Str. 45, D-04277 Leipzig, Germany
E-mail: ibaiperner@aol.com

Maria Petrou
School of Electronic Engineerig, Information Technology and Mathematics
University of Surrey
Guilford, GU2 5XH, UK
E-mail: m.petrou@surrey.ac.uk

Cataloging-in-Publication data applied for

Die Deutsche Bibliothek - CIP-Einheitsaufnahme

Machine learning and data mining in pattern recognition : first international
workshop ; proceedings / MLDM '99, Leipzig, Germany, September 16 - 18, 1999.
Petra Perner ; Maria Petrou (ed.). - Berlin ; Heidelberg ; New York ; Barcelona
; Hong Kong ; London ; Milan ; Paris ; Singapore ; Tokyo : Springer, 1999
 (Lecture notes in computer science ; Vol. 1715 : Lecture notes in artificial
intelligence)
 ISBN 3-540-66599-4

CR Subject Classification (1998): I.2, I.5, I.4

ISBN 3-540-66599-4 Springer-Verlag Berlin Heidelberg New York

© Springer-Verlag Berlin Heidelberg 1999
Printed in Germany

Typesetting: Camera-ready by author
SPIN 10705107   06/3142 – 5 4 3 2 1 0   Printed on acid-free paper

Preface

The field of machine learning and data mining in connection with pattern recognition enjoys growing popularity and attracts many researchers. Automatic pattern recognition systems have proven successful in many applications. The wide use of these systems depends on their ability to adapt to changing environmental conditions and to deal with new objects. This requires learning capabilities on the parts of these systems. The exceptional attraction of learning in pattern recognition lies in the specific data themselves and the different stages at which they get processed in a pattern recognition system. This results a specific branch within the field of machine learning. At the workshop, were presented machine learning approaches for image pre-processing, image segmentation, recognition and interpretation.

Machine learning systems were shown on applications such as document analysis and medical image analysis.

Many databases are developed that contain multimedia sources such as images, measurement protocols, and text documents. Such systems should be able to retrieve these sources by content. That requires specific retrieval and indexing strategies for images and signals. Higher quality database contents can be achieved if it were possible to mine these databases for their underlying information. Such mining techniques have to consider the specific characteristic of the image sources. The field of mining multimedia databases is just starting out. We hope that our workshop can attract many other researchers to this subject.

The workshop is the first workshop of machine learning and data mining in pattern recognition. It was organized by the Leipzig Institute of Computer Vision and Applied Computer Sciences. The aim of the workshop was to bring together researchers from all over the world dealing with machine learning for image processing, image interpretation and computer vision in order to discuss the current state of research and to direct further developments in machine learning for image-related topics. We would like to start a series of MLDM workshops dealing with this specific topic.

It is a pleasure for us to thank the invited speakers for accepting our invitation to give lectures and contribute papers to the proceedings. We would also like to express our appreciation to the reviewers for their precise and highly professional work.

We are grateful to the German Science Foundation for their support of the Eastern European researchers.

We appreciate the help and understanding of the editorial staff at Springer-Verlag, and in particular Alfred Hofmann, who supported the publication of these proceedings in the LNAI series.

Last but not least, we wish to thank all speakers and participants for their interest in the workshop.

September 1999   Petra Perner and Maria Petrou

Workshop Chairs

Petra Perner   Leipzig Institute of Computer Vision and Applied
                            Computer Sciences (IBaI), Germany
Maria Petrou   University of Surrey, UK

Program Committee

Adnan Amin   University of New South Wales / Australia
Bir Bahnu   University of California, Riverside / USA
Terri Caelli   Ohio State University / USA
Janice Glasgow   Queen´s University / Canada
Irwin King   Chinese University / Hong Kong
Erkki Oja   Helsinki University of Technology / Finland
Petra Perner   Leipzig Institute of Computer Vision and Applied
                            Computer Sciences / Germany
Maria Petrou   University of Surrey / UK
Sholom Weiss   IBM, Yorktown Heights / USA

Table of Contents

Invited Papers

Neural Networks Applied to Image Processing and Recognition

Learning in Image Pre-Processing and Segmentation

Image Retrieval

Classification and Image Interpretation

Symbolic Learning and Neural Networks in Document Processing

Data Mining

Learning in Pattern Recognition

M Petrou

School of Electronic Engineering, Information Technology and Mathematics,
University of Surrey, Guildford, GU2 5XH, UK

Abstract. Learning in the context of a pattern recognition system is defined as the process that allows it to cope with real and ambiguous data. The various ways by which artificial decision systems operate are discussed in conjunction with their learning aspects.

1 Introduction

"The measure of all things is the human being". This is according to the Greek philosopher Protagoras. When we develop pattern recognition systems, we assess their quality according to our own criteria. We say that the system made the right decision, or the wrong decision, compared with the decision the corresponding human expert would have made. An expert is a person with special knowledge acquired through a learning process. According to the Oxford English Dictionary, "to learn is to gain knowledge of or skill in, by study, practice or being taught". "Study" here presumably means "self study". All three approaches are slow and time consuming. It is most natural therefore, when we develop an expert system, to try to map on our computer program the ready made knowledge of the expert against whom this system will be compared, instead of trying to make the system learn by its own accord. This approach brings knowledge engineering into the area of pattern recognition. The simplest approach of knowledge engineering is to formulate the knowledge of the expert as a set of rules which are programmed into the system.

The process of teaching our computers has been going on for a few decades now, and it probably followed the same steps as those of teaching a child: first clear and unambiguous instructions are given often through myth and fairy tail. Gradually we allow in the ambiguity, the not so clear cut cases, the reality. So, I would like to propose the following definition for learning in the context of pattern recognition systems: "Learning for a pattern recognition system is the process that allows it to cope with reality".

An example comes from computer vision: The first vision systems presented [6,4] were assuming objects with geometric shapes and perfect edges extracted from images. As the field matured, so research was brought closer to reality. To paraphrase Nevatia [5], who has set the goal for computer vision and ultimately for pattern recognition: "We shall know that we have solved the problem of computer vision, if our system can come up with answers like 'This is a green cow with 5 legs'." This sentence encompasses all three aspects of what a "learnt" machine can do: It can recognise a cow, not just a specific cow. So, it has learned to identify generic objects. It can do that even when the measurements presented to it, ie the identification of colour and the count of the number of legs, are so wrong, that the system most likely never before came across such an instantiation of the object. The reason of Nevatia's aphorism is the fact that a human may come up with a similar answer when presented with the same object. So, the ultimate measure of our success is the human being; but which human being? Are all experts so reliable that we do not question their judgement? Do they always agree with each other? Certainly not, and a "learnt" system must be able to cope with reality in this aspect too.

All the above thoughts lead to the identification of three sources of uncertainty with which a system must **learn** to cope:

- errors in the measurements;
- intraclass variability;
- errors in knowledge elicitation.

In what follows I will give a brief overview of all the approaches commonly used in artificial decision making systems and the learning aspects of them.

2 Rule based systems: The fairy tale age

Systems that operate in this category assume that there are no errors in the measurements and that there are no errors in knowledge elicitation. In other words, we know exactly how an expert makes his judgement, and all we do is we map his expertise on our computer. Such systems use logic in the form:

If condition A + condition B → Decision C

Figure 1 shows schematically such a system for the case of two input measurements. Most geographic information systems (GIS) work that way. They allow intraclass variability in the input measurements and they simply superimpose the "layers" which indicate which conditions are fulfilled where. All the relevant learning used in the system has been done off line, by interviewing the expert and formulating the rules. These systems are very popular because they come up with clear-cut answers. Most users want to get a clear "yes" or a clear "no" from their systems. Ambiguity is often associated with imperfection, and users want systems that are better than themselves!

3 Classical fuzzy systems: Early teens

In rule based systems the exact value of a measurement is not important as long as a condition is fulfilled. In a Fuzzy system [12,13] the actual value becomes important. How close the actual measurement is to the central value for the fulfilment of the condition determines the confidence we have in this measurement. In strict Fuzzy Logic terminology this really determines the membership to the set of values that fulfill the condition, but in practical terms we can talk

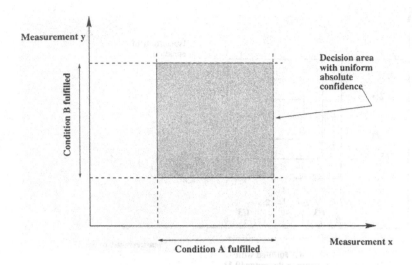

Fig. 1. A rule based reasoning system

about confidence level rather than membership functions. The assignment of confidences to the input measurements automatically requires a mechanism for combining these confidences to infer the confidence in the decision. The most straight forward rule for that, which complies with the non-fuzzy Mathematical Logic and also intuitively makes sense, is the $min - max$ rule for conjunctive and disjunctive reasoning: "A chain is as strong as its weakest link" applies to conjunctive reasoning. "A link is as strong as its strongest component acting in parallel with the rest" applies to disjunctive reasoning. As the system I chose as an example here is a conjunctive system, the min rule was applied in figure 2 to construct the isocontours of constant confidence inside the decision boundary.

This system effectively tries to model the way of thinking of the expert, by telling us not only what the answer is, but also how confident we should be in it. There are two problems with this decision system:

- The confidences assigned to the input data are assigned in a totally arbitrary way: they are usually determined with the help of some triangular functions like those shown in figure 2, or some trapezium functions, ie functions that have plateaus of high confidence in the centre. It is not clear what these functions represent: do they represent the errors in the measuring process, or do they represent the intraclass variability of the measured quantity? Assuming that they represent the intraclass variability, we are at a loss on how to define them. If we assume that they represent the errors in the measurements, then we may be able to derive them by modelling the error process. This approach was adopted in [7].
- Several practical applications showed that the way of combining the confidences using the $min - max$ rule is non-robust and produces results often at odds with experts.

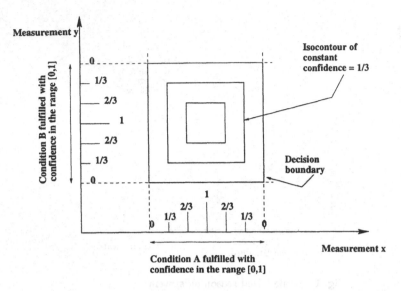

Fig. 2. A fuzzy system that uses the *min* rule for combining information

In spite of the elegance of Mathematical Logic, and in violation of all mathematical rigour, researchers replaced the *min − max* rule by many other options. An excellent review of those can be found in [1]. Each of the combination rules used produces a different shape of isocontours of constant confidence. Figure 3 shows the isocontour of confidence 1/3 when using the rule called "algebraic product" which simply multiplies the confidences in the two input variables to calculate the confidence in the result, and figure 4 shows the isocontour of confidence 1/3 when using the rule called "bounded difference" which combines the two confidences $m(x)$ and $m(y)$ as $\max\{0, m(x) + m(y) - 1\}$. The three rules demonstrated here are all known as T-norms. There are many others.

These systems do not incorporate any aspect of learning, except perhaps the part where one may try to infer the membership functions for the input variables. In most application systems this is not done. In addition, they do not consider the possibility that one of the two factors we combine may play more significant role in the conclusion than the other. So, these systems are static, simple, and still out of touch with reality.

4   Bayesian systems: Coming of age

Bayesian systems use probability theory to decision making (eg [2,3]). Let us say that $P(\theta_i = \omega_j | x, y)$ is the probability with which object θ_i is assigned to class ω_j given the measurements x and y that characterise the object. The foundation stone on which these systems lie is Bayes theorem:

$$P(\theta_i = \omega_j | x, y) = \frac{P(x, y | \theta_i = \omega_j) P(\omega_j)}{P(x, y)} \tag{1}$$

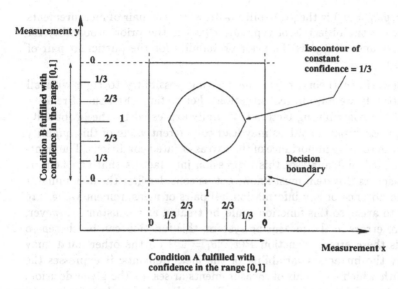

Fig. 3. A fuzzy system that uses the algebraic product to calculate the confidence in the decision.

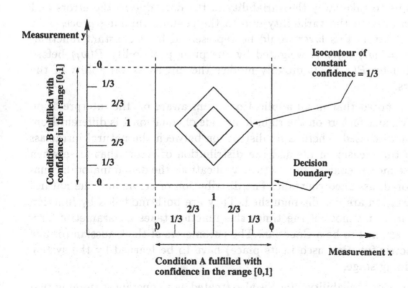

Fig. 4. A fuzzy system that uses the bounded difference to calculate the confidence in the decision.

where $P(x, y|\theta_i = \omega_j)$ is the probability with which the pair of measurements (x, y) arises when the object is of type ω_j, $P(\omega_j)$ is the prior probability for class ω_j to arise and $P(x, y)$ is the prior probability for the particular pair of measurements to arise.

This framework, in theory, offers the exciting possibility to cope with all forms of uncertainty we have in real situations: For a start, the issue of relative importance of the contributing factors is trivially expressed by the probability $P(\theta_i = \omega_j|x, y)$. Each pair of values may lead to different value of this quantity depending on the relative importance of the two associated conditions. The right-hand side of equation 1 analyses this expression into factors that can help us represent all aspects a system must know: Let us consider first the denominator $P(x, y)$. In the absence of any information, all pairs of measurement values are equally likely to arise, so this function could be treated as a constant. However, when there are errors in the measuring system, this function can be chosen so that it models these errors. Function $P(x, y|\theta_i = \omega_j)$ on the other hand, may model directly the intraclass variability of the measurements: it expresses the probability with which each pair of measurements arises for the given decision. This function is multiplied by a constant, $P(\omega_j)$, the prior probability for the given situation to arise. This constant somehow reflects our understanding of the world. We can think of the two major factors, namely $P(x, y|\theta_i = \omega_j)$ and $P(x, y)$ as two layers, similar to the layers used in the GIS to store spatially distributed information. The second layer, that of $P(x, y)$, is somehow a calibration layer which allows us to take away the variability in the data due to the errors and pay attention only to the variability due to the genuine thinking process. At the absence of errors this layer would be represented by a constant function. The $P(x, y|\theta_i = \omega_j)$ layer is weighted by the prior probability $P(\omega_j)$ before it is calibrated by $P(x, y)$. It directly models the intraclass variability of the measurements.

It must be noted that in all applications I am aware of, the interpretation given to the various factors on the right hand side of equation 1 is different from the one I just discussed. There is no distinction between the natural intraclass variability of the measurements and the distribution of errors that arise when we make these measurements. In practical applications the denominator in equation 1 is ignored, assumed constant. The distribution of errors and the natural intraclass variation are not distinguished. They are both modelled by function $P(x, y|\theta_i = \omega_j)$, and most of the times this function takes a parametric form namely it is assumed to be a Gaussian. The parameters of the Gaussian (or any other parametric function used in its place) have to be learned by the system during a training stage.

Often the prior probability $P(\omega_j)$ is also treated as a constant, assuming that all classes (ie all decisions) are equally likely to arise. Then the isocontours of constant confidence in the decision are the same as the isocontours of constant probability of a pair of measurements to arise. When $P(x, y|\theta_i = \omega_j)$ is modelled by a Gaussian with unit covariance matrix, the isocontours are circles. This is the case depicted in figure 5. Note that in the absence of any other class (ie any other decision region), and for a Gaussian distribution, there is no decision boundary. Instead, all pairs of measurements may lead to Decision C but perhaps with extremely low confidence.

The Bayesian approach makes an implicit assumption that the way the brain of the expert operates follows the above basic rule of the mathematical statement of the theorem. It is not clear that this is the case in reality.

Usually the learning part of the system takes place off line using training data and by modelling their probability density functions (eg [9,10]). For reliable results many training data are required.

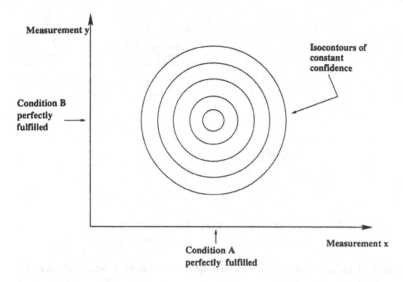

Fig. 5. Isocontours of constant confidence in the decision for a Bayesian system that uses a Gaussian with unit covariance matrix to model the error distributions and the intraclass variability.

5   Neural networks: The age of enlightment

In spite of the elegance of Bayesian systems and the sound mathematical foundation behind them, the necessity to estimate conditional probabilities from training data and the lack of sufficient numbers of such data often leads to the assumption of normal distributions with unreliably estimated mean and variances. So, although the theory in order to be applied does not need any parametric representation of the data, very often it is used in conjunction with Gaussian modelling of the distributions. An approach that does not attempt to model the distributions of the data by any parametric function is that of Neural Networks. Neural networks accept the data as they are and they are trained to learn the decision boundary. They learn to cope with the intraclass variability and the errors in the data without discriminating between the two. The decision boundary is parametrically represented by straight line segments. The values of the parameters of the boundary are determined by the adopted architecture of the network and the training process. The process of thinking of the expert is modelled by a sigmoid function. Figure 6 shows schematically the decision boundary and the isocontours of constant confidence for the simple example considered here.

These systems put strong emphasis on the learning aspect of an expert system.

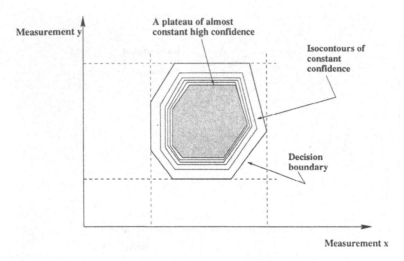

Fig. 6. Isocontours of constant confidence in the decision when a neural network is used.

6 Fuzzy neural networks: New horizons

Neural networks use linear combinations of the input variables fed into a sigmoid function for the final decision. Fuzzy neural networks use fuzzy combination functions instead of linear functions of the input variables. The result is then fed through a sigmoid for the final decision. In most of the cases the $min - max$ rule is used [11] and this in conjunction with the sigmoid function effectively eliminates the need for training as there are no free parameters in the system. The choice of the fuzzy combination rule effectively fixes the shape of the confidence isocontours. Figure 7 shows schematically the decision boundary and the isocontours of constant confidence for the simple example considered here.

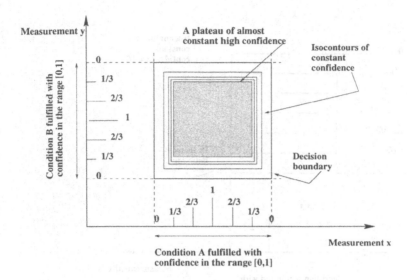

Fig. 7. Isocontours of constant confidence in the decision when a fuzzy neural network is used.

7   Fuzzy systems that can learn: The brute force approach

A trainable fuzzy system considers all possible rules of combination at the disjunctive and conjunctive level and chooses the rules that best model the thinking of the human expert for the particular problem. In addition, one may train the system to recognise the relative importance an expert attaches to the different input variables. This can be done by allowing the membership functions to vary outside the range $[0, 1]$, taking values which reflect the relative importance of the two variables [8]. The maximum value of each membership function as well as the combination rule can be learned during the training process.

Figures 8, 9 and 10 show the isocontour of confidence $1/3$ for a fuzzy system when the combination rule used is the $min - max$ rule, the algebraic product rule, and the generalised bound difference defined by $\max\{0, m(x) + m(y) - \max\{w_x, w_y\}\}$, where w_x and w_y are the maximum values the membership functions of variables x and y take. In the particular example they are chosen to be $w_x = 2$ and $w_y = 1$. By comparing these shapes with figures 2, 3 and 4 respectively, we see that the choice of weights and the choice of combination rules may have a dramatic effect on the shape of the confidence isocontours.

8   Conclusions

In this article I defined the learning of a pattern recognition system as the process that allows it to cope with real data. As the measure of the success of a system is its ability to produce results like a human expert, we may assume that a system

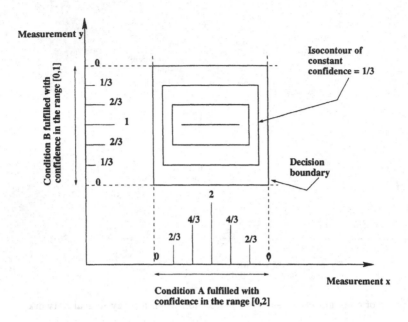

Fig. 8. Isocontours of constant confidence in the decision when a fuzzy system is used with the *min* rule and membership function in the range $[0, 2]$ for the x measurement.

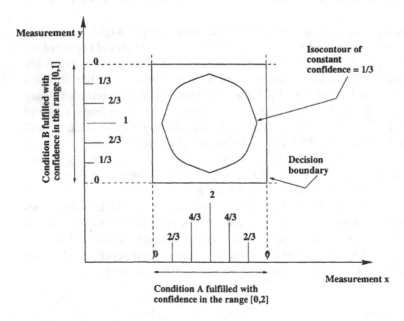

Fig. 9. Isocontour of confidence $1/3$ in the decision when a fuzzy system is used with the algebraic product rule and membership function in the range $[0, 2]$ for the x measurement.

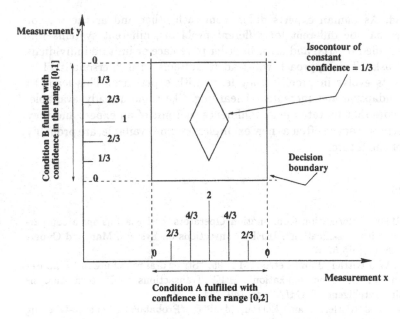

Fig. 10. Isocontour of confidence 1/3 in the decision when a fuzzy system is used with the generalised bounded difference rule and membership function in the range [0, 2] for the x measurement.

is properly trained when its isoconfidence contours in the decision map are the same as those produced by a human expert.

From all the aspects discussed, it becomes clear that:

- It is not easy to separate the intraclass variability from the errors in the measurements. The two processes are usually modelled as a single one.
- The issue of learning the way an expert thinks is equivalent to learning the isocontours of constant confidence in the decision.

The question of learning the isocontours of constant confidence is still an open question. The way the human brain works is clearly a non-linear process. We can only treat it as a black box, the behaviour of which we may try to model by observing its inputs and its outputs. Ideally, a non-parametric modelling should be used. In practice, however, non-parametric digital functions are difficult to handle. One way to deal with the problem is to try various possible parametric models.

Our everyday experience tells us that humans give degrees of confidence in their decisions only when these decisions are near the ambiguity boundary, and that away from that boundary their confidence either drops to zero or rises to its highest value very quickly: Away from the decision boundary the system behaves like a rule-based one. This behaviour is very well captured by the sigmoid function. It is my personal opinion therefore, that trainable fuzzy neural networks that experiment with various combination rules and various architectures are the way ahead. As human experts differ from each other and as the way of their thinking may be different for different problems, different systems will have to be identified by trial and error in order to replace or imitate individuals in particular tasks. This approach will lead to systems with "personality"! In addition, experts evolve in time, ie they learn with experience. This leads to systems with adaptive and incremental learning, like some already available. Systems therefore that imitate the isoconfidence contours of an expert and they update themselves every so often as new examples become available, are probably the systems of the future.

References

1. Bloch, I, 1996. "Information Combination Operators for Data Fusion: a comparative review with classification". IEEE Transactions on System, Man and Cybernetics, vol 26 (1), pp 52–67.
2. Christmas, W J Kittler, J and Petrou, M 1995. "Structural matching in Computer Vision using Probabilistic Relaxation". IEEE Transactions on Pattern Analysis and Machine Intelligence PAMI-17, pp 749–764.
3. Christmas, W J Kittler, J and Petrou, M 1996. "Probabilistic feature-labelling schemes: modelling compatibility coefficient distributions". Image and Vision Computing, Vol 14, pp 617–625.
4. Guzman, A, 1968. "Decomposition of a visual scene into three-dimensional bodies". AFIPS Conference Proceedings 33, pp 291–304, Washington DC: Thompson.
5. Nevatia, R, 1982. Machine Perception. Prentice-Hall, Englewood Cliffs, New Jersey.
6. Roberts, L G, 1965. "Machine perception of three-dimensional solids". Optical and electro optical information processing, J T Tippett et al (eds), pp 159–197, Cambridge Mass, MIT Press.
7. Sasikala, K R, Petrou, M and Kittler, J, 1996. "Fuzzy reasoning with a GIS for decision making in burned forest management". EARSeL Advances in Remote Sensing, Vol 4(4), pp 97–105.
8. Sasikala, K R and Petrou, M, 1999. "Generalised fuzzy aggregation in estimating the risk of desertification of a burned forest". Fuzzy Sets and Systems, to appear.
9. Stassopoulou, A, Petrou, M and Kittler, J, 1998. "Application of a Bayesian network in a GIS based decision making system". International Journal of Geographical Information Sciences, Vol 12, pp 23–45.
10. Stassopoulou, A and Petrou, M, 1998. "Obtaining the correspondence between Bayesian and Neural Networks". International Journal of Pattern Recognition and Artificial Intelligence, Vol 12, pp 901–920.
11. Theisen, M, Steudel A, Rychetsky M and Glesner M, 1998. "Fuzzy logic and neurosystems assisted intelligent sensors". In Sensors update, Vol 3, H Baltes, W Gopel and J Hesse (eds), Wiley-VCH.
12. Zadeh, L A, 1965. Information and Control, vol 8, pp 338–353.
13. Zimmermann, H J, 1985. Fuzzy set theory and its applications. Boston, Kluwer Academic Publishers.

Advances in Predictive Data Mining Methods

Se June Hong and Sholom M. Weiss
IBM T.J. Watson Research Center
P.O. Box 218, Yorktown Heights, NY 10598, USA
sjhong@us.ibm.com and sholom@us.ibm.com

Abstract. Predictive models have been widely used long before the development of the new field that we call data mining. Expanding application demand for data mining of ever increasing data warehouses,
and the need for understandability of predictive models with increased
accuracy of prediction, all have fueled recent advances in automated predictive methods. We first examine a few successful application areas and
technical challenges they present. We discuss some theoretical developments in PAC learning and statistical learning theory leading to the
emergence of support vector machines. We then examine some technical
advances made in enhancing the performance of the models both in accuracy (boosting, bagging, stacking) and scalability of modeling through
distributed model generation.

1 Introduction

An explanatory model summarizes data for the purpose of making sense in terms
of domain knowledge. A predictive model's main concern is the utility of the prediction when applied to the unseen, future cases. Traditionally, accuracy measures have been used almost exclusively in assessing the models for both classification and regression. Although there has been a long history of predictive model
generation from statistics, more recent developments from machine learning area,
including pattern recognition and artificial neural networks, have contributed to
meeting the challenges of data mining ever increasing data warehouses. Predictive modeling, which is perhaps the most-used subfield of data mining, draws
from statistics, machine learning, database techniques, optimization techniques,
and theory of learning. We want the models to be useful and accurate, practical
to generate, and we often prefer models that are understandable.

The proven utility of industrial applications has led to recent advances in
predictive modeling. We will discuss a few application areas that have demonstrated the importance of predictive modeling and have also fueled advances.
Some important advances in learning theory will be considered. The idea of using multiple models to enhance the performance of a model has spawned several
useful approaches with theoretical understanding for their success.

Scaling up to multi-giga bytes of data is one of the most important challenges
of data mining. Besides the traditional sampling techniques, a new emphasis is
being placed on fast disk-based algorithms, sometimes efficiently coupled into
database management systems, as well as parallel and distributed algorithms.
We will discuss these in section 6. Some new directions in the way of measuring

the performance of a predictive model and of comparing different models will be discussed.

2 Challenging applications

It has been well-established that a substantial competitive advantage can be obtained by data mining in general and predictive modeling in particular. There are many success stories of predictive models mined from scientific data, financial data, and banking and insurance business data. Most of these reside in a large data warehouses. For some application area, maximizing accuracy or some other utility measure of the model is of paramount importance, even at the cost of giving up the understandability of a simple model. For some applications, the quality of available data in terms of missing values and noise present extra challenges for model generation. Most of the significant applications have large data volumes. We will briefly examine three challenging application areas: insurance, fraud detection, and text categorization.

2.1 Insurance

Risk assessment is in the core of the insurance business, where actuarial statistics have been the traditional tools of the trade in modeling various aspects of risk such as accident, health claims, or disaster rates, and the severity of these claims. The claim frequency is usually extremely rare and probabilistic by nature. For instance, the auto accident rate of an insured driver is never a clear no-accident class v.s. accident class problem and instead should be modeled as a Poison distribution. The claim amounts usually follow a log-normal distribution which captures the phenomenon of rare but very high damage amounts. Neither of these distributions are well-modeled by conventional modeling tools such as CHAID [1], CART [2], C4.5 [3], SPRINT [4] or classical statistical regression techniques that optimize for traditional normal distributions. In general, different kinds of insurance are better modeled by using different statistical models depending on the fundamental nature of the claims process, requiring a predictive model that can be optimized for different underlying distributions [5].

2.2 Fraud detection

Fraud detection is an important problem because fraudulent insurance claims and credit card transactions alone cost tens of billions of dollars a year just in the US. In the case of credit card fraud, artificial neural-networks have been widely-used by many banks for some time. Attacking this problem is a major effort of many financial services institutions. Frauds are relatively rare, i.e. a skewed distribution that baffles many traditional data mining algorithms unless stratified samples are used in the training set. Some large banks add to the transaction data volume by millions of transactions per day. The cost of processing a fraud case, once detected, is a significant factor against false positive errors while undetected fraud adds to the transaction cost in the loss column. This not only calls for a more realistic performance measure than traditional accuracy, but also influences the decision whether to declare a transaction to be processed as a fraud or not. The pattern of fraudulent transactions varies with time, which requires relatively frequent and rapid generation of new models [6].

2.3 Text mining

Electronic documents or text fields in databases are a large percentage of the data stored in centralized data warehouses. Text mining is the search for valuable patterns in stored text. When stored documents have correct labels, such as the topics of the documents, then that form of text mining is called text categorization.

In many carefully organized text storage and retrieval systems, documents are classified with one or more codes chosen from a classification system. For example, news services like Reuters carefully assign topics to news-stories. Similarly, a bank may route incoming e-mail to one of dozens of potential response sites.

Originally, human-engineered knowledge-based systems were developed to assign topics to newswires [7,8]. Such an approach to classification may have seemed reasonable ten years ago, but the cost of the manual analysis needed to build a set of rules is no longer reasonable, given the overwhelming increase in the number of digital documents. Instead, automatic procedures are a realistic alternative, and researchers have proposed a plethora of techniques to solve this problem.

The use of a standardized collection of documents for analysis and testing, such as the Reuters collection of newswires for the year 1987, has allowed researchers to measure progress in this field. It can be empirically demonstrated that over the course of less than 10 years, substantial improvements in automated performance have been made.

Many automated prediction methods exist for extracting patterns from sample cases [9]. These patterns can be used to classify new cases. In text mining, specifically text categorization, the raw cases are individual documents. These cases can be transformed into a standard model of features and classes. The cases are encoded in terms of features in some numerical form, requiring a transformation from text to numbers. For each case, a uniform set of measurements on the features are taken by compiling a dictionary from the collection of training documents. The frequencies of occurrence of dictionary words in each document are measured. Prediction methods look at samples of documents with known topics, and attempt to find patterns for generalized rules that can be applied to new unclassified documents.

Given a dictionary, sample cases can be described in terms of the words or phrases from the dictionary found in the documents. Each case consists of the values of the features for a single article, where the values could either be boolean, indicating whether the feature appears in the text or does not, or numerical, some function of the frequency of occurrence in the text being processed. In addition, each case is labeled to indicate the classification of the article it represents. Once the data is in a standard numerical encoding for classification, any standard data mining method, such as decision trees or nearest neighbors, can be applied. Beside the issue of binary v.s. word count feature, another secondary characteristics of the dictionary words of interest is the issue of stemmed v.s. raw words, i.e., when compiling the dictionary, the words may be stemmed, i.e. mapped into a common root. For example, plural words may be mapped into their singular form.

A more critical characteristic of the dictionary is its size. How many words should the dictionary hold? The answer to this question depends on many factors including the prediction method and the available computing resources. A universal dictionary of all stemmed words in the document collection can be formed. A feature selection technique is sometimes used to select a small subset of words that are deemed relevant to a particular topic. For example, the Reuters collection has about 22,000 stemmed words. Feature selection for a given topic can yield a subset with less than 1000 words without any loss of performance.

One of the interesting challenges text mining poses is the problem of minimal labeling. Most text collections are not tagged with category labels. Human tagging is usually costly. Starting from some tagged examples, one wishes to develop a text categorization model by asking certain selected examples to be tagged, and one naturally wishes to minimize the number of such requests. Many approaches to this problem are being pursued by theorists as well as practical algorithm developers. Another interesting application of text mining technology is web-mining where a variety of features beyond the original text present a special challenge.

3 Theoretical advances

The theory of predictive modeling has evolved from two research communities: computational learning theory and statistical learning theory. Developments in these areas shed light on what kind of functions, i.e. mapping the feature vectors to the target values, can be learned efficiently with a given set of models [10]. These results give an understanding of model complexity and how it can be used to assess the future performance of models on unseen data. These new concepts are beginning to guide the model search process as well as the model evaluation process for practical cases, complementing traditional techniques from statistics. Because predictive modeling generally assumes that unseen data will be independently and identically distributed (*iid*) as the training data, the theoretical analysis of the model is also confined to the same assumption.

3.1 Support vector machines

Support vector machine has the form of a linear discriminator. A linear discriminator can separate arbitrary partition of $d+1$ points in d dimensions, hence the

VC–dimension is at most $d + 1$ which is its degree of freedom in classical statistical sense. The number of input variables plus one and hence the number of coefficients to be determined for a linear discriminator, however, does not mean the VC–dimension is the same number when the variables are not independent. Here we give a brief sketch of support vector machine model. (For a detailed introduction to the subject, see [11].) Let D be the smallest radius of the sphere that contains the data (example vectors). The points in either side have distances to the separating hyperplane. The smallest such distance is called the *margin* of separation. The hyper plane is called optimal if the margin is maximized. Let ρ be the margin of the optimal hyperplane. The points that are distance ρ away from the optimal hyperplane are called the *support vectors*. It has been shown that the VC–dimension is not greater than $\frac{d^2}{\rho^2} + 1$ and furthermore it is no greater than the number of support vectors. This is important because the VC–dimension of all possible separating hyperplanes for the data is shown to be not a direct function of the dimensionality of the vectors. This implies that one can generate arbitrarily many derived features, e.g. all pairwise products of the original features, as long as the number of support vectors for the optimal hyperplane (in the expanded dimensions) does not increase much. One can see that, although the final form of the model is a linear function, the decision boundary can be of almost arbitrary shape in the original feature space because of the nonlinearity introduced by derived variables.

This understanding leads to a new strategy to search for the support vectors and the coefficients for the optimal hyperplane simultaneously as an optimization problem in the expanded dimensional space. Actually, one need not explicitly compute the values of the derived features if they are chosen in a judicious way. The feature expansion makes use of several popular family of kernel functions, such as polynomial, radial basis functions or sigmoid functions as in the two layer neural network. The search techniques for the optimal hyperplane and the support vectors simultaneously and selecting the right family of feature extension are active areas of research. The support vector machine is a significant new addition for predictive modeling.

4 Use of multiple models

Recent research results in learning demonstrate the effectiveness of combining multiple models of the same or different types for improving modeling accuracy. These methods, variously termed as bagging [12], boosting [13], and stacking [14], have taken different approaches to achieve maximized modeling performance.

Let's look at an example where diverse predictive methods can be applied to obtain a solution. For example, a classification problem that can be solved by either a neural net method or a decision tree or a linear method. Until recently, the typical approach would be to try both methods on the same data, and then select the method with the strongest predictive performance. Stacking offers an alternative approach that combines different models of solutions. In this example, the neural net, the decision tree and the linear solutions are found independently.

For a new case, the answers from all methods are weighted and voted, for example 50% neural net and 25% each for the other methods. How are the appropriate percentages found? They can be readily learned by preparing a new dataset of derived cases, where the features are the answers give by each method and the correct answer is the case label.

Researchers have observed that predictive performance often can be improved by inducing multiple solutions of the same type, for example multiple decision trees. These models are generated by sampling from the same data [12]. The final answer on a new case is determined by giving a vote to each of the multiple decision trees, and picking the answer with the most votes.

Although the techniques for generating multiple models from the same data are independent of the type of model, the decision tree is the most commonly used. How are the trees generated? No change is made to a standard tree induction method. The difference is in the sampling method. In the simplest approach, called bagging [12], a sample of size n is taken with replacement from the original set of n examples. (For very large data, a smaller sample can be taken.) Some examples will be repeated in the sample, others may not occur. The expected proportion of unique examples in any given sample is 63.2%. Thus, it is possible to generate many samples, induce a decision tree from each sample, and then vote the results.

An alternative method of sampling, adaptive resampling, usually performs better than bagging. Instead of sampling all cases randomly, so that each document has a $1/n$ chance of being drawn from the sample, an incremental approach is used in random selection. The objective is to increase the odds of sampling documents that have been erroneously classified by the trees that have previously been induced. Some algorithms use weighted voting, where some trees may be given more weight than others. The "boosting" algorithm, such as AdaBoost [13] uses weighted voting and an explicit formula for updating the likelihood of sampling each case in the training sample. However, it has been demonstrated that unweighted voting and resampling with any technique that greatly increases the likelihood of including erroneous cases is also effective in greatly improving accuracy [12].

Each model has its own bias and variance component of errors. Multiple models of the same kind, e.g. trees, mainly reduce the variance portion of the error, while a mixture of models can reduce the bias effects in participating models as well. Combining multiple models gain primarily by countering the inadequacy of the fixed shape of the decision surface one model in the given family can produce and also by mitigating the inadequacy of search techniques associated with all practical model generation processes. While an ensemble models does not necessarily increase the complexity of the model (in the sense of statistical learning theory), such a combined model does deny what understandability that might have existed in a single model. There are many other ways an ensemble of base models can be employed [15].

5   Scaling up for large data

One of the most pressing challenges of data mining in many application domains is the problem of scaling the model generation algorithms to handle a huge volume of data. Besides traditional sampling techniques, there are numerous new techniques developed in the past decade to address this challenge. In addition to predictive accuracy, efficiency is of paramount concern: computational complexity, data structures, disk-based algorithms, and the degree of interface with database management systems, parallel and distributed algorithms and optimization techniques all play a role in efficient implementations. For many critical applications, relying on some quick (linear in the number of examples) algorithms may not produce a quality predictive model.

Multiple model techniques can be employed to scale up from many samll samples. There are also many examples of parallel implementation of tree generation processes. The SPRINT approach [4], organizes each feature values with their ID and class values in separate disk files for the purpose of rapidly obtaining the necessary contingency tables for the impurity computations. SPRINT develops a GINI-index based, MDL pruned decision tree. As the nodes are split, the split variable's value file is also split into left and right parts, and a hash table is built to quickly decide which branch an example falls through. Experiments have shown that this heavily disk based parallel approach can handle multi millions of examples very efficiently. Other approaches, that embed most of tree generation functions within a DBMS proper, have also been reported.

6   Conclusion

We have presented a brief picture of some notable advances in predictive modeling. There are many other advances of various significance. We will briefly mention just a few more. One of the areas that made much progress in the use of Bayesian networks for prediction purpose. There are new techniques to generate the network from the data itself. A surprising finding is that a simple, naive Bayesian classifier is sometimes very effective and some simple extentions can make them even better [16]. New techniques are being developed that derive understandable rules from neural networks.

References

1. Gallagher C., "Risk Classification Aided by New Software Tool (CHAID -Chi-Squared Automatic Interaction Detector", *National Underwriter Property & Casualty - Risk and Benefits Management*, Vol. 17, No. 19, April 1992.
2. Breiman L., Friedman J.H., Olshen R.A. & Stone C.J., *Classification and Regression Trees*, Wadsworth International Group, 1984.
3. Quinlan J.R., *C4.5 programs for machine learning*, Morgan Kaufmann, 1993.
4. Shafer J., Agrawal R, Mehta M., "SPRINT: A Scalable Parallel Classifier for data Mining", *Procc. of the 22nd ICVLDB*, pp. 544-555, 1996.

5. Apte C., Grossman E., Pednault E., Rosen B., Tipu F., White B, "Insurance Risk Modeling Using Data Mining Technology", *Tech. Report RC-21314*, IBM Research Division, 1998. To appear in *Proc. of PADD99*.

6. Stolfo S.J., Prodromidis A., Tselepis S., Lee W., Fan W. & Chan P., "JAM: Java Agents for Meta-Learning over Distributed Databases", *Proc. of KDDM97*, pp. 74-81, 1997.

7. Hayes P.J. & Weinstein S., "Adding Value to Financial News by Computer", *Proc. of the First International Conference on Artificial Intelligence Applications on Wall Street*, pp. 2-8, 1991.

8. Hayes P.J.,Andersen P.M., Nirenburg I.B., & Schmandt L.M., "TCS: A Shell for Content-Based Text Categorization", *Proc. of the Sixth IEEE CAIA*, pp. 320-326, 1990.

9. Weiss S. & Indurkhya N., *Predictive Data Mining: A Practical guide*, Morgan Kaufmann, 1998.

10. Hosking J.R.M., Pednault E.P.D. & Sudan M., "A Statistical Perspective on Data Mining", *Future Generation Computer Systems: Special issue on Data Mining*, Vol. 3, Nos. 2-3, pp. 117-134., 1997.

11. Vapnik V.N., *Statistical Learning Theory*, Wiley, 1998

12. Breiman L., "Bagging Predictors",*Machine Learning*, Vol. 24, pp.123-140, 1996.

13. Freund Y. & Schapire R., "Experiments with a New Boosting Algorithm", *Proc. of the International Machine Learning Conference*, Morgan Kaufmann, pp. 148-156, 1996.

14. Wolpert D., "Stacked Generalization", *Neural Networks*, Vol. 5, No. 2, pp. 241-260, 1992.

15. Dietterich, T.D., "Machine learning Research: Four Current Directions", *AI Magazine*, Vol. 18, No. 4, pp. 97-136, 1997.

16. Domingos P. & Pazzani M., "on the Optimality of the Simple Bayesian Classifier under Zero-One Loss", *Machine Learning*, Vol. 29, pp. 103-130, 1997.

Multi-valued and Universal Binary Neurons: Learning Algorithms, Application to Image Processing and Recognition

Igor N.Aizenberg[*], Naum N.Aizenberg[*], Georgy A.Krivosheev[**]

[*] For communications: Minaiskaya 28, kv. 49, Uzhgorod, 294015, Ukraine
E-mail: ina@karpaty.uzhgorod.ua

[**] For communications: Paustovskogo 3, kv. 430, Moscow, Russia
E-mail: albatros@glasnet.ru

Abstract. Multi-valued and universal binary neurons (MVN and UBN) are the neural processing elements with complex-valued weights and high functionality. It is possible to implement an arbitrary mapping described by partial-defined multiple-valued function on the single MVN and an arbitrary mapping described by partial-defined or fully-defined Boolean function (which can be not threshold) on the single UBN. The fast-converged learning algorithms are existing for both types of neurons. Such features of the MVN and UBN may be used for solution of the different kinds of problems. One of the most successful applications of the MVN and UBN is their usage as basic neurons in the Cellular Neural Networks (CNN) for solution of the image processing and image analysis problems. Another effective application of the MVN is their use as the basic neurons in the neural networks oriented to the image recognition.

1. Introduction

An intensive developing of the neural networks as a high-speed parallel processing systems during last years makes their application to image processing, analysis and recognition very attractive. E.g., many of image processing algorithms in spatial domain may be reduced to the same operation, which it is necessary to perform over all the pixels of image. For example, many of the algorithms of linear and nonlinear filtering in spatial domain are reduced exactly to the processing within the local window around each pixel of the image.

Since a local processing within a local window around the pixel is not recursive, and may be organized simultaneously for all the pixels, and independently each other, it is natural to organize this process using some kind of neural network. The most appropriate neural network for solution of the considered problems is the Cellular Neural Network (CNN). CNN has been introduced in the pioneer paper of Chua and Yang [1] as special high-speed parallel neural structure for image processing and recognition, and then intensively developed. Many results from simple filters for binary images [1-2] to algorithms for processing of the color images [3] and even to design of the CNN universal machine (CNNUM) [4], were carried out during the nine-years period of development of CNN theory and its applications. CNN is a locally connected network (each neuron is connected with an only limited number of other ones - only with neurons from its nearest neighborhood). Depending on the type of neurons that are basic elements of the network it is possible to distinguish classical (or continuous-time) CNN (CTCNN) [1], discrete-time CNN (DTCNN) [5] (oriented especially on binary image processing), CNN based on multi-valued neurons (CNN-MVN) [6] and CNN based on universal binary neurons (CNN-UBN) [7]. Disadvantages of the CTCNN are limitation of the types of nonlinear filters that may be implemented and very complicate learning algorithms. Disadvantage of the DTCNN is a limited functionality. Such a limitation is defined by functionality of the threshold neuron or traditional perceptron. It could implement only the threshold Boolean functions. It is well known that number of threshold Boolean functions is very small (e.g., only about 2000 Boolean functions of 4 variables from 65536 are the threshold functions). A good solution of the problem is application of the universal binary neuron (UBN) instead of the threshold neuron. UBN [7] has a universal functionality. It means that any (not only threshold) Boolean function could be implemented on the single UBN. CNN-UBN makes possible an implementation of the image processing algorithms that are defined not only by threshold, but by any Boolean function. A problem of precise edge detection and its solution using CNN-UBN will be considered below.

Multi-valued neural element (MVN), which is based on the ideas of multiple-valued threshold logic [8], has been introduced in [6]. Different kinds of networks, which are based on the MVN, have been proposed [6, 9-12]. Successful application of these networks to simulation of the associative memory [6, 9-12], image recognition and segmentation [11, 12], time-series prediction [10, 11] confirms their high efficiency. Solution of the image recognition problems using neural networks became very popular during last years. Many corresponding examples are available (e.g., [13, 14]). On the other hand many authors consider image recognition reduced to the analysis of the some number of orthogonal spectrum coefficients on the different neural networks [14, 15]. Here we would like to consider the original approach to image recognition based on the following background: 1) high functionality of the MVN and quick convergence of the learning algorithm for them; 2) well-known fact about concentration of the signal energy in the small number of low-frequency spectral coefficients [16]. Some types of the MVN-based neural networks were proposed during last years for solution of the problem of image recognition in associative memory: cellular network [9], network with random connections [10, 11] and Hopfield-like network [12]. A disadvantage of the both networks is impossibility of the recognition of shifted or rotated image, also as image with changed dynamic range. To break these disadvantages and to more effective using of multi-valued neurons features, we would like to propose here new type of the network, learning strategy and data representation (frequency domain will be used instead of spatial one).

To solve all the attractive applied problems that have been just mentioned above it is necessary to have quickly converged learning algorithms for MVN and UBN. Exactly such algorithms will play a main role in the paper.

2. Multi-valued and Universal Binary Neurons

Universal Binary Neuron (UBN) [7] performs a mapping that may be described by arbitrary Boolean function of n variables. Multi-Valued Neuron (MVN) [6] performs a mapping that may be described by full-defined or partial-defined threshold k-valued function (function of k-valued logic), where k is in general arbitrary positive integer.

Common basic mathematical background of the UBN and MVN is the following. An arbitrary Boolean function of n variables or k-valued function of n variables is represented by $n+1$ complex-valued weights $w_0, w_1, ..., w_n$:

$$f(x_1, ..., x_n) = P(w_0 + w_1 x_1 + ... + w_n x_n) \qquad (1)$$

where $x_1, ..., x_n$ are the variables, of which performed function depends (neuron inputs) and P is the activation function, which is defined in the following way.

1) For Multi-Valued Neuron:

$$P(z) = \exp(i2\pi j/k), \text{ if } 2\pi (j+1)/k > \arg(z) \geq 2\pi j/k \qquad (2a)$$

or with integer-valued output:

$$P(z) = j, \text{ if } 2\pi(j+1)/k > \arg(z) \geq 2\pi j/k, \qquad (2b)$$

where $j=0, 1, ..., k-1$ are the values of the k-valued logic, i is imaginary unity, $z = w_0 + w_1 x_1 + w_n x_n$ is the weighted sum, $arg(z)$ is the argument of the complex number z. (values of the function and of the variables are coded by the complex numbers, which are k-th power roots of unity: $e^j = \exp(i2p\,j/k)$, $j \in \{0,1,...,k-1\}$, i is imaginary unity. In other words values of the k-valued logic are represented by k-th power roots of unity: $j \rightarrow \varepsilon^j$);

2) For Universal Binary Neuron

$$P(z) = (-1)^j, \text{ if } (2\pi (j+1)/m) > \arg(z) \geq (2\pi j/m), \qquad (3)$$

where m is the positive integer, j is non-negative integer $0 \leq j < m$, $z = w_0 + w_1 x_1 + w_n x_n$ is the weighted sum, $arg(z)$ is the argument of the complex number z. Evidently, functions (2)–(3) separate the complex plane on k sectors (2a, 2b) and m sectors (3), respectively. The equations (2) – (3) are illustrated by Fig.1-2.

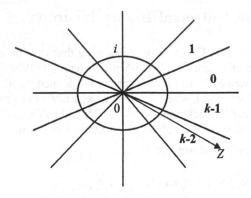

$$P(z) = \varepsilon^{k-2}$$

Fig. 1. Definition of the function (2)

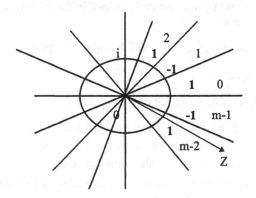

$$P(z) = 1$$

Fig. 2. Definition of the function (3)

Moving to the Complex domain is a keyword moment. It is possible by such a way to extend neuron functionality. Let us consider example. Let $n=2$ and we would like to implement on the single neuron non-threshold XOR-function $f(x_1, x_2) = x_1 \oplus x_2$. Let $m=4$ in (3), therefore we separate Complex plane into 4 sectors (Fig.2). Our XOR function of 2 variables is implemented on the single universal binary neuron by the weighted vector $W=(0, 1, i)$, where i is imaginary unity. Any network is not needed for solution of this popular problem. The Table 1 and Fig. 3 illustrate this fact.

Table 1. Implementation of the XOR function on the single neuron.

X_1	X_2	$z = w_0 + w_1 x_1 + w_2 x_2$	$P(z) = f(x_1, x_2)$
1	1	$1 + i$	1
1	-1	$1 - i$	-1
-1	1	$-1 + i$	-1
-1	-1	$-1 - i$	1

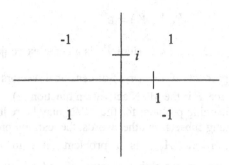

Fig. 3. Implementation of the XOR function on the single neuron (see also Table 1), m=4 in (3).

3. Learning Algorithms for MVN and UBN

Let us consider learning of the MVN. Then it will be shown that learning of the UBN us reducing to the learning of the MVN.

The learning of a threshold element may be presented by the following way. Let we have a learning set $A = A_1 \bigcup A_{-1}$, where A_1 is a subset of the neuron's inputs, on which output has to be equal to 1, A_{-1} is a subset of the neuron's inputs, on which output has to be equal to -1. A learning is reduced to the search of a hyperplane, which separates the subsets of a learning set in the space. The coefficients of a hyperplane equation will be the synaptic weights implementing a corresponding mapping.

Taking into account that MVN implements a k-valued mapping, it is easy to conclude that MVN's learning set consists of k classes. Let now $k>2$ is some integer. Let us consider $(n+1)$ - dimensional vectors $X = (1, x_1, ..., x_n)$, $x_1, ..., x_n \in \{\varepsilon^0, \varepsilon, ..., \varepsilon^{k-1}\}$, where $\varepsilon = i2\pi / k$ is a primitive k-th power root of a unity. Let A_j is a learning subset $\{X_1^{(j)}, ... X_{N_j}^{(j)}\}$ of the input neuron states corresponding to the output value j (ε^j in the complex-valued form). In such a case we can present the global learning set as $A = \bigcup_{0 \le j \le k-1} A_j$. Certainly, some of the sets A_j may be empty, and $A_i \bigcap A_j = \varnothing$ for any $i \ne j$.

Definition 1. The sets $A_0, A_1, ..., A_{k-1}$ are called *k-separated*, if it is possible to find such a permutation $R = (\alpha_0, \alpha_1, ..., \alpha_{k-1})$ consisted from the elements of the set $E_k = \{0, 1, ..., k-1\}$, and such a weighting vector $W = (w_0, w_1, ..., w_n)$, that

$$P(X,\overline{W}) = \varepsilon^{\alpha_j} \tag{4}$$

for each $X \in A_j$, $j = 0, 1, ..., k\text{-}1$. Here $\overline{W}$ is a complex-conjugated to W vector, $(X,\overline{W})$ is a scalar product of the $(n+1)$-dimensional vectors within the $(n+1)$-dimensional unitary space, P is the MVN activation function (2).

It is clear that the learning problem for the MVN may be reduced to the problem of k-separation of learning subsets. In other words, the learning problem for the given learning subsets $A_0, A_1, ..., A_{k-1}$ is a problem, how to find a permutation $(\alpha_0, \alpha_1, ..., \alpha_k)$, and a weighting vector $W = (w_0, w_1, ..., w_n)$, which satisfy the condition (4).

The learning is reduced to obtaining the sequence S_w of the weighting vectors $W_0, W_1, ...$. Each vector corresponds to single iteration of learning. A convergence of learning means that beginning from the some number m_0: $W_{m_0} = W_{m_0+1} = ...$, and (4) also as (1) are true. We will consider here two learning rules, but first of all let us consider a global scheme of learning algorithm. Two strategies may be used. It will be shown below that they are equivalent, moreover, other equivalent strategies may be proposed.

Strategy 1 (Sequential sorting of the learning subsets).

Step 1. The starting weighting vector W_0 is chosen as an arbitrary vector (e.g., its components may be the random numbers or may be equal to zero); $j=0$;

Step 2. Checking of the (4.1.1) for the elements of learning subsets $A_0, ..., A_j$:

if (4.1.1) is true for all of them *then go to* the step 4 *else go to* the step 3;

Step 3. Obtaining of the vector W_{m+1} from the vector W_m by the learning rule (considered below); *go to* the step 2;

Step 4. $j = j+1$; *if* $j = k$ *then* learning is finished successfully, *else go to* the step 2.

Strategy 2. (Consideration of all the learning subsets together).

X_s^j is the s-th element of the learning set A belonging to the learning subset A_j. Let N is a cardinality of the set A.

Step 1. The starting weighting vector W_0 is chosen as an arbitrary vector (e.g., its components may be the random numbers or may be equal to zero); $s=1$; $l=0$;

Step 2. Checking of the (4.1.1) for the element $X_s^{j_s}$ of learning subset A_{j_s}:

if (4.1.1) is true for it *then go to* the step 4 *else begin* $l=1$; *go to* the step 3 *end*;

Step 3. Obtaining of the vector W_{m+1} from the vector W_m by the learning rule (considered below); *go to* the step 2;

Step 4. $s = s+1$; *if* $s \leq N$ *then go to* the step 2
else if $l=0$ *then* the learning is finished successfully
else begin $s=1$; $l=0$; *go to* the step 2; *end*.

l is a flag of successful learning for some vector X_s^j in Strategy 2. If current vector W satisfy (4.1.1) for the vectors from learning set then l=0, if the vector W does not satisfy (4.1.1) for some vector X_s^j then l=1.

A learning rule is of course a keyword point of learning algorithm with both strategies just proposed. It should ensure an effective correction of the weights, and lead to the convergence as soon as possible. We will consider here two linear learning rules. Both of them may be considered as generalization of the corresponding perceptron learning rules. A generalization means the following. If perceptron output for some element of the learning set is incorrect (1 instead of -1, or -1 instead of 1) then the weights should be corrected by some rule to ensure an inversion of the sign of weighted sum. Therefore, it is necessary to move the weighted to the opposite subdomain (respectively from "positive" to "negative", or from "negative" to "positive"). For MVN, which performs a mapping described by k-valued function we have exactly k domains. Geometrically they are the sectors on the complex plane. If the desired output of MVN on some vector from the learning set is equal to ε^q then the weighted sum should to fall into the sector number q. But if the actual output is equal to ε^s then the weighted sum has fallen into sector number s (see Fig. 4). A learning rule should correct the weights to move the weighted sum from the sector number s to the sector number q.

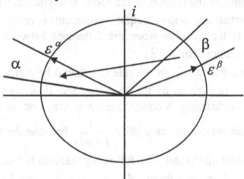

Fig. 4. Problem of the MVN learning

3.1 Learning rule 1

The learning rule should transform the current weighting vector W_m to the vector W_{m+1}. The first learning rule is described by the following equation

$$W_{m+1} = W_m + \omega_m C_m \varepsilon^\alpha \overline{X} \qquad (5)$$

where $\overline{X}$ is the complex-conjugated vector of the neuron's input signals (the current vector from the learning set), ε^{α} is the desired neuron's output, C_m is the scale coefficient, ω is the correction coefficient. Such a coefficient must be chosen from the point of view that the weighted sum should move exactly to the desired sector, or at least as close, as possible to it after the correction of weights according to the rule (5). For choice of the ω the following three cases should be considered. Let $\varepsilon^{\beta} = (X, \overline{W}_m)$ is the actual neuron's output, i is an imaginary unit.

Case 1. $\omega = -i\varepsilon$, if $\varepsilon^{\beta} = \varepsilon^{\alpha+1}$ for $k=2$ and $k=3$, or $\varepsilon^{\alpha+1} \prec \varepsilon^{\beta} \prec \varepsilon^{\alpha+[k/4]}$ for $k \geq 4$.

Case 2. $\omega = 1$, if $\varepsilon^{\alpha+[k/4]+1} \prec \varepsilon^{\beta} \prec \varepsilon^{\alpha+3[k/4]-1}$ for $k \geq 4$ (for $k < 4$ such a case is impossible).

Case 3. $\omega = i$, if $\varepsilon^{\beta} \prec \varepsilon^{\alpha+2}$ for $k=3$, or $\varepsilon^{\alpha+3[k/4]} \prec \varepsilon^{\beta} \prec \varepsilon^{\alpha+k-1}$ for $k \geq 4$ (for $k=2$ such a case is impossible).

Here $[k/4]$ is an integer part of $k/4$ and a relation noted by $\prec$ is defined like this: $\varepsilon^p \prec \varepsilon^q \Leftrightarrow p(\mathrm{mod}\, k) \leq q(\mathrm{mod}\, k)$.

The case 1 corresponds to the motion to the "right" side from the actual sector, if the difference between actual and desired output's arguments is not more than $\pi/2$. The case 3 corresponds to the motion to the "left" side from the actual sector, if the difference between actual and desired output's arguments is not more than $\pi/2$. The case 2 corresponds to the situation when the difference between actual and desired output's arguments is more than $\pi/2$.

A role of scale coefficient C_m in the rule (5) should be clarified. This coefficient may be changed during process of the learning, and it is possible to control the learning process by its changing. A control means an acceleration of the convergence. Anywhere C_m should contain the multiplier $\dfrac{1}{(n+1)}$ because the weighting vector W is exactly $(n+1)$-dimensional vector. The following theorem is true.

Theorem 1. Let the learning subsets A_0, A_1, ..., A_{k-1} are k-separated according to the Definition 1. Then such an integer number m_0 $(1 \leq m_0 \leq k!)$ exists that

$$W_{m_0+1} = W_{m_0+2} = ... = W_{m_0+3} = ..., \text{ where } W_{m_0+1} = W, \text{ and permutation } R = R_{m_0}$$

satisfy the equation (4). In other words: If the learning subsets A_0, A_1, ..., A_{k-1} are k-separated for the given value of k, then the learning algorithm with the rule (5) is converged, and requests for the convergence not more than $k!$ iterations (the extreme upper estimate).

3.2 Learning rule 2

The second learning rule is a generalization of the error-correction rule for the threshold neuron [17] on the multi-valued case. Error-correction rule for the MVN is described by the following equation:

$$W_{m+1} = W_m + C_m (\varepsilon^q - \varepsilon^s) \, \overline{X} \qquad (6)$$

where W_m and W_{m+1} are the current and the next weighting vectors, $\overline{X}$ is the vector of the neuron's input signals (complex-conjugated), ε is the primitive k-th power root of a unity (k is chosen from (2)), C_m is the scale coefficient, q is the number of the "correct" (desired) sector, s is the number of the sector to which actual value of the weighted sum has fallen. A role of scale coefficient C_m is the same that for the learning rule (5). The following theorem is true.

Theorem 2. If the learning subsets A_0, A_1, ..., A_{k-1} are k-separated then the learning algorithm with the learning rule (6) is converged. The maximal number of the iterations, which may be needed for the convergence, is equal to $k!$.

3.3 Learning for the UBN

Learning for the UBN may be reduced to the learning of the MVN. This fact is followed from the next theorem.

Theorem 3. If the Boolean function $f(x_1,...,x_n)$ is P-realizable, and the predicate P is defined by the equality (3), then such a partial-defined m-valued function $\tilde{f}(x_1,...,x_n)$ exists that it is m-valued threshold function. The function $\tilde{f}$ may be implemented on the MVN, and any weighting vector of one of the functions f and $\tilde{f}$ is common for both functions.

Two learning rules for the UBN learning are based on the Theorem 3 and learning rules 1 and 2 for the MVN. An incorrect output of the UBN for some input vector X from the learning set means that a weighting sum has fallen into an "incorrect" sector. It is evident from the equality (3), which establishes an activation function of UBN, and Fig. 2 that if the weighted sum gets into the "incorrect" sector, both of the neighborhood sectors are "correct" in such a case because $P(z_1) = P(z_2) = -P(z)$, $z \in (s)$ $z_1 \in (s+1)$, $z_2 \in (s-1)$ (see Fig. 6).

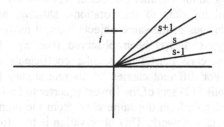

Fig. 5. Definition of the "correct" sector for UBN learning

Thus, the weights should be corrected to direct the weighted sum into one of the neighborhood sectors. A natural choice of the "correct" sector (left or right) is based on the consideration to what of them a current value of weighted sum is closer. To correct the weights we can use the same linear learning rules (5) and (6) that have been used for MVN learning.

Evidently a choice of the correction coefficient ω for the learning rule (5) will be the following:

$$\begin{cases} -i\varepsilon, & \text{if } Z \text{ must be "moved" to the right sector} \\ i, & \text{if } Z \text{ must be "moved" to the left sector} \end{cases} \tag{7}$$

where ε is a primitive m-th root of unity. The number of the "correct" (desired) sector for the learning rule (6) is defined like follows:

$$q = s - 1 \pmod{m}, \text{ if } Z \text{ is closer to } (s-1) \bmod m \text{ -th sector} \tag{8a}$$

$$q = s + 1 \pmod{m}, \text{ if } Z \text{ is closer to } (s+1) \bmod m \text{ -th sector}, \tag{8b}$$

where z is an actual value of weighted sum, s is a number of sector, to which the actual value of weighted sum has fallen, q is a number of the "correct" (desired) sector. The following theorem is true.

Theorem 4. The UBN learning algorithm with the rules (5)-(7) or (6)-(8) is converged, if the corresponding Boolean function may be implemented on the UBN with the given value of m in (3). Number of iterations will not more than $m!$.

Let us consider some applications of the MVN, UBN and therefore of the learning algorithms for them.

4. MVN-Based Neural Network for Image Recognition

Consider N classes of objects, which are presented by images of n x m pixels. The problem is formulated into the following way: we have to create recognition system based on a neural network, which makes possible successful identification of the objects by fast learning on the minimal number of representatives from all classes.

To make our method invariant to the rotations, shifting, and to make possible recognition of other images of the same objects we will move to frequency domain representation of objects. It has been observed (see e.g., [14-16]) that objects belonging to the same class must have similar coefficients corresponding to low spectral coefficients. For different classes of discrete signals (with different nature and length from 64 until 512) sets of the lowest (quarter to half) coefficients are very close each other for signals from the same class from the point of view of learning and analysis on the neural network. This observation is true for different orthogonal transformations. In the terms of neural networks to classify object we have to train a neural network with the learning set contained the spectra of representatives of our classes. Then the weights obtained by learning will be used for classification of unknown objects.

We propose the following structure of the MVN based neural network for the solution of our problem. It is single-layer network, which has to contain the same number of neurons as the number of classes we have to identify. Each neuron has to recognize pattern belongency to its class and to reject any pattern from any other class. Taking into account that single MVN could perform arbitrary mapping, it is easy to conclude that exactly such a structure of the network is the most effective.

To ensure more precise representation of the spectral coefficients in the neural network they have to be normalized, and their new dynamic range after normalization will be [0, 511]. We will use phases of a lower part of the Fourier transformation coefficients for the frequency domain representation of our data. We are basing here on such a property of Fourier transformation that phase contains more information about the signal than amplitude (this fact is investigated e.g., in [18].

The best results have been obtained experimentally, when for classification of the pattern as belongs to the given class we reserved the first $l=k/2$ (from the $k=512$) sectors on the complex plane (see (2ab)).

The proposed structure of the MVN based network and approach to solve of the recognition problem has been evaluated on the example of face recognition. Experiments have been performed on the software simulator. We used MIT faces data base [19], which was supplemented by some images from the data base used in our previous work on associative memories (see [10-11]). So our testing data base contains 64 x 64 portraits of 20 persons (27 images per person). Fragment of the data base is presented in Fig.7 (each class is presented by single image).

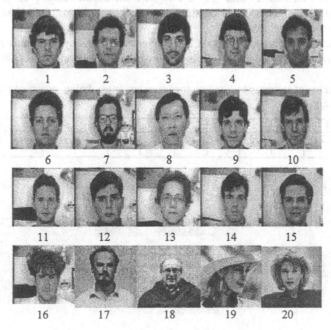

Fig. 7. Testing image data base

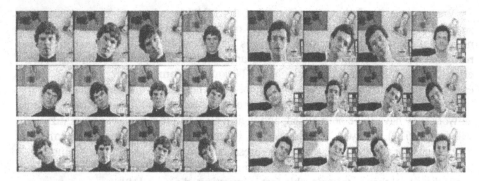

Fig. 8. Class 1: 100% successful recognition.   **Fig. 9.** Class 2: 100% successful recognition

According to the structure proposed above, our single-layer network contains twenty MVNs (the same number, as number of classes). For each neuron we have the following learning set: 16 images from the class corresponding to given neuron, and 2 images for each other class (so 38 images from other classes). Let describe the results. The best results have been obtained for 405 inputs of the network, or for 405 spectral coefficients, which are inputs of the network, and beginning from this number the results stabilized. Phase of spectral coefficients has been chosen according to "zigzag" rule. For all classes 100% successful recognition has been gotten (see e.g., Fig. 8-10). For classes "2" and "13" 2 images from another class ("13" for "2", and "2" for "13") also have been identified as "its", but this mistake has been easy corrected by additional learning.

To estimate a precision ensured by the learning, Table 2 contains numbers of sectors (from 512), to which the weighted sum has been fallen for class No 17.

Table 2. Number of sectors, which to weighted sum has fallen during recognition of the images presented in Fig. 10

Image	1	2	3	4	5	6	7	8	9	10	11	12
Sector	126	122	130	129	120	135	118	134	151	126	107	119

Fig. 10. Class "17" - 100% successful recognition

5. Precise Edge Detection Using CNN-UBN

As it was mentioned above, CNN-UBN is a very nice mean to implement the image processing algorithms described by arbitrary (including non-threshold) Boolean functions. Such a kind of image processing is called cellular neural Boolean filtering (CNBF) [20]. CNBF is a spatial domain filter, which operates within a local 3x3 window. It may be defined by the Boolean function of 9 variables:

$$f\begin{bmatrix} x_1 & x_2 & x_3 \\ x_4 & x_5 & x_6 \\ x_7 & x_8 & x_9 \end{bmatrix} = f(x_1, x_2, x_3, x_4, x_5, x_6, x_7, x_8, x_9). \tag{9}$$

Processing of the gray-scale image by CNBF is organized via direct separation of the image on the binary planes, their independent processing by filter (9) and final integration to the resulting image.

The following Boolean functions describe the edge detection problem for upward jumps, downward ones and global ones (upward and downward jumps together), respectively:

$$f\begin{bmatrix} x_1 & x_2 & x_3 \\ x_4 & x_5 & x_6 \\ x_7 & x_8 & x_9 \end{bmatrix} = x_5 \& (\overline{x}_1 \vee \overline{x}_2 \vee \overline{x}_3 \vee \overline{x}_4 \vee \overline{x}_6 \vee \overline{x}_7 \vee \overline{x}_8 \vee \overline{x}_9). \tag{10}$$

$$f\begin{bmatrix} x_1 & x_2 & x_3 \\ x_4 & x_5 & x_6 \\ x_7 & x_8 & x_9 \end{bmatrix} = \overline{x}_5 \& (x_1 \vee x_2 \vee x_3 \vee x_4 \vee x_6 \vee x_7 \vee x_8 \vee x_9) \tag{11}$$

$$f\begin{bmatrix} x_1 & x_2 & x_3 \\ x_4 & x_5 & x_6 \\ x_7 & x_8 & x_9 \end{bmatrix} = \begin{aligned} & x_5 \& (\overline{x}_1 \vee \overline{x}_2 \vee \overline{x}_3 \vee \overline{x}_4 \vee \overline{x}_6 \vee \overline{x}_7 \vee \overline{x}_8 \vee \overline{x}_9) \vee \\ & \vee \overline{x}_5 \& (x_1 \vee x_2 \vee x_3 \vee x_4 \vee x_6 \vee x_7 \vee x_8 \vee x_9) \end{aligned} \tag{12}$$

Applying the learning algorithm (5)-(7) or (6)-(8) to these functions we obtain the weighting templates for their implementation on the UBN and CNN-UBN, respectively. For example, the learning algorithm (5)-(7) gives the following weights starting from the random weighting vectors:

for function (10), m=4 in (3), 32 iterations:

$$W = (-6.3 \quad -5.6) \begin{bmatrix} (-0.82,\ 0.32) & (-0.95,\ -016) & (-0.04,\ 0.01) \\ (0.25,\ -1.4) & (-0.32,\ -0.05) & (-0.03\ 0.01) \\ (0.0,\ 0.10) & (0.63,\ 0.60) & (-0.02\ 0.01) \end{bmatrix} ;$$

for function (11), m=4 in (3), 12 iterations:

$$W = (-1.7 \quad -1.5) \begin{bmatrix} (-0.91,\ 0.74) & (-0.78,\ -0.99) & (-0.1,\ -0.04) \\ (-0.06,\ -0.08) & (1.4,\ 1.6) & (-0.86\ -0.96) \\ (-0.15,\ -0.07) & (-0.06,\ -0.05) & (-0.142\ -0.03) \end{bmatrix} ;$$

for function (12); m=4 in (3), 16 iterations:

$$W = (-0.55 \quad -0.82) \begin{bmatrix} (13.0,\ -25.0) & (0.75,\ 6.4) & (0.66,\ 2.9) \\ (1.2,\ 4.6) & (-1.3,\ 1.3) & (-2.0\ 2.0) \\ (-2.9,\ 1.3) & (-1.9,\ 4.4) & (1.0\ 4.3) \end{bmatrix} .$$

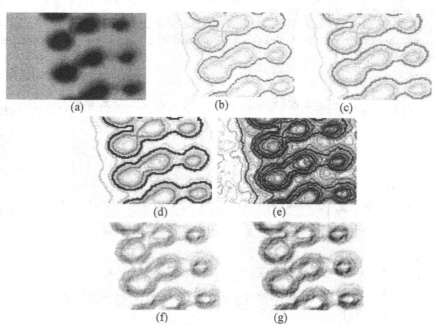

(a) - original image; (b) - processing by function (10), (upward edges); (c) - processing by function (11), (downward edges); (d) - processing by function (12), (global edges); (e) - image from the Fig. (c) corresponding to downward edges with amplified contrast; (f) - processing by Sobel operator for comparison; (g)-processing by Prewitt operator for comparison.

Fig. 11. Edge detection on the lectronic microscope image

References

1. Chua L.O. and Yang L., "Cellular neural networks: Theory", *IEEE Transactions on Circuits and Systems.* Vol. 35, No 10 (1988), 1257-1290

2. "Proc. of the First *IEEE International Workshop on Cellular neural networks and their applications (CNNA-90)* " Budapest (1990).

3. Lee C.-C. and.Pineda de Gyvez J "Color Image Processing in a Cellular Neural -Network Environment", IEEE *Trans. On Neural Networks,* vol. 7, No 5, (1996), 1086-1088.

4. Roska T. and Chua L.O. "The CNN Universal Machine: An Analogic Array Computer", *IEEE Transactions on Circuits and Syst. - II,* vol. 40. (1993), 163-173.

5. Harrer H. and Nossek J.A. "Discrete-time cellular neural networks", *International Journal of Circuit Theory and Applications,* Vol.20, (1992), 453-467.

6. Aizenberg N.N., Aizenberg I.N "CNN based on multi-valued neuron as a model of associative memory for gray-scale images", *Proc. of the 2-d IEEE International Workshop on Cellular Neural Networks and their Applications, Munich, October 12-14* (1992), 36-41.

7. Aizenberg I.N. "Processing of noisy and small-detailed gray-scale images using cellular neural networks" *Journal of Electronic Imaging,* vol. 6, No 3, (1997), 272-285.

8. Aizenberg N.N., Ivaskiv Yu.L *Multiple-Valued Threshold Logic.* Naukova Dumka, Kiev, (1977) (in Russian)

9. Aizenberg N.N., Aizenberg I.N. "Fast Convergenced Learning Algorithms for Multi-Level and Universal Binary Neurons and Solving of the some Image Processing Problems", *Lecture Notes in Computer Science,* Ed.-J.Mira, J.Cabestany, A.Prieto, Vol. 686, Springer-Verlag, Berlin-Heidelberg (1993), 230-236.

10. Aizenberg N.N., Aizenberg I.N.. Krivosheev G.A. "Multi-Valued Neurons: Learning, Networks, Application to Image Recognition and Extrapolation of Temporal Series", *Lecture Notes in Computer Science,* Vol. 930, (J.Mira, F.Sandoval - Eds.), Springer-Verlag, (1995), 389-395.

11. Aizenberg N.N., Aizenberg I.N., Krivosheev G.A. "Multi-Valued Neurons: Mathematical model, Networks, Application to Pattern Recognition", *Proc. of the 13 Int.Conf. on Pattern Recognition, Vienna, August 25-30, 1996, Track D,* IEEE Computer Soc. Press, (1996), 185-189.

12. Jankowski S., Lozowski A., Zurada M. "Complex-Valued Multistate Neural Associative Memory", *IEEE Trans. on Neural Networks,* Vol. 7, (1996), 1491-1496.

13. Petkov N., Kruizinga P., Lourens T. "Motivated Approach to Face Recognition", *Lecture Notes in Computer Science,* Vol. 686, (J.Mira, F.Sandoval - Eds.), Springer-Verlag, (1993), 68-77.

14. Lawrence S., Lee Giles C., Ah Chung Tsoi and Back A.D. "Face Recognition: A Convolutional Neural-Network Approach", *IEEE Trans. on Neural Networks,* Vol. 8, (1997), pp. 98-113.

15. Foltyniewicz R. "Automatic Face Recognition via Wavelets and Mathematical Morphology", *Proc. of the 13 Int. Conf. on Pattern Recognition, Vienna, August 25-30, 1996, Track B,* IEEE Computer Soc. Press, (1996), 13-17.

16. N.Ahmed, K.R.Rao "Orthogonal Transforms for Digital Signal Processing", Springer-Verlag (1975).

17. Haykin S. *Neural Networks. A Comprehensive Foundation.* Macmillan College Publishing Company, New York, 1994.

18. Oppenheim A.V. and. Lim S.J "The importance of phase in signals", *Proc. IEEE,* Vol. 69, (1981), pp. 529-541.

19. Turk M. and Petland A. "Eigenfaces for Recognition", Journal of Cognitive Neuroscience, Vol. 3, (1991).

20. Aizenberg I.N., Aizenberg N.N., Agaian S., Astola J., Egiazarian K. "Nonlinear cellular neural filtering for noise reduction and extraction of image details", *SPIE Proceedings,* Vol. 3646, 1999, pp.100-111.

A Dynamics of the Hough Transform and Artificial Neural Networks

Atsushi Imiya and Kazuhiko Kawamoto

Deptartment of Information and Image Sciences, Chiba University
1-33 Yayoi-cho, Inage-ku, Chiba 263-8522, Japan

Abstract. The least-squares method efficiently solves the model fitting problems, if we assume model equations. However, to the model fitting for a collection of models, the classification of data is required as preprocessing. We show that the randomized Hough transform achieves both the model fitting by the least-squares method and the classification of sample points by permutation simultaneously. Furthermore, we derive a dynamical system for the line detection by the Hough transform, which achieves grouping of sample points as the permutation of data sequence. The theoretical analysis in this paper verifies the reliability of the Hough-transform based template matching for the detection of shapes from a scene.

1   Introduction

The least-squares method (LSM) efficiently solves the model fitting problems if we assume model equations. For instance, the method detects a line from noisy data. For the fitting of many lines on a plane, the classification of data as preprocessing is required. However, the classification of data is possible after models are determined. Therefore, the classical model fitting by LSM could not detect a collection of lines. Conversely, the Hough transform detects all lines in a collection of lines from noisy data. The randomized Hough transform is formulated as a parallel distributed model which estimates parameters of planar lines and spatial planes, which are typical basic problems in computer vision. Furthermore, many problems in computer vision are formulated as model fitting problems in higher dimensional spaces. These problems are expressed in the framework of the least-squares method for the parameter estimation [1].

If we assume a class of models, for example, planar lines, planar conics, spatial curves, and a class of curves, the Hough transform detects all elements in a class of models in a sense. This property implies that the Hough transform is acceptable as an engine for the knowledge discovery from an image database. Furthermore, the other important property of the Hough transform is grouping of sample data using a class of models. Therefore, an extension of the Hough transform will be an essential tool for data mining in machine vision. In this paper, we aim to contribute the theoretical foundation of the Hough transform from viewpoints of control theory and dynamical systems. Our paper verifies the ability and reliability of the Hough transform. We derive a dynamics which is equivalent to the inference by the sampling and voting process. This process solves least-square problems in machine vision.

The family of ascent equation

$$\dot{x} = \nabla \phi \tag{1}$$

provides a framework for the minimization of the least-squares method [2, 3]. In machine vision $\phi = tr(\boldsymbol{XA})$ is a typical expression of the energy function. Brockett introduces a dynamical system for a matching problem which is motivated by a basic problem in computer vision, matching for the motion analysis. He has extended and examined mathematical properties of these dynamical systems. We continue his primal motivations applying his primal idea to the Hough transform. Furthermore, the mathematical properties of of the random sampling and voting procedures for computer vision are examined as a dynamical system.

In reference [6], Oja *et.al.* introduced a combination of self-organization map (SOM) [4, 5] and the accent equation for the least square fitting. The method possesses the same mechanism with the randomized Hough transform, since the method is also based on the sampling and voring process. The present paper also shows the relations among the principal component analysis (PCA) as a method to solve LSM [8, 9, 10], SOM, a class of dynamical system. Our SOM permits algebraic manifold as feature space, that is, our accumulator space are manifolds based on the algebraic properties of the parameters which should be estimated.

2 Model Fitting and LSM

Setting $x = (x, y)^\top$ to be a vector in two-dimensional Euclidean space $\mathbf{R}^2$, the homogeneous coordinate of vector x is expressed as $n = (x, y, 1)^\top$ which expresses a point on the projective plane. For a nonzero real number λ, the the homogeneous coordinates n and λn express the same point x, that is, a homogeneous coordinate $n = (\alpha, \beta, \gamma)^\top$ such that $n \neq (0, 0, 0)^\top$ defines a point $(\alpha/\gamma, \beta/\gamma)^\top$. Therefore, there exist one-to-one mapping between points on $\mathbf{R}^2$ and points on the positive hemisphere S_+^2 in three-dimensional Euclidean space $\mathbf{R}^3$. We define the homogeneous coordinate n of a vector $x \in \mathbf{R}^k$ for $k \geq 3$ as $n = (x^\top, 1)^\top$. We denote the Euclidean length of vector x in k-dimensional Euclidean space $\mathbf{R}^k$ for $k \geq 1$ as $|a|$.

A line on two-dimensional Euclidean plane $\mathbf{R}^2$ is expressed as

$$n^\top a = 0 \tag{2}$$

where parameter vector $a = (a, b, c)^\top$ is normalized to the unit length, that is, $|a| = 1$. Therefore, the solution of the line fitting problem for noisy data $\{x_i\}_{i=1}^n$ is the vector which minimizes the criterion

$$\sum_{\alpha=1}^n w(i)(n_\alpha^\top a)^2 \to \min, \tag{3}$$

where $w(i)$ is a sequence of weights such that $w(i) \geq 0$ and $\sum_{i=1}^{n} w(i) = 1$. The solution is minimizes the functional

$$J(a) = \sum_{i=1}^{n} w(i)(n_i^\top a)^2 - \lambda(1 - |a|^2). \tag{4}$$

Therefore, the solution is the eigenvector which associates to the smallest eigenvalue of

$$Ma = \lambda a, \text{ s.t. } M = \sum_{i=1}^{n} w(i)n_i n_i^\top. \tag{5}$$

In the following, we assume $w(i) = 1/n$.

Setting

$$N = (n_1, n_2, \cdots, n_m)^\top \tag{6}$$

a system of equations,

$$n_\alpha^\top a = 0, \ \alpha = 1, 2, \cdots m, \tag{7}$$

is expressed as

$$Na = o. \tag{8}$$

Furthermore, because $n_\alpha^\top a = 0$ and $n_\beta^\top a = 0$ imply that a unit vector a is orthogonal to both n_α and n_β, we have the equality

$$a = \frac{n_\alpha \times n_\beta}{|n_\alpha \times n_\beta|}. \tag{9}$$

Since samples are noisy, that is, in applications, we should deal with the system of equations,

$$n_\alpha^\top a = \varepsilon_\alpha, \ \alpha = 1, 2, \cdots, n. \tag{10}$$

where ε_α is a small number, we adopt the average of a for many combination of column vectors of N. There are $_mC_2$ possibilities for the selection of two column vectors from N.

If we normirize b to -1, the parameter of a line minimizes the functional

$$J(a, c) = \left| y - A \begin{pmatrix} a \\ c \end{pmatrix} \right|^2, \ A = - \begin{pmatrix} x_1, & x_2, & \cdots, & x_n \\ 1, & 1, & \cdots, & 1 \end{pmatrix}^\top, \tag{11}$$

for $y = (y_1, y_2, \cdots, y_n)^\top$. Since $\operatorname{rank} A = 2$, the solution is given as

$$\begin{pmatrix} a \\ c \end{pmatrix} = A^- y, \tag{12}$$

where

$$A^- = \begin{pmatrix} A_2^{-1} & O \end{pmatrix}, \text{ s.t. } A_2 = - \begin{pmatrix} x_i, & 1 \\ x_j, & 1 \end{pmatrix}. \tag{13}$$

A generalization of this property derives the following proposition [11].

Proposition 1 *Assuming that matrices P_k and O are a $k \times k$ permutation matrix and the $(m - n) \times n$ null matrix, respectively, for a $m \times n$ matrix A such that $m > n$ and $rank A = n$, vector a which is defined as*

$$a = \left(A_n^{-1} \, O\right) y \qquad (14)$$

for

$$A_n = (P_n \, O) \, P_m A \qquad (15)$$

minimizes a criterion $|y - Aa|^2$.

The proposition implies that if the $m \times n$ system matrix is column full-rank,

1. selecting n equations from the system of equations, and
2. solving this nonsingular equation,

we obtain the solution of the least square optimization. There are ambiguities for the selection of P_n and P_m. These ambiguites of P_n and P_m enables us to derive a randomized algorithm. If we randomly select column vectors, this method also derives an extension of the randomize Hough transform. We show a simple example for the application of this proposition.

Example 1 *Let a system of equations be*

$$\begin{pmatrix} 1/2 \; 1/2 \\ 2/3 \; 1/3 \\ 1/4 \; 3/4 \end{pmatrix} \begin{pmatrix} a \\ b \end{pmatrix} = \begin{pmatrix} 1 \\ 1 \\ 1 \end{pmatrix}. \qquad (16)$$

Since the rank of the system matrix is 2, we have the following three systems of equations,

$$\begin{pmatrix} 1/2 \; 1/2 \\ 2/3 \; 1/3 \end{pmatrix} \begin{pmatrix} a \\ b \end{pmatrix} = \begin{pmatrix} 1 \\ 1 \end{pmatrix},$$

$$\begin{pmatrix} 1/2 \; 1/2 \\ 1/4 \; 3/4 \end{pmatrix} \begin{pmatrix} a \\ b \end{pmatrix} = \begin{pmatrix} 1 \\ 1 \end{pmatrix}, \qquad (17)$$

$$\begin{pmatrix} 2/3 \; 1/3 \\ 1/4 \; 3/4 \end{pmatrix} \begin{pmatrix} a \\ b \end{pmatrix} = \begin{pmatrix} 1 \\ 1 \end{pmatrix}.$$

The solutions of these equations are all $(a, b)^\top = (1, 1)^\top$.

3 A Mathematical Aspect of the Hough Transform

3.1 The Hough Transform as LMS

The Hough transform for the line detection achieves both the classification of sample points and the model fitting concurrently. Therefore, in this section, we formulate the randomized Hough transform as the LSM for the model fitting problem.

Let m lines exist on Euclidean plane $\mathbf{R}^2$ and sample-points P be separated to clusters of points such as

$$P = \bigcup_{i=1}^{m} P_i, \text{ s.t. } P_i = \{x_{ij}\}_{j=1}^{n(i)}. \tag{18}$$

Assuming that points in each cluster distribute in the neighborhood of a line, the line fitting problem for a collection of lines is achieved minimizing the functional

$$J(a_1, \cdots, a_m) = \sum_{i=1}^{m} \left\{ \sum_{j=1}^{n(i)} w_i(j)(n_{ij}^\top a_i)^2 - \lambda_i(1 - |a_i|^2) \right\}, \tag{19}$$

where $w_i(j) \geq 0$ and $\sum_{i=1}^{m}\sum_{j=1}^{n(i)} w_i(j) = 1$. This minimization problem yields a system of eigenvalue equations

$$M_i a_i = \lambda_i a_i, \text{ s.t. } M_i = \sum_{j=1}^{n(i)} w_i(j) n_{ij} n_{ij}^\top. \tag{20}$$

for $i = 1, 2, \cdots, m$. Furthermore, the solutions are the eigenvectors which associate to the smallest eigenvalues of each problem. We assume that both $w(i)$ and $w_i(j)$ are $1/n$. Furthermore, we assume that in each cluster there exists k points, that, is $k = n(i)$ and $k \times m = n$.

Setting

$$N = (n_1, n_2, \cdots, n_n)^\top, \tag{21}$$

eq. (4) is expresed as

$$J(a) = |Na|^2 - \lambda(1 - |a|^2). \tag{22}$$

in the matrix form for the noisy data. If there exist m lines, after clustering sample-points, we have the equation,

$$N_i a_i = o, i = 1, 2, \cdots m, \tag{23}$$

where

$$N_i = (n_{i(1)}, n_{i(2)}, \cdots, n_{i(k)})^\top \tag{24}$$

If we do not know any clusters of sample-points, the model fitting problem is expressed as

$$(T\bar{n})^\top \bar{a} = 0, \tag{25}$$

where T is an appropriate permutation matrix and

$$\bar{n} = (n_1^\top, n_2^\top, \cdots, n_n^\top)^\top, \ \bar{a} = (\bar{a}_1^\top, \bar{a}_2^\top, \cdots, \bar{a}_m^\top)^\top, \ \bar{a}_i = (\underbrace{a_i^\top, a_i^\top, \cdots, a_i^\top}_{k's})^\top.$$

$$\tag{26}$$

Therefore, the parameters minimize the functional

$$J(a, T) = |(T\bar{n})^\top \bar{a}|^2 - \sum_{i=1}^{m} \lambda_i(1 - |a_i|^2). \tag{27}$$

This property implies that the classification of sample data is equivalent to the permutation of elements of $\bar{n}$. There exist many possibilities for the selection of a permutation T, if we do not know the estimate of $\{a_i\}_{i=1}^m$. These expressions of the line fitting problem conclude that the Hough transform achieves both the permutation of data matrix $\bar{n}$ and the computation of the solution which satisfies eq. (25) concurrently.

3.2   Dynamics of the Hough Transform

First, we consider the problem to determine a r-dimensional linear subspace in $\mathbf{R}^n$, where $1 < r < n$, which approximate the distribution of data-set $\{y_i\}_{i=1}^k$, the mean of which are zero, $\frac{1}{k}\sum_{i=1}^k y_i = 0$. The orthogonal projection matrix P such that $rank P = r$ which minimizes the criterion

$$\varepsilon^2 = tr(PM), \quad M = \frac{1}{k}\sum_{i=1}^k y_i y_i^\mathsf{T}, \tag{28}$$

determines the r-dimensional linear subspace which approximate the distribution of $\{y_i\}_{i=1}^k$.

Since matrices P and M are symmetry matrices, there exist orthogonal matrices U and V which diagonalize P and M, respectively. If we set

$$P = UFU^\mathsf{T}, \quad M = VDV^\mathsf{T}, \tag{29}$$

where F is a diagonal matrix whose entries are 0 or 1 such that $tr F = r$, and D is a diagonal matrix. Equation (29) derives

$$\varepsilon^2 = tr(WFW^\mathsf{T}D), \quad W = V^\mathsf{T}U, \tag{30}$$

since

$$\begin{aligned} tr(PM) &= tr(UFU^\mathsf{T}VDV^\mathsf{T}) \\ &= tr(V^\mathsf{T}UFU^\mathsf{T}VD). \end{aligned} \tag{31}$$

Therefore, our problem is mathematically equivalent to the determination of an orthogonal matrix which minimizes the criterion defined by eq. (30).

The gradient flow for W

$$\frac{d}{dt}W = -[FWDW^\mathsf{T}]W, \tag{32}$$

where $[X,Y] = XY - YX$, is the continuous version of the gradient decent equation to search an orthogonal matrix which minimizes the criterion defined by eq. (30). Furthermore, setting

$$G = WFW^\mathsf{T}, \tag{33}$$

eq. (32) is equivalent to the double bracket equation,

$$\frac{d}{dt}G = -[G,[D,G]]. \tag{34}$$

If $n = 3$ and $r = 1$, our equation determines a line on a plane using the homo-geneous coordinate system.

For the detection of many lines on a plane, the criterion for the minimization is

$$
\begin{aligned}
\varepsilon^2 &= |(\boldsymbol{T\bar{n}})^\top \bar{a}|^2 \\
&= tr(\boldsymbol{ATMT}^\top),
\end{aligned}
\tag{35}
$$

where $\boldsymbol{A} = \bar{a}\bar{a}^\top$ and $\boldsymbol{M} = \bar{n}\bar{n}^\top$. Let $\boldsymbol{S}$ be an orthogonal matrix which digonalizes $\boldsymbol{A}$ such that

$$
\boldsymbol{A} = \boldsymbol{S}(\boldsymbol{I} \otimes \mathrm{Diag}(1,0,0))\boldsymbol{S}^\top.
\tag{36}
$$

Since $\boldsymbol{A}$ is the covariance matrix, matrix $\boldsymbol{A}$ is expressed as the Kroneker product of the identity matrix and $\mathrm{Diag}(1,0,0)$ using an appropriate coordinate system, where m is the number of lines which exist on a plane. Equation (35) is equivalent to

$$
tr(\boldsymbol{TUFU}^\top \boldsymbol{T}^\top \boldsymbol{SDS}^\top) = tr(\boldsymbol{WFW}^\top \boldsymbol{D}),
\tag{37}
$$

if we set $\boldsymbol{D} = \boldsymbol{I} \otimes \mathrm{Diag}(1,0,0)$ and $\boldsymbol{W} = \boldsymbol{S}^\top \boldsymbol{TU}$. This expression of the criterion for the detection of many lines implies that the line detection trough the Hough transform is also achieved by the gradient flow. The double brocket dynamics has clarified mathematical property of the Hough transform which concurently detects many lines on a plane from noisy data.

3.3 SDP and the Hough Transform

The Hough transform is also expressed as the following Problem 1.

Problem 1. Find $\boldsymbol{A}$ such that $\boldsymbol{A} \succeq \boldsymbol{O}$ which minimizes

$$
f(\boldsymbol{A}) = (\boldsymbol{D}, \boldsymbol{A})
\tag{38}
$$

with the constraint

$$
(\boldsymbol{I}, \boldsymbol{WFW}^\top) = m,
\tag{39}
$$

where $\boldsymbol{X} \succeq \boldsymbol{O}$ means that $\boldsymbol{X}$ is a positive semidefinite matrix.

This problem is equivalent to the following Problem 2.

Problem 2. Find $\boldsymbol{T}$ such that $\boldsymbol{T} = \boldsymbol{T}^\top = \boldsymbol{T}^2$ which minimizes

$$
f(\boldsymbol{T}) = (\boldsymbol{M}, \boldsymbol{T})
\tag{40}
$$

with the constraint

$$
(\boldsymbol{I}, \boldsymbol{T}) = m.
\tag{41}
$$

These are expressions of the semidefinite programming problem. Therefore, the interior point method, which is a gradient decent method for convex program-ming problem, solves these problems. This property also implies that the Hough transform is a dynamical system which detect many lines concurrently.

4 On-Line Algorithms

In this section, we derive on-line algorithms which is admissible to the detection of parameters from time dependent sequences of samples. For solving line fitting problem using a dynamical system, we need to precollect all samples and to predetermine the number of lines. Therefore, this method is not applicable to time-varying data. However, for example, for the detection of piesewise-linear time varying signals from a sequence of sample points, as we have dealt with in the reference [12], we need an on-line algorithm which does not assume any predetection of the all samples and predetermination of the number of lines. The main part of the Hough transform is the computation of parameter from samples. LSM- and ANN-based algorithms do not require the number of lines as a parameter of algorithms. This idea is also applicable to the on-line detection of models, if samples are sequentially measured and randomly selected.

4.1 The Random Sampling and Voting Process

As we have described in section 2, from a pair of noisy samples, we have the estimation of parameter as

$$a_{ij} = \frac{n_i \times n_j}{|n_i \times n_j|} \tag{42}$$

for all n_i and n_j such that $i \neq j$. For noisy data, the average of a_{ij}

$$a = \frac{1}{{}_nC_2} \sum_{i<j} a_{ij} \tag{43}$$

might provide a good estimate of parameter of a line.

If we can predetermine the number of lines or the number of vectors $\{a_i\}_{i=1}^m$ using an appropriate method, we can separate P into a collection of point-sets $\{P_i\}_{i=1}^m$ which satisfy the relation

$$P = \bigcup_{i=1}^m P_i. \tag{44}$$

Furthermore, for any pairs of points x_α and x_β in each P_i the number of $(n_\alpha \times n_\beta)/|n_\alpha \times n_\beta|$ is ${}_nC_2$ if $|P_i| = n$. Therefore, for randomly selected pairs of sample points, if the number of duplications for a vector a_0 is sufficiently large, we can conclude that there exists a collection of points which lines on a line $a_0^\top n = 0$. Therefore, after a sufficient number of iterations, each element in $\{a_i\}_{i=1}^m$, has sufficiently large number of duplications, we conclude that there exists a collection of point sets which lie on lines $a_i^\top n = 0$, for $i = 1, 2, \cdots, m$. This property derives the following algorithm for the estimate of parameter vectors from noisy data.

Algorithm 1

1 : Select randomly x_i and x_j.

2 : Solve the system of equations as $a_k = \frac{n_i \times n_j}{|n_i \times n_j|}$

3 : Vote 1 to a_k in the accumulator space.

4 : Repeat **1** to **3** for an appropriate number of times and detect peaks in the accumulator space.

5 : Set $P_j = \{x | f(a_k, n) = 0\}$ for all peaks $\{a_j\}_{j=1}^m$.

This procedure estimates a separation of a point set P collecting many evidences, since we can assume that samples lie on lines. Furthermore, the procedure determines a permutation matrix collecting many evidences.

Next, we estimate the accuracy of solutions which Algorithm 1 yields. Assuming that $|P_i| = p$ and the dimension of the parameter is q for $p \gg 2$, the number of the combinations of the equations which yield the valid solution is $_pC_2$ for each parameter. Furthermore, the number of the combination of 2 equations from n samples is $_nC_2$. Therefore, the probability for obtaining valid solutions is $_pC_2/_nC_2$, since we assume that there exist m models and $p \times m(= n)$ sample points. This property implies that the probability of valid solutions is

$$P_t =_p C_2/(m \times_n C_2), \tag{45}$$

and the probability of invalid solutions is

$$P_f = \frac{1 -_p C_2/_n C_2}{_n C_2 -_p C_2}. \tag{46}$$

Henceforward, we have the inequality $P_t \gg P_f$ if $n \gg m$. This property implies that, after the sufficient number of iterations, Algorithm 1 achieves both the classification of data and the estimation of parameters concurrently.

For the estimation of parameters, it is possible to use eigenvalues of the correlation matrices of randomly selected data. This idea derives the following algorithm.

Algorithm 2

1 : Select randomly $\{x\}_{i=1}^p$, where p is an appropriate positive integer larger than 3.

2 : Compute $M_j a_{jk} = \lambda_{jk} a_{jk}$ for $M_j = \frac{1}{p} \sum_{j=1}^p n_j n_j^\top$, such that $|a_{jk}| = 1$.

3 : Vote 1 to a_{jp} in the accumulator space.

4 : Repeat **1** to **3** for an appropriate number of times and detect peaks in the accumulator space.

5 : Set $P_j = \{x | a_j^\top n = 0\}$ for all peaks $\{a_j\}_{j=1}^m$.

4.2 ANN and the Hough transform

The principal component analyzer(PCA) proposed by Oja [6, 7, 8] estimates an orthogonal projection P to a linear subspace which approximates the distribution of data points in higher dimensional vector spaces. He proposed the dynamical system,

$$\tilde{W}(k) = W(k-1) - \gamma(k)(n(k)n(k)^{\top})W(k-1)$$
$$W(k) = \tilde{W}(k)K(k)^{-1} \qquad (47)$$
$$K(k) = (\tilde{W}(k)^{\top}\tilde{W}(k))^{1/2}.$$

This dynamical system basically solves the model fitting problems by LSM. If we assume that $rank P = 1$ the dimension of space is one. This means that the PCA detects a line which approximates a distribution of planar points, the mean of which is zero.

For the computation of the eigenvector associated with the smallest eigenvalues, we can adopt PCA base method. However, for the application of PCA, we need the large number of samples. Therefore, introducing the control of voting area in the accumulator space, we develop an algorithm which does not require large number of samples. This idea derive the following self-organization based algorithm.

Algorithm 3

1 : Select randomly $\{x_i\}_{i=1}^{p}$, where p is the number of the dimensions of parameters.

2 : Compute

$$a_j := \begin{cases} a_j - \gamma_j \dfrac{\partial}{\partial a_j} J(a_j), & \text{if } a_j \in N(j) \\ a_j, & \text{otherwise,} \end{cases}$$

for

$$J(a_j) = \sum_{i=1}^{p}(n_i^{\top}a_j)^2,$$

where $N(j)$ is the topological neighborhood of point a_j.

3 : Repeat **1** to **2** for an appropriate number of times and detect peaks in the accumulator space.

4 : Set $P_j = \{x | a_j^{\top} n = 0\}$ for all peaks $\{a_j\}_{j=1}^{m}$.

The algorithm is same as the SOM-based algorithm proposed by Oja. In the Kohonen's SOM, $N(j)$ is called the topological neighborhood, since there is no metric in the accumulator space. However, in our framework, $N(j)$ is the geometric neighborhood on S_+^2 in $\mathbf{R}^3$ for the detection of planar lines, since our parameters are computed as unit vectors and the accumulator space is positive unit semisphere in three-dimensional Euclidean space. This algorithm shows that the SOM-based Hough transform is mathematically equivalent to the successive application of PCA to randomly selected sets of samples.

5   Application in Machine Vision

5.1   Positive Unit Semisphere

Let S^{n-1} be the unit sphere of $\mathbf{R}^n$ consisting of all points x with distance 1 from the origin. For $n = 1$, $S^0 = [-1, 1]$. Furthermore, the positive half-space is defined by

$$\mathbf{R}_+^n = \{x | x_n > 0\}, \ n \geq 1. \tag{48}$$

Now, by setting

$$H_+^{n-1} = S^{n-1} \bigcap \mathbf{R}_+^n, \ n \geq 1, \tag{49}$$

the positive unit semi-sphere is defined by

$$S_+^{n-1} = S_+^{n-2} \bigcup H_+^{n-1}, \ n \geq 1. \tag{50}$$

5.2   Reconstruction of Polyhedron

The plane detection is mathematically expressed in the same manner with the line detection. For a sample point $x = (x, y, z)^\top$, which define a plane if we define $n = (x^\top, 1)^\top$ the parameter satisfies the relation

$$ax + by + cz + d = 0. \tag{51}$$

Therefore, setting $D = \mathrm{Diag}(1, 0, 0, 0)$, we have the same equation with the line detection.

Furthermore, for a real number $\lambda \neq 0$ such that $(\lambda a, \lambda b, \lambda c, \lambda d)^\top$ determines the same plane. This implies that we can normalize the length of vector $(a, b, c, d)^\top$ to unity. Therefore, setting

$$\alpha = \frac{a}{\sqrt{a^2 + b^2 + c^2 + d^2}} \quad \beta = \frac{b}{\sqrt{a^2 + b^2 + c^2 + d^2}}$$

$$\gamma = \frac{c}{\sqrt{a^2 + b^2 + c^2 + d^2}} \quad \delta = \frac{d}{\sqrt{a^2 + b^2 + c^2 + d^2}} \tag{52}$$

a vector $(\alpha, \beta, \gamma, \delta)^\top$ determines a point on S_+^3. This means that our model fitting problem is mathematically the determination of a point on S_+^3, since there is one-to-one mapping between planes and points on S_+^3.

Once a set of planes $\{\mathbf{P}_i\}_{i=1}^m$ is determined from samples $\{x\}_{i=1}^n$, the intersection of half spaces $\{\mathbf{H}_i\}_{i=1}^m$

$$\mathbf{C} = \bigcap_{i=1}^n \mathbf{H}_i \tag{53}$$

determines a convex polyhedron from samples. Therefore, the dynamics proposed in the previous section reconstructs a convex polyhedron. Assuming $o \in \mathbf{C}$, for plane $\mathbf{P}_i$, half space $\mathbf{H}_i$ contains o. Therefore, $\mathbf{H}_i$ is defined as

$$\mathbf{H}_i = \{x | a_i^\top n \leq 0\}, \tag{54}$$

since a_i is a point on the positive unit semisphere, that is $d > 0$.

5.3 Detection of Curves

In this section, x and y express real arguments of polynomials which take real values. Let

$$\mathcal{P}_2^k = \{p_i(x,y)\}_{i=1}^k \tag{55}$$

be a set of independent monomials of x and y and let

$$\mathcal{A}^k = \{a \mid a = \{a_i\}_{i=1}^k\} \tag{56}$$

be a set of all n-tuple real numbers, where at least one of a_i is nonzero. Then, setting

$$P(x,y) = \sum_{i=1}^k a_i\, p_i(x,y), \tag{57}$$

a set

$$\mathcal{C}_2(\mathcal{P}_2^k, \mathcal{A}^k) = \{\, (x,y)^\top \mid P(x,y) = 0\} \tag{58}$$

defines a family of curves on the plane for $a \in \mathcal{A}^n$. Here, the suffix 2 of $\mathcal{C}_2(\mathcal{P}_2^n, \mathcal{A}^k)$ indicates a set of algebraic curves of two real arguments. We show an example of a set of monomials and algebraic curves defined by these monomials.

Example 2 *If elements of* $\mathcal{P}_2^6$ *are*

$$\begin{aligned}
p_1(x,y) &= 1, & p_2(x,y) &= 2x, \\
p_3(x,y) &= 2y, & p_4(x,y) &= x^2, \\
p_5(x,y) &= 2xy, & p_6(x,y) &= y^2,
\end{aligned} \tag{59}$$

we obtain

$$P(x,y) = ax^2 + 2bxy + cy^2 + 2dx + 2ey + f. \tag{60}$$

Then, $\mathcal{C}_2(\mathcal{P}_2^6, \mathcal{A}^6)$ *determines the family of conics in the Euclidean plane if at least one of* a, b, *and* c, *and* f *are not zero.*

The following theorem are held for $\mathcal{A}^k$.

Theorem 1 *An element of* $\mathcal{A}^k$ *corresponds to a point in the n-dimensional vector space.*

From theorem 1, we define a coefficient vector of $P(x,y)$ as

$$a = (a_1, a_2, \cdots, a_k)^\top. \tag{61}$$

For a positive real value λ, $\lambda P(x,y) = 0$ and $-\lambda P(x,y) = 0$ define the same curve. Conversely, once a point a on S_+^{k-1} is fixed, we can obtain a curve of $\mathcal{C}_2(\mathcal{P}_2^k, \mathcal{A}^k)$. This leads to the following theorem.

Theorem 2 *There is one-to-one mapping between* $\mathcal{C}_2(\mathcal{P}_2^k, \mathcal{A}^n)$ *and* S_+^{k-1}.

This theorem also yields an algorithm for the detection of planar algebraic curves. Setting

$$n = (p_1(x,y), p_2(x,y), \cdots, p_k(x,y))^\top \tag{62}$$

and $|a| = 1$, eq. (57) are equivalent to

$$n^\top a = 0. \tag{63}$$

Therefore, the estimation of a curve and a collection of curves from samples $\{(x_i, y_i)^\top\}_{i=1}^n$ is achieved by the same dynamics proposed in the section 3.

5.4 Detection of Conics

The conic fitting is achieved estimating a 3×3 positive definite matrix S which minimizes the criterion

$$\varepsilon^2 = tr(MS) \tag{64}$$

where both M and S are positive definite since M is the covarinace matrix of $\{(x_i^\top, 1)^\top\}_{i-1}^n$. For the detection of conics, parameter matrix S is in the form

$$S = \begin{pmatrix} a\,b\,d \\ b\,c\,e \\ d\,e\,f \end{pmatrix} \tag{65}$$

5.5 Detection of Linear Manifolds

In this section, we aim to extend a criterion which detects planar lines to a criterion which detects linear manifolds in Euclidean space. A line in n-dimensional Euclidean space is expressed as

$$x = a + td, \ |d| = 1. \tag{66}$$

Since k lines which pass through a point a determine a k-dimensional linear manifolds as

$$x = a + \sum_{i=1}^{k} t_i d_i, \ |d_i| = 1, \tag{67}$$

where $\{d_i\}_{i=1}^{k}$ is a collection of linear independent vectors. This expression is equivalent to

$$Qx = a, \tag{68}$$

where Q is the orthogonal projection to the orthogonal complement of the linear subspace spanned by $\{d_i\}_{i=1}^{k}$, if we select a as $a^\top d_i = 0$.

Therefore, for a collection of sample points $\{x_\alpha\}_{\alpha=1}^{k}$, setting $K = [Q, a]$ and $n_\alpha = (x_\alpha^\top, 1)^\top$, Q and a are determined as the solutions which minimize the criterion

$$J(Q, a) = \sum_{\alpha=1}^{m} |Kn_\alpha|^2 + \lambda\{(n - k) - tr(Q^\top Q)\}, \tag{69}$$

since Q is the orthogonal projection to a $(n - k)$-dimensional linear subspace. If we have s linear manifolds, we have the criterion such that

$$J(Q, T, a) = \sum_{\alpha=1}^{m} |KT\bar{n}_\alpha|^2 + \sum_{j=1}^{s} \lambda_j\{(n - k) - tr(Q_j^\top Q_j)\}, \tag{70}$$

where

$$Q = \mathrm{Diag}(Q_1, Q_2, \cdots, Q_s). \tag{71}$$

Here, we assume that $s \times t = m$ where t is the number of sample points lie on each manifold.

5.6 Flow Field Detection

Setting $f(x, y, t)$ to be a time dependent gray-scale image, the optical flow u is the solution of the linear equation

$$f^{\mathsf{T}} u = 0, \ f = \left(\frac{\partial f(x, y, t)}{\partial x}, \frac{\partial f(x, y, t)}{\partial y}, \frac{\partial f(x, y, t)}{\partial t} \right)^{\mathsf{T}}, \ u = (u, v, 1)^{\mathsf{T}} \quad (72)$$

for

$$\frac{df(x, y, t)}{dt} = f^{\mathsf{T}} u, \ u = \frac{\partial x}{\partial t}, \ v = \frac{\partial y}{\partial t}. \quad (73)$$

For a gray-scale image, the derivatives $\frac{\partial f(x,y,t)}{\partial x}$, $\frac{\partial f(x,y,t)}{\partial y}$, and $\frac{\partial f(x,y,t)}{\partial t}$ are approximated by $(f(x+1, y, t) - f(x, y, t))$, $(f(x, y+1, t) - f(x, y, t))$, and $(f(x, y, t + \Delta) - f(x, y, t))$, where Δ is the sampling interval accoding to the argument t, respectively. Assuming that the flow vector u is constant in an area, the flow vector in this area is the solution of the minimization problem

$$\sum_{\alpha=1}^{n} (f_{\alpha}^{\mathsf{T}} u)^2 \rightarrow \min, \quad (74)$$

with the constrain $u_3 = 1$ for $u = (u_1, u_2, u_3)^{\mathsf{T}}$. Therefore, methods described in the previous sections are valid for the detection of the flow filed. Setting the eigenvector associated to the minimum eigenvalue of covariance matrix M,

$$M = \frac{1}{n} \sum_{\alpha=1}^{n} f_{\alpha} f_{\alpha}^{\mathsf{T}} \quad (75)$$

to be $(A, B, C)^{\mathsf{T}}$, our solution is

$$u = (\frac{A}{C}, \frac{B}{C}, 1)^{\mathsf{T}}. \quad (76)$$

For the detection of flow field in a scene, we can apply the same dynamics to each area in parallel.

6 Conclusions

The least-squares method efficiently solves the model fitting problem, if we assume a model equation. However, for the fitting for a collection of models, the classification of data is required as preprocessing. We showed that the random sampling and voting method, which is an extension of the randomized Hough transform, achieves both the classification of sample points and the model fitting concurrently. Furthermore, we expressed the classification of data for the model fitting problems in machine vision as the permutation of matrices which are defined by data. We showed that these frameworks derive the energy minimization problems.

The dynamical system which we have obtained derives an off-line algorithm, because the algorithm starts to solve the problem after detecting all data. However, the Hough transform basically derives both on-line and off-line algorithms. The next stage of our research is the derivation of off-line algorithms. The most simple on-line algorithm is derived by decomposing the covariance matrix into column vectors. Since this primitive algorithm is not so elegant, the ANN approach might derive an elegant on line algorithms.

References

1. Kanatani, K., Statistical optimization and geometric inference in computer vision, *Philosophical Transactions of the Royal Society of London, Series A*, **356** 1997, 1308-1320.
2. Brockett, R. W., Least square matching problem, *Linear Algebra and its Applications*, **122/123/124**, 1989, 761-777.
3. Brockett, R.W., Dynamical system that sort list, diagonalize matrices, and solve linear programming problems, *Linear Algebra and its Applications*, **146**, 1991, 79-91.
4. Kohonen, T., *Self-organization and Associative Memory, 2nd Ed*, Springer, Berlin, 1988
5. Ritter, H. and Schulten, K., Convergence Properties of Kohonen's topological conservation maps: fluctuations, stability, and dimensional selection, Biological Cybernetics, **60** 1988, 59-71.
6. Oja, E., Xu, L., and Kultanen, P., Curve detection by an extended self-organization map and related RHT method, Proc. International Neural Network Conference, **1**, 1990, 27-30.
7. Xu, L., Oja, E. and Suen, C.Y., Modified Hebbian learning for curve and surface fitting, *Neural Networks*, **5**, 1992, 441-457.
8. Oja, E. Principal components, minor components, and linear neural networks, *Neural Networks*, **5**, 1992, 927-935.
9. Diamantaras, Y. and Kung, S.Y., *Principal Component Neural Networks: Theory and Applications*, John Wiley & Sons, New York, 1996.
10. Karhunen, J. and Joutsenalo, J., Generalizations of principal components analysis, optimization problem, and neural networks, *Neural Networks*, **8**, 1995, 549-562.
11. Rao, C.R. and Mitra, S.K., *Generalized Inverse of Matrices and its Applications*, John Wiley & Sons, New York. 1971.
12. Imiya, A., Detection of piecewise-linear signals by the randomized Hough transform, *Pattern Recognition Letters*, **17** 1996 771-776.

Applications of Cellular Neural Networks for Shape from Shading Problem

Mariofanna Milanova[1], Paulo E. M. Almeida[2], Jun Okamoto Jr.[1] and Marcelo Godoy Simões[1]

[1] Department of Mechanical Engineering – Escola Politécnica – USP
Av. Prof. Mello Moraes, 2231 - São Paulo 05508-900, SP – BRAZIL
FAX : +55-11-813-1886
milanova@lyra.mcca.ep.usp.br, {jokamoto, mgs}@usp.br

[2] Department of Research and Postgraduate / CEFET – MG
Av. Amazonas, 7675 - Belo Horizonte 30510-000, MG – BRAZIL
FAX : +55-31-319-5212
paulo@dppg.cefetmg.br

Abstract. The Cellular Neural Networks (CNN) model consist of many parallel analog processors computing in real time. CNN is nowadays a paradigm of cellular analog programmable multidimensional processor array with distributed local logic and memory. One desirable feature is that these processors are arranged in a two dimensional grid and have only local connections. This structure can be easily translated into a VLSI implementation, where the connections between the processors are determined by a cloning template. This template describes the strength of nearest-neighbour interconnections in the network. The focus of this paper is to present one new methodology to solve Shape from Shading problem using CNN. Some practical results are presented and briefly discussed, demonstrating the successful operation of the proposed algorithm.

1 Introduction

The contrast between artificial and natural vision systems is due to the inherent parallelism and continuous time and signal values of the latter. In particular, the cells of the natural retina combine photo transduction and collective parallel processing for the realization of low-level image processing operations (feature extraction, motion analysis, etc.), concurrently with the acquisition of the image. Having collected spatio-temporal information from the imagery, there exist spatial representations of this information. The Cellular Neural Network paradigm is considered as a unifying model for spatio-temporal properties of the visual system [1],[2].

Many visual tasks are related to visual reconstruction and can be treated as optimization problems. Examples are shape from shading, edge detection, motion analysis, structure from motion and surface interpolation. These ill-posed, inverse problems yield a solution through minimization techniques. From Poggio [4] (see

Table 1), it can be observed that various early and intermediate level computer vision tasks are obtained by energy minimization of various functionals.

As shown by Koch [5], quadratic variational problems can be solved by linear, analog electrical or chemical networks using regularization techniques, additive models or Markov random fields (MRF) approaches. However, quadratic variational principles have limitations. The main problem is the degree of smoothness required for the unknown function that has to be recovered. For instance, the surface interpolation scheme outlined above smoothes over edges and thus fails to detect discontinuities.

Table 1. Problems and the Corresponding Functionals

Problem	Regularization principle
Edge detection	$\iint \left[(Sf-i)^2 + \lambda(f_{xx})^2 \right] dx$
Area based Optical flow	$\iint \left[(i_x u + i_y v + i_t)^2 + \lambda(u_x^2 + u_y^2 + v_x^2 + v_y^2) \right] dxd$
Contour based Optical Flow	$\int \left[(V.N - V^N)^2 + \lambda \left(\dfrac{dV}{dx} \right)^2 \right]$
Surface Reconstruction	$\iint \left[(S.f - d^2 + \lambda(f_{xx} + 2f_{xy}^2 + f_{yy}^2)) \right] dxdy$
Spatio-temporal approximation	$\iint \left[(S.f - i)^2 + \lambda(\nabla f.V + ft)^2 \right] dxdydt$
Color	$\| I^y - Ax \|^2 + \lambda \| Pz \|^2$
Shape from Shading	$\iint \left[(E - R(f,g))^2 + \lambda(f_x^2 + f_y^2 + g_x^2 + g_y^2) \right] dxdy$
Stereo	$\int \left\{ \left[\nabla^2 G * (L(x,y) - R(x+d)x,y),y)) \right]^2 + \lambda(\nabla d)^2 \right\} dxdy$
Contours	$\int E_{snake}(v(s)) \; ds$

Hopfield and Tank have shown that networks of nonlinear analog "neurons" can be effective in computing the solution of optimization problems (traveling salesman problem, stereo matching problem, etc. [20]).

The focus of this paper is to present a new methodology to solve Shape from Shading problem. For that purpose, a regularization technique is used, based on Markov random fields (MRF) modeling and energy minimization via the iterated relaxation algorithm. We started from mathematical viewpoint (i.e., statistical regularization based on MRF) and mapping the algorithm onto an analog network

(CNN). Robust shape recovering is achieved by using spatio-temporal neighborhood for modeling pixel interactions.

This paper is organised as follows. In Section 2, the architecture of CNN is briefly reviewed. In Section 3, a new method for surface reconstruction is proposed. Experimental results are presented in Section 4 and section 5 concludes the paper.

2 Architecture of Cellular Neural Networks

Cellular Neural Networks (CNN) and the CNN universal machine (CNN–UM) were introduced in 1988 and 1992, respectively [1]-[3].The most general definition of such networks is that they are arrays of identical dynamical systems, the cells, that are only locally connected [2]. In the original Chua and Yang model, each cell is a one-dimensional dynamic system. It is the basic unit of a CNN. Any cell is connected only to its neighbour cells, i.e. adjacent cells interact directly with each other. Cells not in the immediate neighbourhood have indirect effect because of the propagation effects of the dynamics in the network. The cell located in the position (i,j) of a two-dimensional $M \times N$ array is denoted by C_{ij}, and its r-neighbourhood N^r_{ij} is defined by

$$N^r_{ij} = \{C_{kl} \mid \max\{|k\text{-}i|,|l\text{-}j|\} \leq r; 1\leq k \leq M, 1\leq l \leq N\} \tag{1}$$

where the size of the neighbourhood r is a positive integer number.

Each cell has a state x, a constant external input u, and an output y. The equivalent block diagram of a continuous time cell is shown in Figure 1.

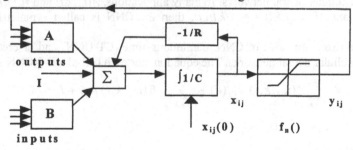

Fig. 1. Block diagram of one cell

The first-order non-linear differential equation defining the dynamics of a cellular neural network can be written as follows:

$$C\frac{\partial x_{ij}(t)}{\partial t} = -\frac{1}{R}x_{ij}(t) + \sum_{C_{kl} \in N^r_{ij}} A(i,j;k,l)\, y_{kl}(t) + \sum_{C_{kl} \in N^r_{ij}} B(i,j;k,l)\, u_{kl} + I \tag{2}$$

$$y_{ij}(t) = \frac{1}{2}\left(\left|x_{ij}(t)+1\right| - \left|x_{ij}(t)-1\right|\right)$$

where x_{ij} is the state of cell C_{ij}, C and R conform the integration time constant of the system, and I is an independent bias constant. From [2], $y_{ij}(t) = f(x_{ij}(t))$, where f can be any convenient non-linear function.

The matrices $A(.)$ and $B(.)$ are known as cloning templates. $A(.)$ acts on the output of neighbouring cells and is referred to as the feedback operator. $B(.)$ in turn affects the input control and is referred to as the control operator. Of cause, $A(.)$ and $B(.)$ are application dependent. A constant bias I and the cloning templates determine the transient behaviour of the cellular non-linear network. In general, the cloning templates do not have to be space invariant, they can be, but it is not a necessity. A significant feature of CNN is that it has two independent input capabilities: the generic input and the initial state of the cells. Normally they are bounded by

$$|u_{ij}(t)| \leq 1 \quad and \quad |x_{ij}(0)| \leq 1 \tag{3}$$

Similarly, if $|f(.)| \leq 1$ then $|y_{ij}(t)| \leq 1$.

When used as an array processing device, the CNN performs a mapping

$$\left. \begin{array}{c} x_{ij}(0) \\ u_{ij}(t) \end{array} \right\} : F \Rightarrow y_{ij}(t) \tag{4}$$

where F is a function of the cloning template (A, B, I).

The functionality of the CNN array can be controlled by the cloning template A, B, I, where A and B are $(2r+1) \times (2r+1)$ real matrices and I is a scalar number in two-dimensional cellular neural networks. In many applications, $A(i,j;k,l)$ and $B(i,j;k,l)$ are space invariant. If $A(i,j;k,l) == A(k,l;i,j)$, then the CNN is called symmetrical or reciprocal.

There are two main cases of CNN: continuous–time (CT-CNN) and discrete-time (DT-CNN) cellular neural networks. The equations for each cell of a DT-CNN are

$$x_{ij}^{(k)} = \sum_{C_{kl} \in N^r_{ij}} A(i,j;k,l)\, y_{kl}(k) + \sum_{C_{kl} \in N^r_{ij}} B(i,j;k,l)\, u_{kl} + I_{ij}$$

$$y_{ij}^{(k)} = f(x_{ij}(k-1)) \tag{5}$$

$$f(x) = \mathrm{sgn}(x)$$

A special class of two-dimensional cellular neural network is described by ordinary differential equations of the form (see [2], [10]).

$$\frac{\partial x_{ij}(t)}{\partial t} = -a_{ij} x_{ij}(t) + \sum T_{ij,kl}\, sat(x_{kl}(t)) + I_{ij} \tag{6}$$

$$y_{ij}(t) = sat(x_{ij}(t))$$

where $1 \leq i \leq M$, $1 \leq j \leq N$, $a_{ij} = 1/RC > 0$, and x_{ij} and y_{ij} are the states and the outputs of the network, respectively, and $sat(.)$ represents the activation function.

We consider zero inputs ($u_{ij} \equiv 0$ for all i and j) and a constant bias vector $I = [I_{11}, I_{12}, ..., I_{MN}]^T$.

Under these circumstances, we will refer to (6) as a zero-input non-symmetric cellular neural network where the n neurones are arranged in a M x N array (with $n = M$ x N) and the interconnection structure is restricted to local neighbourhoods of radius r.

System (6) is a variant of the recurrent Hopfield model with activation function $sat(.)$. There are also several differences from the Hopfield model: 1) The Hopfield model requires that T is symmetric. We do not make this assumption for T here. 2) The Hopfield model is allowed to operate asynchronously, but the present model is required to operate in a synchronous mode. 3) In a Hopfield network used as an associative memory, the weights are computed by a Hebb rule correlating the prototype vectors to be stored, while the connections in the Cellular Neural Network are only local. For example, a CNN of the form (11) with M=N=9 and r=3, has 2601 total interconnections, while a fully connected NN with n=81 will have a total of 6561 interconnections.

The most popular application for CNN has been in image processing, essentially because of their analog feature and sparse connections, which are conductive to real-time processing [1], [8], [9].

A two dimensional CNN can be viewed as a parallel non-linear two-dimensional filter and have already been applied for noise removal, shape extraction, edge detection, etc.

3 Solving the Shape from Shading Problem by Means of CNN

3.1 The Shape from Shading Problem

Shape from shading (SFS) refers to the process of reconstructing, from a unique monocular 2D image, its corresponding 3D shape. The success of SFS depends on two factors: 1) a suitable imaging model that specifies the relationship between surface shape and image brightness and 2) a good numerical algorithm for the reconstruction of shape from the given image.

In SFS research , the image model is specified through a reflectance map $R(p,q)$, with $p=dz/dx$ and $q=dz/dy$ being the partial derivatives of height z with respect to image coordinates and called the surface gradients at (x,y). With the reflectance map determined, the SFS problem becomes one of finding the best way to reconstruct a surface z(x,y), satisfying the image irradiance equation

$$I(x,y) = \eta.n.L = R(p,q) = \eta \frac{1 + pp_s + qq_s}{(1+p^2+q^2)^{1/2}(1+p^2+q_s^2)^{1/2}} \qquad (7)$$

$$p = z_{ij} - z_{i,j+1} \quad and \quad q = z_{ij} - z_{i+1,j}$$

where η is called the albedo such that $0 < \eta < 1$, and it represents the deviation in reflectance properties due to pigmentation or markings on the surface; $I(x,y)$ is the image intensity at position (x,y), and n is the surface normal represented by

$$n = \frac{(-p,-q,1)}{(1+p^2+q^2)^{1/2}} \tag{8}$$

L is a vector representing the incident light, calculated by

$$L = \frac{(-p_s,-q_s,1)}{(1+p_s^2+q_s^2)^{1/2}} \tag{9}$$

Shape from shading is precisely an inverse rendering or inverse graphics problem: given the image $I(x,y)$, find the surface S, the albedo η and the light L that satisfy equation (7).

Equation (7) (or image irradiance equation) can be viewed as a non-linear partial differential equation for the surface function $z = z(p,q)$. Unfortunately, thinking of it in this way is not very useful for real images. Standard methods of numerical integration of differential equations (e.g., characteristic strip method) in practice fail. These methods are inherently too sensitive to noise and boundary conditions.

An alternative formulation is to think of shape from shading as an optimization problem where one attempts to minimize the average error between intensity and irradiance on an energy function, as showed on equation (10). The optimization approach is generally more flexible for including additional constraints and is more robust to image noise and modeling errors. Typical energy functions are derived and discussed in [11],[12][13], [14], [15],[16].

$$E = \sum_i \sum_j (I(x,y) - R(p,q))^2 + \lambda \sum_i \sum_j (p^2_x + p^2_y + q^2_x + q^2_y) +$$
$$+\mu \sum_i \sum_j ((z_x - p)^2 + (z_y - q)^2) \tag{10}$$

Here, the first term corresponds to the intensity error, the second term is the regularization term (smoothness measure of the surface) and the third term is the integrability term.

Grimson [17] proposed interpolation schemes to obtain depth values throughout the image, that correspond to fitting a thin flexible plate through the observed data points. These interpolation schemes can be described in terms of standard regularization theory [5]. The energy function $E(z)$ is derived from the inverse problem

$$B.z = I + n \tag{11}$$

where the data I (intensity) and the linear operator B are known, n represents noise process, and z has to be computed by

$$E(z) = |Bz - I|^2 + \alpha |Sz|^2 \tag{12}$$

In the above equation, the first term gives a measure of the distance of the solution to the data and the second term corresponds to the regularization needed to make the problem well posed. S is a linear operator associated with a membrane plate, depending on the kind of smoothing desired and α is a regularization parameter. B is a diagonal matrix with elements equal to 1 at those locations where the depth is known and 0 at all others.

$E(z)$ can be reformulated as

$$E(V) = \frac{1}{2}\sum_{ij}T_{ij}V_iV_j + \sum_i V_i I_i \tag{13}$$

by identifying the matrix T with $2(B^TB + \alpha S^TS)$, V with z, I with $-2B^Tz$ and dropping the constant term z^Tz.

For the case of quadratic regularization principles, $E(V)$ is positive definite quadratic, and therefore the system will always converge to the unique energy minimum. However , the quadratic smoothness term uniformly suppresses changes in surface shape, irrespective of changes in intensities.

Regarding the use of neural networks in shape from shading, we are aware of previous work [18], [19]. According to Yu and Tsai [12], we can use neural network techniques to solve many problems which have already been solved by the relaxation process.

A number of researchers have used the optimization capability of the Hopfield model for specific early-vision optimization problems [6],[7]. Hopfield's idea was to solve combinatorial optimization problems by allowing the binary variable to vary continuously between 0 and 1 and to introduce terms in the energy function that forced the final solution to one of the corners of the hypercube $[0,1]^N$. Briefly, let the output variable $y_i(t)$ for neuron i have the range $0 < y_i(t) < 1$ and be a continuous and monotonic increasing function of the internal state variable $x_i(t)$ of the neuron i : $y_i = f(x_i)$. The output is then given as (with a sigmoid-like function):

$$y_i = \frac{1}{2}(1 + \tanh\frac{xi}{x_0}) = \frac{1}{1 + e^{-2x_i/x_0}} \tag{14}$$

where x_0 determines the steepness of the gain function.

Hopfield interprets the expression (13) as the Lyapunov function of the network. As shown by Bose and Liang [21], CNN is an analog Hopfield network in which the connections are limited to units in local neighborhood of individual units with bi-directional signal paths.

The dynamics of the CNN are described by the system of non-linear ordinary differential equations showed on equation (6) and by an associated computation energy function (called the Lyapunov function) which is minimized during the computation process. The resulting changing equation that determines the rate of change x_{ij} is

$$C_{ij}\frac{\partial x_{ij}(t)}{\partial t} = -\frac{x_{ij}(t)}{R_i} + \sum T_{ij,kl}y_{ij}(t) + I_{ij} \tag{15}$$

where $y_{ij}(t) = f(x_{ij}(t))$.

The sign-type non-linearity showed in (6) is replaced by a sigmoidal non-line linearity. In this case, the system becomes a continuously valued dynamical system where gradients are well defined and classical optimization algorithms can be applied.

The Lyapunov function, $E(t)$, of the CNN is given by

$$E(t) = -\frac{1}{2}\sum_{(i,j)}\sum_{(k,l)}T_{ij,kl}y_{ij}(t)y_{kl}(t) + \frac{1}{2R_x}\sum_{(i,j)}y_{ij}(t)^2 - \sum_{(i,j)}Iy_{ij}(t) \qquad (16)$$

By using an appropriately defined energy function, stability of the CNN can be proved in the same way as an analog or continuous Hopfield network. Hopfield and Tank [20] investigated the analogy between finding a solution to a given optimization problem and setting an appropriate Lyapunov function corresponding to the additive neural model.

The analog network has two advantages. First, the function E is Lyapunov, while for a digital network it is not. Second, deeper minima of energy have generally larger basins of attraction. A randomly selected starting state has a higher probability of falling inside the basins of attraction of a deeper minimum.

3.2   A New Algorithm for Shape from Shading

Here we propose another method for surface reconstruction, based on the interactions between neighborhood pixels provided by the CNN and MRF paradigms. Since SFS is an intensity-driven process, the random field of intensity in small area is assumed to have MRF properties, i.e, a Gibbs distribution and a neighborhood structure. The spatio-temporal neighborhood of the pixel (or site) is given as in CNN structure.

The raw observation is at pixel level (site or node), where $s=(i,j)$ is given by changes in the intensity function (image irradiance equation) by the function

$$o_s = I(i,j) - R(i,j) \qquad (17)$$

According to Geman [22], Koch [5] and Luthon [9], one way to calculate Z and observe is to minimize an energy or cost function E consisting of two terms

$$E = E_a(z) + E_b(z) \qquad (18)$$

The model energy $E_a(z)$, embedding a priori modeling of spatio-temporal interactions between sites, is a regularization term similar to smoothness constraints classically used to solve ill-posed problems. The attachment energy $E_b(z)$ is the intensity error .

The energy function can be rewritten as

$$E = \sum_{i,j}\left[\begin{array}{l}k_a(z_{ij} - z_{i+1,j})^2 + k_a(z_{ij} - z_{i,j+1})^2 + k_a(z_{ij} - z_{i-1,j})^2 + \\ +k_a(z_{ij} - z_{i,j-1})^2 + k_b\left|I_{ij} - R_{ij}\right|\end{array}\right] \qquad (19)$$

The minimum energy may be computed using either stochastic relaxation algorithms, like simulated annealing [22], or deterministic algorithms, such as iterated conditional models (ICM) [23]. Here, the iterative method ICM is used.

The minimum of E with respect to all z_{ij} corresponds to the null partial derivatives

$$\forall_{ij} \frac{\partial E}{\partial z_{ij}} = 0 \Leftrightarrow k_a \nabla^2 z_{ij} - k_b \left| I_{ij} - R_{ij} \right| = 0 \qquad (20)$$

where

$$\nabla^2 z_{ij} = 4z_{ij} - z_{i+1,j} - z_{i-1,j} - z_{i,j+1} - z_{i,j-1} \qquad (21)$$

The resulting differential equation that determines the rate of change z_{ij} is

$$C \frac{\partial z_{ij}}{\partial t} = k_a \nabla^2 z_{ij} - k_b \left| I_{ij} - R_{ij} \right| \qquad (22)$$

ICM relaxation runs over field z, that is scanned pixel by pixel. At each node, a local decision is taken

$$z_{ij}^{(k+1)} = k_a (4z^{(k)}_{ij} - z^{(k)}_{i+1,j} - z^{(k)}_{i-1,j} - z^{(k)}_{i,j+1} - z^{(k)}_{i,j-1}) + k_b \left| I_{ij} - R^{(k)}_{ij} \right| \qquad (23)$$

This relaxation iterates until convergence is achieved at each one of the neighborhood systems defined in the field z. A relative energy decrease criterion $\Delta E / E < \varepsilon$ is used to determine a convergent state.

4   Experimental Results

To verify and to demonstrate the correctness of the approach just proposed, the algorithm has been applied to some typical images in the area of image processing to perform SFS. The CNN architecture was simulated by means of the ICM relaxation algorithm above described. This algorithm iteratively increases the consistency among the states and constraints on the nodes, so that a better state, i.e., a less energetic state, can be reached at each iteration. When the algorithm converges, this means that a minimum of the correspondent energy function was found, and actual values for image depth were obtained.

For purposes of comparing the results obtained here and others in the literature, some images found on previously published papers were used. They are gray scale images with intensity values ranging from 0 to 255, and sizes varying around 300x300 pixels. First, a semispherical object illuminated from the view point is used. Figure 2 shows the original image on the left and the corresponding depth map obtained by our algorithm on the right. After, a mannequin face image is shown in figure 3. The average number of steps needed to make the relaxation algorithm to converge was found to be between 3 and 4 iteration steps.

In these experiments, the light source direction was estimated by using the techniques shown in [16]. In effect, our algorithm is very robust with respect to imprecision on the values of light source direction. It allows some range of variation in these values without reproducing significant variations on the calculated depth values. This feature can be evaluated by the experiment showed on figure 4.

As can be regarded in the figures, the algorithm has reached quite good results. In fact, the results are very close to those showed in [15]. Nevertheless, our algorithm is essentially parallel and very affordable to hardware implementation. These characteristics are the most important contribution of this work, because they allow SFS to be performed in real-time, when implemented on adequate massively parallel machines or analog VLSI dedicated circuits.

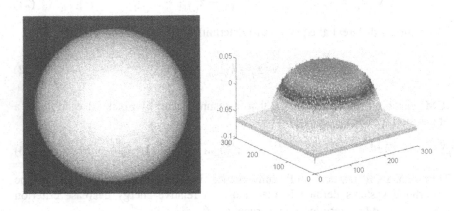

Fig. 2. A semispherical object and its 3D shape (input image on the left, results on the right)

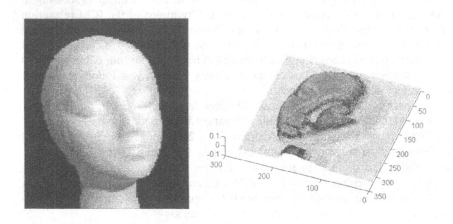

Fig. 3. A mannequin face and its 3D shape (input image on the left, results on the right)

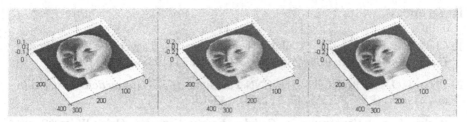

Fig. 4. Demonstration of the robustness of the algorithm proposed with respect to variations on the light source direction values. (a) Depth map of the mannequin face (figure 3, on the left), with $P = Q = 1.0$; (b) Idem, with $P = 1.0$, $Q = 0.0$; (c) Idem, with $P = 0.0$, $Q = 1.0$.

5 Conclusions

Some considerations about the common nature of various problems in early vision were made, concerning an optimization approach and finding a minima of an energy (Lyapunov) function of a representation model. The CNN architecture was described and found to be very suitable to perform such an optimization process, based on its intrinsic properties of evolution to a global minimal energy state.

The SFS problem was described, in terms of the variables involved and possible approaches to its solution. It was derived an energy function whose minimum value corresponds to the solution of the SFS problem, based on the concepts of spatial neighborhood and MRF. It was also showed that a CNN architecture is very affordable to implement such regularization techniques, because of the local nature of the interconnections between its neurons.

Finally, some experimental results of the algorithm proposed were showed and could be compared with others found on the literature. It can be seen that the results obtained here are similar to the old ones, but the new approach is very affordable to parallelism and analog VLSI implementation, allowing the SFS solution to be performed in real-time, if adequately implemented.

Acknowledgements

The research reported in this article was supported by FINEP, by means of the Artificial Intelligence Net at RECOPE project, and FAPESP.

References

1. Chua, L.O. and Yang, L. "Cellular Neural Networks: Theory and Applications", *IEEE Trans. on Circuits and Systems, (CAS)*, Vol.35 (1988), 1257-1290

2. Chua, L.O. and Roska, T. "The CNN Paradigm. *IEEE Transactions on Circuits and Systems* (Part I)", CAS-40, 3 (1993), 147-156

3. Roska, T. and Vandewalle, J. *Cellular Neural Networks.* (John Wiley&Sons), (1993)

4. Poggio, T., Torre, V. and Koch, C. "Computational Vision and Reqularisation Theory", *Nature*, Vol. 317 (1985), 314-319

5. Koch, C., Marroquin, J. and Yuille, A. "Analog Neural Networks in Early Vision", *Proc. Natl. Acad. Sci. USA*, Vol. 83 (1986), 4263-4267

6. Wechsler, H. *Computer Vision*, Academic Press, Inc, (1990)

7. Pajares, G., Cruz, J. and Aranda, J. "Relaxation by Hopfield Network in Stereo Image Matching", *Patter Recognition*, Vol. 31, No 5 (1998), 561-574

8. Radvanti A. "Structural Analysis of Stereograms for CNN Depth Detection", *IEEE Trans. Circuits Syst. I*, Vol. 46 (1999), 239-252

9. Lithon, F. and Dragomirescu, D."A Cellular Analog Network for MRF-Based Motion Detection", *IEEE Trans. Circuits Syst. I*, Vol 46 (1999), 281-293

10. Liu, D. and Michel,A. "Sparsely Interconnected Neural Networks for Associative Memories with Applications to Cellular Neural Networks". *IEEE Transactions on Circuits and Systems Part II Analog and Digital Signal Processing*, Vol. 41, No. 4 (1994), 295-307

11. Horn, B.K.P. "Obtaining Shape from Shading Information". In *The Psychology of Computer Vision*, Winston, P.H., (Ed.). New York, McGraw-Hill, (1975), 115-155

12. Yu, S.S. and Tsai, W.H. "Relaxation by the Hopfield Neural Network", *Pattern Recognition* , No. 25(2), (1992), 197-209

13. Horn, B.K.P. "Local Shading Analysis", *IEEE Trans. Pattern Anal. Machine Intelligence*, Vol. PAMI-16, No. 2 (Mar 1984), 170-184

14. Pentland, A.P., "Linear Shape from Shading", *Int. J. Comput. Vision*, Vol. 4 (1990), 153-162

15. Tsai, P.S. and Shah, M. "Shape from Shading using Linear Approximation", *Research Report*, University of Central Florida, (1995)

16. Zheng, Q. and Chellapa, R. "Estimation of Illuminant Direction, Albedo, and Shape from Shading", *IEEE Trans. Pattern Anal. Machine Intelligence*, Vol. 13, No. 7 (Jul 1991), 680-702

17. Grimson, W.E.L. *From Images to Surfaces: A Computational Study of the Human Early Visual System*, MIT Press, Cambridge, MA, (1981)

18. Lehky and Sejnowski. "Network Model of Shape from Shading: Neural Function Arises from both Receptive and Projective Fields", *Nature*, Vol. 333 (Jun 1988), 452-454

19. Wei, G. and Hirzinger, G. "Learning Shape from Shading by a Multilayer Network", *IEEE Trans. On Neural Networks*, Vol. 7, No. 4 (Jul 1996), 985-995

20. Hopfield, J. and Tank, D. "Neural Computation of Decisions in Optimization Problems", *Biological Cybernetics*, Vol.52 (1985), 141-152

21. Bose, N.K. and Liang, P. *Neural Network Fundamentals with Graphs, Algorithms and Applications* , McGraw-Hill Series in Electrical and Computer Engineering, (1996)

22. Geman, S. and Geman, D. "Stochastic Relaxation, Gibbs Distributions, and the Bayesian Restoration of Images", *IEEE Trans. Patter Anal. Machine Intelligence*, Vol. PAMI-6, No. 6 (Nov 1984), 721-741

23. Besag, J. "On the Statistical Analysis of Dirty Pictures", *J. R. Statist. Soc. B*, Vol. 48, No. 3 (1986), 259-302

Unsupervised Learning of Local Mean Gray Values for Image Pre-processing

Herbert Jahn

Deutsches Zentrum für Luft- und Raumfahrt e.V. (DLR)
Institut für Weltraumsensorik und Planetenerkundung
Rutherfordstraße 2
D-12489 Berlin, Germany
herbert.jahn@dlr.de

Abstract. A parallel-sequential unsupervised learning method for image smoothing is presented which can be implemented with a Multi Layer Neural Network. In contrast to older work of the author which has used 4-connectivity of processing elements (neurons) leading to a very big number of recursions now each neuron of network layer t+1 is connected with $(2M+1)*(2M+1)$ neurons of layer t guaranteeing a significant reduction of network layers with the same good smoothing results.

1   Introduction

Image pre-processing and especially edge preserving smoothing is a necessary step before other tasks such as edge detection, feature grouping (segmentation), object recognition and scene analysis can be envisaged. In the past the author has shown how various image features can be smoothed with the same recursive non-linear algorithm [1 – 4]. That algorithm can be implemented with a generalized discrete time Cellular Neural Network (CNN) [5] allowing parallel processing of the image data. Because of the cellular structure each neuron is only connected with its Voronoi neighbors (4-neighbors in regular square grids). Therefore, the smoothing process is slow and many iterations are needed. Implementation of the algorithm with a network of Multi Layer Neural Network type [6, 7] is not feasible because too many network layers are necessary.

To reduce the number of network layers a neuron of layer t+1 must be connected with many neurons of layer t in order to guarantee averaging over large regions. The network structure must resemble that of the human visual system [8] where one neuron can be connected with thousands of other neurons allowing pre-processing in few post-retinal layers.

Therefore, here a generalization of the older approach is made. Now a neuron of layer t+1 is connected with $(2M+1)*(2M+1)$ neurons of layer t. Generalizing [3] the approach is limited to the case of (edge preserving) gray value smoothing in images with regular square grid structure.

In contrast to the well-known Multi Layer Perceptrons [6, 7] which represent *supervised learning*, the algorithm presented here is an *unsupervised learning* algorithm. The local mean gray value representing the undisturbed image is learned. The weights used in the network have not to be learned (e.g. with a backpropagation type method). They are signal-driven, i.e. they adapt to the image structure and statistics. Such an approach is useful because pre-processing must be very fast (as in the human visual system where it is done pre-attentively) and it must adapt to a big variety of possible images.

In section 2 a short introduction to the old approach (using the 4-neighborhood) is given. The new method then is presented in section 2. Some results are given in section 3.

2   Old smoothing algorithm

Be $g_{i,j}$ (i=0,...,N_x-1; j=0,...,N_y-1) the input image. As neighborhood of a pixel (i,j) the 4-neighborhood N_4(i,j) with the neighbors (i,j-1), (i,j+1), (i-1,j), (i+1,j) of pixel (i,j) is used. Then the recursive averaging scheme is

$$g_{i,j}(t+1) = g_{i,j}(t) + \frac{1}{5} \sum_{k,l \in N_4(i,j)} w_{i,j;i+k,j+l}(t) \cdot [g_{i+k,j+l}(t) - g_{i,j}(t)] \tag{1}$$

with the initial condition $g_{i,j}(0) = g_{i,j}$. In (1) $g_{i,j}(t)$ is the smoothed gray value at recursion level t. Without the adaptive weights w the (linear) algorithm blurs edges and converges for $t \rightarrow \infty$ against a constant gray value. To guarantee edge preservation the weights are chosen as a non-increasing function $s(x)$ (with $s(0) = 1$ and $s(\infty) = 0$) of the edge strength

$$x_{i,j;i'j'}(t) = \frac{|g_{i,j}(t) - g_{i',j'}(t)|}{\mu_{i,j;i'j'}(t)} . \tag{2}$$

The parameter $\mu_{i,j;i'j'}$ in (2) is an adaptive threshold which depends on the image variability in the vicinity of 4-neighbored pixels (i,j) and (i',j') (see [3]). If the image noise is not very strong then a signal-independent value $t_{i,j;i'j'} = \mu(t)$ can be used. As function $s(x)$ the function

$$s(x) = \frac{1}{1 + x^2} \tag{3}$$

was chosen up to now. This function can be interpreted as proportional to the probability density of 4-neighboured gray value differences. In case of function (3) that probability density is the Cauchy distribution which has an infinite variance allowing big gray value differences to occur. Experimental results show that function (3) gives good smoothing results for many images even when the gray value differences do not obey a Cauchy distribution (e.g. figure 5) showing a certain robustness of function (3).

With (3) the weights can be written as

$$w_{i,j;i',j'}(t) = \frac{\mu^2(t)}{\mu^2(t) + \left|g_{i,j}(t) - g_{i',j'}(t)\right|^2 + \varepsilon}. \tag{4}$$

These weights prevent averaging across edges because w becomes small if $\left|g_{i,j} - g_{i',j'}\right|$ is big. The value ε in (4) prevents the denominator to become zero.

The time-discrete non-linear dynamical system can be implemented with a network structure as shown in figure 1. Each neuron (i,j) of layer $t+1$ is connected with neurons (i,j) and $(i',j') \in N_4(i,j)$ of layer t.

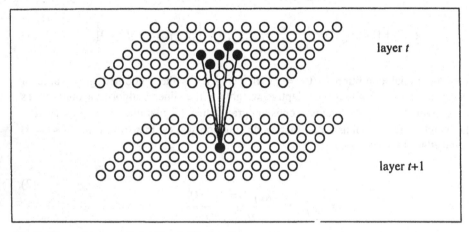

Fig. 1. Network connectivity (4-neighborhood)

The non-linear unsupervised learning algorithm (1), (4) gives good results but needs many iterations because in each step the averaging is extended over five pixels at most. Therefore, to reduce the number of network layers a generalization of (1) with an extension of the neural connectivity is needed.

3   New smoothing algorithm

Now the averaging is extended to a $(2M+1) * (2M+1)$ window centered at pixel (i,j). To apply the weights (4) to differences $|g_{i,j} - g_{i',j'}|$ of 4-neighbored pixels inside the $(2M+1) * (2M+1)$ window the linear averaging algorithm

$$\bar{g}_{i,j} = \frac{1}{(2M+1)^2} \sum_{k,l=-M}^{M} g_{i+k,j+l} \tag{5}$$

is considered first. (5) can also be written as

$$\overline{g}_{i,j} = \frac{1}{(2M+1)^2}\{g_{i,j} + \sum_{k=1}^{M}[g_{i+k,j} + g_{i-k,j} + g_{i,j+k} + g_{i,j-k}]$$

$$+ \sum_{k,l=1}^{M}[g_{i+k,j+l} + g_{i+k,j-l} + g_{i-k,j+l} + g_{i-k,j-l}]\}.$$

(6)

Another equivalent notation using the differences of 4-neighbored pixels is

$$\overline{g}_{i,j} = g_{i,j} + \sum_{k=1}^{M} a_k \cdot [(g_{i+k,j} - g_{i+k-1,j}) + (g_{i-k,j} - g_{i-k+1,j})]$$

(7)

$$+ \sum_{l=1}^{M} b_l \cdot [(g_{i,j+l} - g_{i,j+l-1}) + (g_{i,j-l} - g_{i,j-l+1})]$$

$$+ \sum_{k,l=1}^{M} c_{k,l} \cdot [(g_{i+k,j+l} - g_{i+k,j+l-1}) + (g_{i+k,j+l} - g_{i+k-1,j+l})$$

$$+ (g_{i+k,j-l} - g_{i+k,j-l-1}) + (g_{i+k,j-l} - g_{i+k-1,j-l})$$

$$+ (g_{i-k,j+l} - g_{i-k,j+l-1}) + (g_{i-k,j+l} - g_{i-k-1,j+l})$$

$$+ (g_{i-k,j-l} - g_{i-k,j-l-1}) + (g_{i-k,j-l} - g_{i-k-1,j-l})]$$

Because of symmetry it follows that $a_k = b_k$, $c_{k,l} = c_{l,k}$. In formula (7) each difference of 4-neighbored gray values appears only once. Figure 2 shows the connections for M=2.

If (7) is rearranged so that it can be compared with (6) than the following recursion formulas for the coefficients a_k and $c_{k,l}$ are obtained:

$$c_{M,M} = 0.5$$

(8)

$$c_{k,M} = 0.5 \cdot (1 + c_{k+1,M}) \qquad (k=M-1,\dots,1)$$

$$c_{l,l} = 0.5 + c_{l,l+1} \qquad (l=M-1,\dots,1)$$

$$c_{k,l} = 0.5 \cdot (1 + c_{k,l+1} + c_{k+1,l}) \qquad (k=l-1,\dots,1)$$

$$a_1 = M \cdot (M+1)$$

$$a_{k+1} = a_k - 2 \cdot c_{k,l} - 1 \qquad (k=1,\dots,M-1)$$

Together with the symmetry relations the formulas (8) allow the computation of the coefficients a_k, b_k, $c_{k,l}$ for every value of M.

Now, if in (7) $g_{i',j'}$ is replaced by $g_{i',j'}(t)$, $\overline{g}_{i,j}$ by $g_{i,j}(t+1)$, and if the differences $g_{i',j'}(t) - g_{i'',j''}(t)$ are multiplied with the weights $w_{i',j';i'',j''}$ (4) then (7) generalizes the learning algorithm (1). This new smoothing algorithm gives results of the same quality as that of (1) but, depending on M, with less iterations. Therefore, the algorithm can be implemented with a network of multi layer type with few layers (see figure 3 for the new network structure).

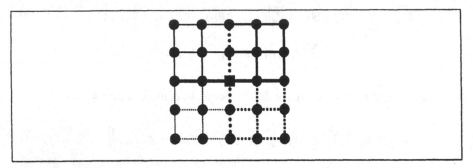

Fig. 2. Connections in eq. (7)

▬▬▬	Row 1 in eq. (7)	··············	Row 4 in eq. (7)
··········	Row 2 in eq. (7)	─────	Row 5 in eq. (7)
▬▬▬	Row 3 in eq. (7)	·················	Row 6 in eq. (7)

Because linear recursive averaging is stable and the weights (4) fulfill the condition $w < 1$ it can be shown that the non-linear algorithm is stable too. But, for constant μ it converges very slowly, sometimes with slowly decaying oscillations. For $\mu = 0$ holds $w = 0$ which means $g_{i,j}(t+1) = g_{i,j}(t)$. Therefore, choosing $\mu(t) \to 0$, convergence of (7) can be accelerated. Experiments have shown that the sequence

$$\mu^2(t) = \mu^2(0) \cdot \left(1 - \frac{t}{t_C}\right) \tag{9}$$

gives good results. At $t = t_C$ there is $\mu = 0$ and $g_{i,j}(t)$ has reached its final state.

Converging of (7) can also be accelerated if the sums in (7) are multiplied with a multiplier $\alpha(t)$ with $\alpha(t) \to 0$ as it is often done in learning algorithms. But, this was not yet studied in connection with (7) because (9) gives good results.

To stop the iteration $g_{i,j}(t+1) = g_{i,j}(t) + \Delta\, g_{i,j}(t)$ $(t = 0, 1, 2, ...,t_C)$ earlier a stopping criterion can be be introduced. Here the criterion

$$\underset{i,\,j}{MAX} \left| g_{i,j}(t+1) - g_{i,j}(t) \right| < 1 \tag{10}$$

was used.

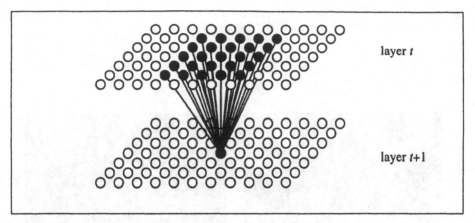

Fig. 3. Network connectivity (5*5- window, M = 2)

4 Results

The method was applied to various images. A few results are presented here. First, some general remarks. The adaptive threshold used in [3] (which takes into account the image variability) is necessary if there is strong noise. In most images with low or medium noise the image independent threshold $\mu(t)$ (9) is sufficient and is used here. For given M the quality of the smoothing strongly depends on the parameters $\mu(0)$ and t_c of $\mu(t)$ (9). The bigger these parameters are the smoother is the result. To obtain good values of these parameters a simulated image (figure 4a) with a background, a square in it, and additive noise with SNR = 2 in the left half and SNR = 4 in the right half was chosen. The visual criterion applied is a good separability of the square from the background together with good noise reduction. Figures 4b (smoothed image), 5a (Roberts edge operator applied to the original image), and 5b (Roberts edge operator applied to the smoothed image) demonstrate the quality of the method. The parameters are M = 1, $\mu(0) = 3.5$, $t_c = 60$. The stopping criterion was fulfilled after t_{max} = 36 iterations. Using bigger windows nearly the same result can be obtained with less iterations, e. g. for M = 3 only 22 iterations are necessary.

The next image shows a 512 x 512 part of the Lena image. The same parameters (M = 1, $\mu(0) = 3.5$, $t_c = 60$) as used before give the result of figures 6 and 7 (t_{max} = 33 iterations). One can see that there is an efficient noise reduction, that the texture in the hat is mainly smoothed out (which can be prevented with a smaller value of t_c), and that small but essential details (e. g. the eye lashes) are retained.

Another example is the Pentagon image. With the same parameters and t_{max} = 33 iterations the results of figures 8 and 9 are obtained. Again there is a good noise reduction and perhaps a little bit too smooth result.

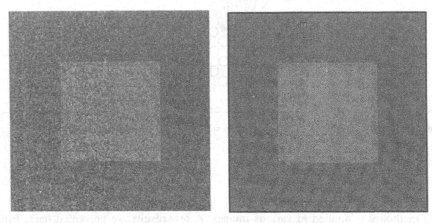

Fig. 4. Background with square a) Original image b) Smoothed image

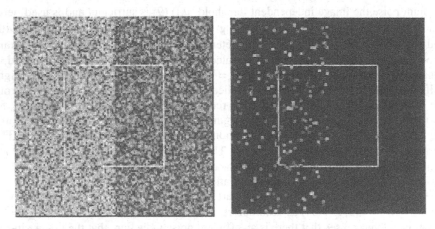

Fig. 5. a) Roberts operator (original image) b) Roberts operator (smoothed image)

Fig. 6. Lena a) Original image   b) Smoothed image

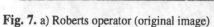

Fig. 7. a) Roberts operator (original image)   b) Roberts operator (smoothed image)

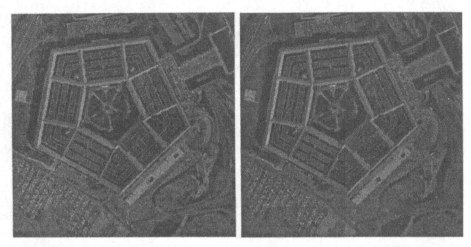

Fig. 8. Pentagon a) Original image   b) Smoothed image

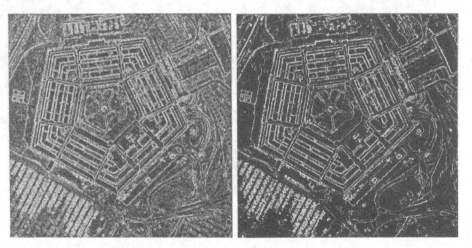

Fig. 9.   a) Roberts operator (original image)   b) Roberts operator (smoothed image)

The last example is an image of the Austrian alps (region Vorarlberg). With the same parameters as before after 35 iterations the results of figures 10 and 11 are obtained. One can see that without smoothing there is almost no structure in the Roberts edge image. But even with smoothing there are too many edge points. Bigger values of the parameters $\mu(0)$ and t_c can make it better. But the question is how optimal parameters can be chosen. This must be investigated in the future.

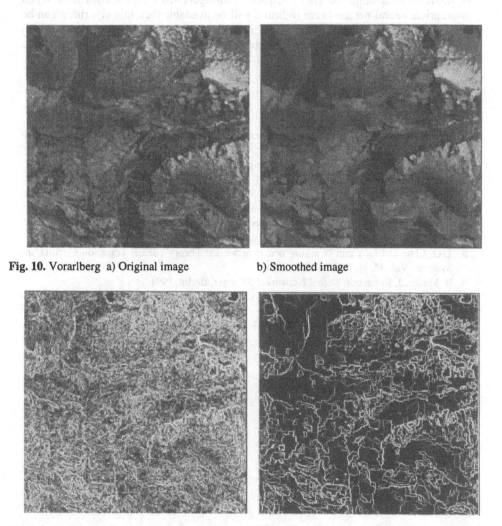

Fig. 10. Vorarlberg a) Original image   b) Smoothed image

Fig. 11.   a) Roberts operator (original image)   b) Roberts operator (smoothed image)

5 Conclusions

It was shown that efficient edge preserving smoothing in images of different kind can be provided by a simple parallel – sequential unsupervised learning algorithm. When appropriate neural net hardware in future will be available then this algorithm can be implemented with a few network layers if sufficient big smoothing windows (M>1) are used. Very fast and efficient edge detection and image segmentation then seem to come nearer.

References

1. H. Jahn; "Image preprocessing and segmentation with a cellular neural network"; SPIE Proceedings, Vol. **3304**, pp. 120-131, 1998
2. H. Jahn; "Dot pattern clustering using a cellular neural network"; SPIE Proceedings **3346**, pp. 298-307, 1998
3. H. Jahn; A Neural Network for Image Smoothing and Segmentation; Lecture Notes in Computer Science **1451**, pp. 329-338, 1998
4. H. Jahn, W. Halle; "Texture segmentation with a neural network"; SPIE Proceedings, Vol. **3646**, "Nonlinear Image Processing X", pp. 92 – 99, 1999
5. L.O. Chua and L. Yang; "Cellular neural networks: Theory"; IEEE Trans. on Circuits and Systems, Vol. **35**, pp. 1257 – 1272, 1988
6. B. Müller, J. Reinhardt; Neural Networks; Springer, Berlin, 1991
7. B. Kosko; Neural Networks and Fuzzy Systems; Prentice-Hall Inc., Englewood Cliffs, New Jersey, 1992
8. D. Hubel; Eye, Brain, and Vision; Scientific American Library, New York, 1995

Neural Networks in MR Image Estimation from Sparsely Sampled Scans

M. Reczko[1], D. A. Karras[2], V. Mertzios[1], D. Graveron-Demilly[3], D. van Ormondt[4]

[1]DEMOCRITUS University of Thrace, Xanthi, Greece
[2]University of Piraeus, Dept. Business Administration, Ano Iliupolis, 16342 Athens, Greece, e-mail: dakarras@www.hotmail.com
[3]Laboratoire de RMN, CNRS, UPRESA 5012, Universite LYON I-CPE, France
[4]Delft University of Technology, Applied Physics Department, P.O Box 5046, 2600 GA Delft, The Netherlands

Abstract. This paper concerns a novel application of machine learning to Magnetic Resonance Imaging (MRI) by considering Neural Network models for the problem of image estimation from sparsely sampled k-space. Effective solutions to this problem are indispensable especially when dealing with MRI of dynamic phenomena since then, rapid sampling in k-space is required. The goal in such a case is to reduce the measurement time by omitting as many scanning trajectories as possible. This approach, however, entails underdetermined equations and leads to poor image reconstruction. It is proposed here that significant improvements could be achieved concerning image reconstruction if a procedure, based on machine learning, for estimating the missing samples of complex k-space were introduced. To this end, the viability of involving Supervised and Unsupervised Neural Network algorithms for such a problem is considered and it is found that their image reconstruction results are very favorably compared to the ones obtained by the trivial zero-filled k-space approach or traditional more sophisticated interpolation approaches.

1. Introduction

MRI scans are sampled along trajectories in k-space [1]. Ideally, these trajectories are chosen to completely cover the k-space according to the Nyquist sampling criterion. The measurement time of a single trajectory can be made short. However, prior to initiating a trajectory, return to thermal equilibrium of the nuclear spins needs to be awaited. The latter is governed by an often slow natural relaxation process that is beyond control of the scanner and impedes fast scanning. Therefore, the only way to reduce scan time in MRI is to reduce the overall waiting time by using fewer trajectories, which in turn should individually cover more of k-space through added curvatures. This fast scanning approach in MRI is indispensable when dynamic phenomena are considered, as for instance in functional MRI. Although, however, such trajectory omissions achieve the primary goal, i.e. more rapid measurements, they entail undersampling and violations of the Nyquist criterion thus, leading to concomitant problems for image reconstruction.

The above rapid scanning in MRI problem is highly related with two other ones. The first is the selection of the optimal scanning scheme in k-space, that is the problem of finding the shape of sampling trajectories that more fully cover the k-space using fewer number of trajectories. The second one is associated with image estimation from fewer samples in k-space, that is the problem of omitting as many trajectories as possible without attaining worse results concerning image reconstruction.

Regarding the former issue, mainly three alternative shapes of sampling trajectories have been considered in the literature and are used in actual scanners, namely, Cartesian, radial and spiral [2]. The last two of them are shown in fig. 1, presenting different advantages and disadvantages.

Both Cartesian and radial trajectories are straight lines. However, the former start at edge of k-space where the signal is weakest, whereas the latter start at the centre of k-space where the signal is strongest. An obvious advantage of Cartesian scanning is that all sample positions coincide with a uniform rectangular grid, allowing very fast image reconstruction simply using the Inverse 2D FFT. Advantages of radial scanning are: less sensitivity to motion of the patient and the ability to deal with possible very fast decays of signals. A disadvantage of radial scanning is that the data are not amenable to direct application of the Inverse 2D FFT, which significantly slows down the reconstruction process. In this case, the image can be obtained by using the Projection Reconstruction approach [2], the linogram method [2] or the SRS-FT [2] approach. Finally, spiral trajectories, being strongly curved, cover much more k-space than Cartesian and radial trajectories do. As a result, fewer spirals are needed to satisfy the Nyquist sampling criterion everywhere.

Concerning the second issue, the main result of the scan trajectories omissions is that we have fewer samples in k-space than needed for estimating all pixel intensities in image space. Therefore, there is an infinity of MRI images that satisfy the sparse k-space data and thus, the reconstruction problem becomes ill-posed. Additionally, omissions usually cause violation of the Nyquist sampling condition. Theses problems might be amended by using the so called Bayesian reconstruction approach recently proposed by two of the authors [2], through regularizing the problem invoking general prior knowledge in the context of Bayesian formalism. The algorithm amounts to minimizing the following objective function [2],

$$| \underline{S} \text{-} T \, \underline{L} |^2 / (2\sigma^2) + (3/2) \sum_{x,y} \log \{ \alpha^2 + (^x\Delta_{xy})^2 + (^y\Delta_{xy})^2 \} \tag{1}$$

with regards to $\underline{L}$, which is the unknown image to be reconstructed that fits to the sparse k-space data given in $\underline{S}$. The first term comes from the likelihood term and the second one from the prior knowledge term of the well known Bayesian formulation [2]. In the above formula, $T((k_x, k_y),(x,y)) = e^{-2\pi i (xk_x + yk_y)}$ represents the transformation from image to k-space data (through 2-D FFT). The second term symbols arise from the imposed 2D Lorentzian prior knowledge. $^x\Delta_{xy}$ and $^y\Delta_{xy}$ are the pixel intensity differences in the x- and y- directions respectively and α is a Lorentz distribution-width parameter.

Although the Bayesian reconstruction approach tackles the problem of handling missing samples in k-space, it exhibits, however, some disadvantages. First, the validity of the assumption that the gaussian probability distributions involved in this method are adequate for formulating the probability distributions occurred in any MRI image is an issue under question. Second, the fact that Bayesian formulation of the problem treats it as being an optimization problem could lead to inferior reconstruction results. Indeed, as it was discussed above, after the Bayesian formulation of the reconstruction task in MRI, the conjugate gradient method is applied to the corresponding objective function in order to find its optima. Conjugate gradients, which is a local optimization technique, has been invoked here as the optimization procedure of preference since a huge number of variables is actually involved (all N X N image pixels). It is well known, however, that local optimization procedures can usually get stack to some local optima of the objective function, been unable to find the desired global optimum. Their performance depends on the initial values of the design variables. On the other hand, even if global optimization techniques were invoked there would be no guarantee, in the general case, that the global optimum could be reached. Therefore, the optimization formulation of the MRI reconstruction from missing samples cannot ensure the quality of the resulted image by its own, but it depends, instead, on the quality of the initial conditions for the design variables. Third, the fact, again, that the Bayesian reconstruction approach leads to a formulation in terms of an extremely huge optimization problem has as another consequence the need for immense computing power and storage requirements. The above disadvantages worsen things when 3-D Bayesian MRI reconstruction is considered, especially in the case of functional MRI. In this case a lot of slices should be acquired in order to have a 3-D reconstruction and the problem of reducing scan time by omitting scanning trajectories becomes of primary importance.

The previous discussion makes obvious that another more effective methodology for handling the reconstruction problem in the sparse sampled k-space is needed and this is exactly the motivation for the research presented here. The methodology herein suggested is based on the attempt to fill in the missing complex values in k-space from their neighboring complex values. This approach transforms the original problem into an interpolation one in the complex domain. While linear interpolators have already been used in the literature [3-5], the novelty of this paper lies on the fact that it deals with nonlinear interpolation in k-space. The obvious advantages of the interpolation approach compared to the Bayesian formalism are the capability for faster reconstruction since it avoids optimization procedures during reconstruction, the need for less computing power and fewer storage requirements as well as the avoidance of any model assumption about the probability distributions. This last point is ensured because of the application of Artificial Neural Network (ANN) models in the complex domain interpolation task herein involved. The reconstruction results achieved by both supervised architectures of the MLP type and unsupervised ones of the Kohonen type are very promising and very favorably compared to the reconstruction results obtained by traditional interpolation techniques as well as by the simplest "interpolation" procedure, that is by zero-filling the missing samples in k-space.

The organization of this paper is as follows. In section 2 the proposed methodology is illustrated. In section 3 the experimental study exhibiting the comparisons of the various interpolation techniques herein involved in MRI reconstruction is presented and the results obtained are discussed. Finally, section 4 concludes the paper.

2. The Neural Network Approach for Estimating the Missing Samples in K-Space

The proposed interpolation procedure for predicting missing complex values in the k-space from their surroundings is outlined in the following steps.

- The k-space data of an N X N MRI image is raster scanned by a $(2M+1)$ X $(2M+1)$ sliding window containing the associated complex k-space values. The estimation of the complex number in the center of this window from the rest of the complex numbers comprising the sliding window is the goal of the proposed interpolation procedure. Each position of the previously defined sliding window in k-space is, therefore, associated with a desired output pattern comprised of the complex number in k-space corresponding to the window position, and an input pattern comprised of the complex numbers in k-space corresponding to the rest $(2M+1)$ X $(2M+1)$ -1 window points. This scheme is used in the MLP case, while in the Kohonen's Self Organizing Feature Map (SOFM) case there is only an input pattern with $(2M+1)$ X $(2M+1)$ complex number components.

- Each such pattern is then, normalized according to the following procedure. First, the absolute values of the complex numbers in the input pattern are calculated and then, their average absolute value $|z_{aver}|$ is used to normalize all the complex numbers belonging both in the input and the desired output patterns. That is, if z_1 is such a number then this normalization procedure transforms it into the $z_1/|z_{aver}|$. This pair of normalized input and desired output patterns of complex k-space values can be next used in the training procedure of the ANN interpolation architecture. On the other hand, in the case of test patterns we apply the same procedure. That is, the average absolute value $|z_{aver}|$ for the complex numbers of the test input pattern is first calculated and used to normalize them. Afterwards, these normalized complex values $z_i/|z_{aver}|$ feed the ANN interpolation technique to predict the sliding window central normalized complex number z^{norm}_{centre}. The corresponding unnormalized complex number is simply $z^{norm}_{centre} \cdot |z_{aver}|$.

- The next step is the production of training patterns for the ANN interpolators. To this end, we compile a set of representative MRI images as training pictures and their corresponding k-space data. Then, by randomly selecting sliding windows from the associated k-spaces and producing the corresponding input and desired output training pairs of patterns as previously defined, we construct the set of training patterns. The assumption that underlies such an approach of training

ANN interpolators is that there are regularities in every sliding window associated k-space data, the same for any MRI image, which can be captured by the ANNs. Unlike Bayesian reconstruction, however, this can be achieved without any prior assumption for the model of their probability distributions.

- In the sequel, the ANN interpolators are trained using the previously defined learning sets. In the case of the MLP based complex interpolator both input and desired output patterns are involved. Each complex number, component of either an input or an output pattern, is associated with two adjacent neurons of the MLP input or output layer respectively, having its real part assigned to the left neuron of the pair and its imaginary part to the right one. The same assignments for the complex numbers belonging to the input training patterns are met in the case of the Kohonen's SOFM. However, since this is an unsupervised architecture there is no desired output response employed in its training phase. Instead, the SOFM is comprised of a L X P array of output neurons that map the probability distribution of the $(2M+1)$ X $(2M+1)$ complex numbers of any input pattern, preserving the topological conditions of the input pattern space. That is, the training phase of the SOFM attempts to assign every input pattern to a neuron of the map so that the quantization error becomes as small as possible.

- After completion of the above defined training procedure both ANN interpolators can be evaluated by applying them to the sparse k-space data corresponding to a completely unknown set of MRI images. This application involves the following procedure.

1. The $(2M+1)$ X $(2M+1)$ sliding window raster scans the sparse k-space data starting from the center. Its central point position moves along the perimeter of rectangles covering completely the k-space, having as center of gravity the center of the k-space array and having distance from their two adjacent ones of 1 pixel. It can move clockwise or counterclockwise or in both directions. For every position of the sliding window, the corresponding input pattern of $(2M+1)$ X $(2M+1) - 1$ or $(2M+1)$ X $(2M+1)$ complex numbers is derived following the above described normalization procedure.

2. Subsequently, this normalized pattern feeds the ANN interpolator, either MLP or SOFM. In the case of MLP, the wanted complex number corresponding to the sliding window center is found as $z_{centre} = z_{MLP}^{out} \cdot |z_{aver}|$, where z_{MLP}^{out} is the MLP output and $|z_{aver}|$ the average absolute value of the complex numbers comprising the unnormalized input pattern. In the case of SOFM, for the winning neuron corresponding to the test input pattern, its associated weight vector $\underline{W}^{win}$ might be considered as a good representative of the cluster of input patterns that correspond to it. Then, the wanted complex number z_{centre} is equal to $z_{centre} = (W^{win}_{x0}, W^{win}_{y0})$, where $W^{win}_{x0}, W^{win}_{y0}$ are the weights corresponding to the central values of the input pattern and the associated central point $(x0, y0)$ of the sliding window. Following this procedure, the unknown complex number that corresponds to the current sliding window position can be interpolated from its neighboring points values.

3. For each rectangle covering the k-space, the previously defined filling in process takes place so that it completely covers its perimeter, only once, in both

clockwise and counterclockwise directions. The final missing complex values are estimated as the average of their clockwise and counterclockwise obtained counterparts.

3. Experimental Study

An extensive experimental study has been conducted in order to evaluate the above described ANN interpolation methodology. All the interpolation methods involved have been applied to a large MRI image database which has been downloaded from the Internet, namely, the Whole Brain Atlas http://www.med.harvard.edu/ AANLIB/home.html (copyright © 1995-1999 Keith A. Johnson and J. Alex Becker). There exists the permission that portions of that database might be individually downloaded, copied, and cited for the personal and educational purposes of individuals and organizations in their work, provided that proper attribution and context are given. We have used 3 images, shown in figure 2, for training the ANN interpolators, and 4 images, shown in figures 3-8, for testing them. All these images have 256 by 256 dimensions. The k-space data for these images have been produced by applying the 2D FFT to them. Radial and spiral trajectories have been used to scan the resulted 256 X 256 complex array of k-space data. In the case of radial scanning 4 X 256 = 1024 radial trajectories are needed to completely cover k-space. On the other hand, in the case of spiral scanning 60 spirals are enough for attaining a good image reconstruction. In order to apply the interpolation techniques involved in this study, the k-space has been sparsely sampled using 128 only radial trajectories in the former case and 30 only spiral trajectories in the latter. Regarding the sliding window raster scanning the k-space, the best results were obtained using a 5 X 5 window for the MLP case and a 3 X 3 in the SOFM case.

Concerning ANN architectures, the best results for the MLP based interpolator have been achieved using an architecture of 48 input neurons, 10 hidden ones and 2 output neurons. On the other hand, concerning the SOFM interpolator the best results have been obtained using an architecture of 18 input neurons and 25 X 10 output neurons in the map. These ANN interpolators have been trained using 3600 training patterns. Apart from the neural interpolators there was experimentation using two traditional interpolation techniques, namely, the linear and the cubic one. Moreover, the simplest "interpolation" approach, namely filling in the missing samples in k-space with zeroes and then reconstructing the image, has been invoked. All these methods (2 neural, 2 traditional and the zero-filling based reconstruction) have been implemented in the MATLAB programming language and all simulations have been carried out using the MATLAB programming platform.

Concerning the measures involved to quantitatively compare the performance of the various interpolation techniques, we have employed the usually used Sum of Squared Errors (SSE) between the original MRI image pixel intensities and the corresponding pixel intensities of the reconstructed image. Additionally, another quantitative measure has been used, which expresses performance differences in terms of the RMS error in dB. This is outlined in the following MATLAB code and has been proposed in [5]

```
lambda=(image_recon(:)'*image_orig(:))/(image_recon(:)'
*image_recon(:));

residu=image_orig-lambda*image_recon;

dB=10*log10((image_orig(:)'*image_orig(:))/(residu(:)'*
residu(:)));
```

The quantitative results obtained by the different interpolation methods involved are outlined in table 1, except for the results of the two traditional interpolation techniques. These latter methods have always given worse results than the zero-filling reconstruction. For instance, for the test image of figure 5 the cubic interpolation gives 2.7E3 for the SSE and 15.02 dB for the comparison with the original image, which are obviously worse than the ones obtained by zero-filling reconstruction. Concerning reconstruction performance qualitative results, they are all shown in figures 3-8. Both quantitative and qualitative results clearly demonstrate the superiority of the proposed ANN interpolation approach in terms of MRI image reconstruction performance.

Test	sampled	zero-filled		Kohonen network		MLP	
Picture	trajectories	SSE	dB	SSE	dB	SSE	dB
tc1 (Fig. 3)	128 radial	3.71E3	15.26	3.57E3	15.55	3.02E3	16.69
tc1 (Fig. 4)	30 spiral	1.61E4	3.76	1.48E4	4.57	9.62E3	8.17
tl4 (Fig. 5)	128 radial	2.49E3	15.51	2.19E3	16.54	1.62E3	18.73
tl4 (Fig. 6)	30 spiral	1.03E4	4.11	9.19E3	5.34	5.72E3	8.6
dg1 (Fig. 7)	128 radial	3.38E3	10.04	2.99E3	10.99	2.24E3	12.94
038 (Fig. 8)	128 radial	2.47E3	14.32	2.1E3	15.65	1.49E3	17.95

Table 1. The quantitative results with regards to reconstruction performance of the various methodologies involved

Fig. 1. Spiral (left) and radial (right) scanning trajectories in k-space (white area). For the spiral sampling, out of 60 trajectories covering the complete k-space, the first 30 trajectories are omitted, while for the radial 128 trajectories have been sampled.

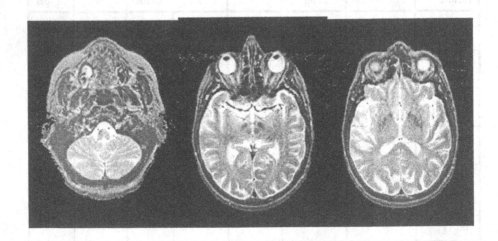

Fig. 2. Training images, normal brain, 3 slices out of the complete database (http://www.med.harvard.edu/AANLIB/cases/caseM/mr1/008.html, 024.html, 028.html)

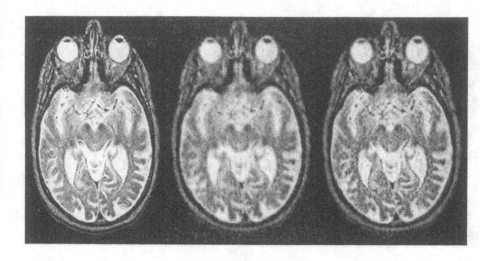

Fig. 3. A Test Image illustrating a brain slice with Alzheimer's disease (http://www.med.harvard.edu/AANLIB/cases/case3/mr1-tc1/020.html), the sparse-sampled k-space (nr=128) –zerofilled image reconstruction and the BP-interpolated image

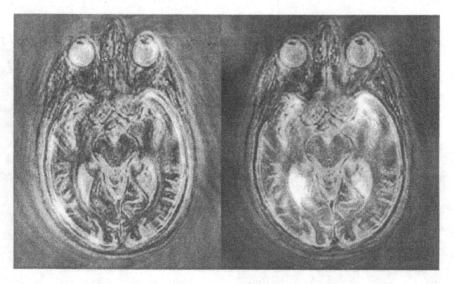

Fig. 4. Same test image, the sparse-sampled on 30 spiral trajectories-zerofilled image reconstruction and the BP-interpolated image

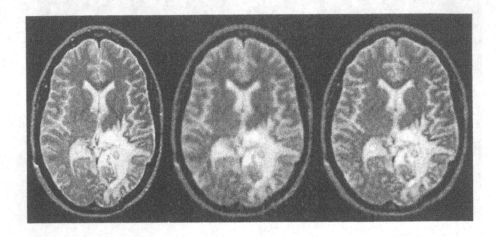

Fig. 5. A Test Image showing a brain with Glioma (brain-tumor)-TlTc-SPECT (http://www.med.harvard.edu/AANLIB/cases/case1/mr1-tl4/029.html), the zerofilled image reconstruction and the BP-interpolated image

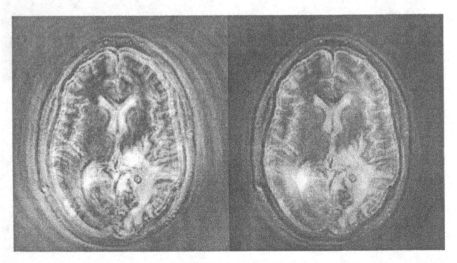

Fig. 6. Same test image-sparse-sampled on 30 spiral trajectories, zerofilled image reconstruction and the BP-interpolated image

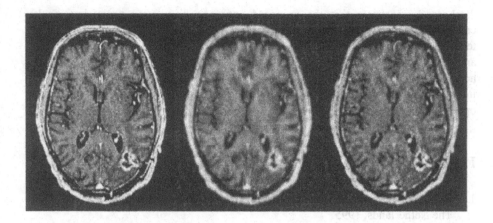

Fig. 7. A Test Image-Glioma (brain-tumor)-FDG-PET (http://www.med.harvard.edu/AANLIB cases/caseSLU/mr1-dg1/060.html, the zerofilled image reconstruction and the BP-interpolated image

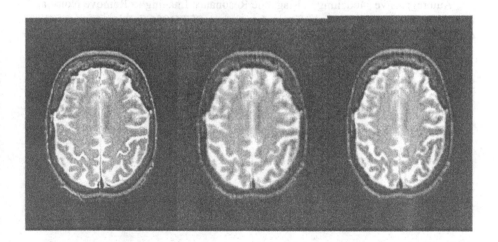

Fig. 8. A Test image showing a normal brain slice 38- (http://www.med.harvard.edu/ AANLIB/cases/caseM/mr1/038.html), the zerofilled image reconstruction and the BP-interpolated image

4. Conclusions and Future Trends

A new methodology has been developed for reconstructing MRI images from sparsely sampled k-space data using MLP and SOFM interpolation for estimating the missing samples. A detailed experimental study on a well organized MRI image database demonstrates that the proposed approach gives very promising results concerning reconstruction performance compared to some traditional interpolation techniques. A comparison with Bayesian MRI reconstruction is under development and the results will be presented in another occasion. What is more interesting, however, is to achieve a combination of these two approaches since ANN interpolation can supply Bayesian reconstruction with a better starting point for the optimization process.

References

1. Basic Principles of MR Imaging, published by Philips Medical Systems, Best, The Netherlands, 1995.
2. G.H.L.A. Stijnman, D. Graveron-Demilly, F.T.A.W. Wajer and D. van Ormondt: MR Image Estimation from Sparsely Sampled Radial Scans "Proc. ProRISC/IEEE Benelux workshop on Circuits, Systems and Signal Processing, Mierlo (The Netherlands), 1997" , 603-611
3. M.R. Smith, S.T. Nichols, R.M. Henkelman, and M.L. Wood: Application of Autoregressive Modelling in Magnetic Resonance Imaging to Remove Noise and Truncation Artifacts, Magn. Reson. Imaging, 4, 257 (1986).
4. P. Barone and G. Sebastiani: A New Method of Magnetic Resonance Image Reconstruction with Short Acquisition Time and Truncation Artifact Reduction, IEEE Trans. Med. Imaging, 11, 250 (1992).
5. I. Dologlou, F.T.A.W. Wajer, M. Fuderer, D. van Ormondt: Spiral MRI Scan-Time Reduction through Non-Uniform Angular Distribution of Interleaves and Multichannel SVD Interpolation, in "Proc. ISMRM, 4th Meeting, New York, 1996", p. 1489.

Extraction of Local Structural Features in Images by Using a Multi-scale Relevance Function

Roman M. Palenichka and Maxim A. Volgin

Inst. of Physics & Mechanics, Lviv, Ukraine
pal@ah.ipm.lviv.ua

Abstract. Extraction of structural features in radiographic images is considered in the context of flaw detection with application to industrial and medical diagnostics. The known approache, like the histogram-based binarization yield poor detection results for such images, which contain small and low-contrast objects of interest on noisy background. In the presented model-based method, the detection of objects of interest is considered as a consecutive and hierarchical extraction of structural features (primitive patterns) which compose these objects in the form of aggregation of primitive patterns. The concept of relevance function is introduced in order to perform a quick location and identification of primitive patterns by using the binarization of regions of attention. The proposed feature extraction method has been tested on radiographic images in application to defect detection of weld joints and extraction of blood vessels in angiography.

1 Introduction

Detection of defect indications in noisy radiographic images is a topic of current research in non-destructive evaluation of materials and products in industrial diagnostics systems. Similar problems arise in medical imaging in detection of various abnormalities in a human body. The poor quality of radiographic images is due to the physical nature of the radiography method as well as small size of the flaws (abnormalities) and their poor orientation relatively to the size and thickness of the evaluated part (or a human organ).

The basic approach to detection of such flaws is the computation of difference image between the original image and the evaluated background image from the original one. Then, the resulting binary segmentation of flaws is made by application of a thresholding operation to the obtained difference image. In the framework of this approach, termed as a dynamic thresholding, the known methods differ by the manner of evaluation of the background intensity and threshold selection for binary segmentation [1-6]. Usually, the threshold value in all these methods is determined from local or global histograms based on the two-mode histogram assumption [3-5]. Another and a relatively new approach to flaw detection is the multi-resolution image analysis by using a wavelet representation [7-9]. This method has the advantage of being able to detect efficiently different in size and location local objects as candidates for the flaws. The use of statistical approach to threshold determination allows object detection on different resolution levels. However, it still has the disadvantage of the previously mentioned methods of differentiation in case of low-contrast objects on noisy background because it does not consider shape constraints of local objects as well as an explicit model of intensity function. Good results have been reported by using a model-based statistical approach to segmentation and detection of local objects in images with robust statistical estimation of the underlying model parameters [9-15].

Recently, artificial neural networks (ANN) and the rule-based learning of object recognition became popular in applications to industrial and medical diagnostics systems

[16-19]. The learning method using a case-based reasoning with incremental learning seems to be a promising approach to flaw (abnormality) detection problem as well [20]. Structural information of local objects important for recognition can be represented by an attribute graph and compared with available cases in the database by the graph matching. The ANN turn out to be an inefficient technique because they do not provide a meaningful image analysis at a variety of object shapes, noise and various positions of objects. The problem solution in the diagnostic imaging requires a structural description of various objects and correct interpretation of detected local objects of interest.

The method suggested in this paper has the following advantages for extraction of local structural features. A model-based approach is used which exploits multi-scale morphological representation of objects composed of primitive patterns. The concept of a multi-scale relevance function has been introduced for time-efficient solution of object detection problems. It allows quick location and identification (recognition) of primitive patterns both during the learning and the recognition stages. The primitive pattern is considered in a broad sense, namely, as the image structural feature consisting of a respective binary primitive (a thresholded version of the primitive pattern) and intensity attributes, which yield a concise description of image intensity properties.

The paper is organized so, that after the brief introduction in Section 1, the underlying structural model of local objects on a background is described in Section 2. The application of the introduced relevance function to learning and detection of primitive patterns is described in Section 3. This section describes also a novel algorithm of local binary segmentation. The experimental results on extraction of structural features with application to object detection on radiographic images are described in Section 4 and concluding remarks are given in Section 5.

2 Structural Composite Model of Image Local Objects

2.1. Structural model of local isolated objects on a background

A distinctive feature of the composite image model is the separate modeling of planar shape of the objects of interest and the intensity function on these planar objects. The shape features of the objects of interest have primary relevance in the current application to detection of local objects, whereas intensity features are considered as their attributes (e.g., local contrast, edge smoothness, intensity flatness, etc.). In order to describe explicitly the planar shape of the objects, the notions and operations of mathematical morphology have been used [21]. The domain model for local isolated objects on a background is generated by means of such concepts as *generating sets* $\{G_k\}$ and *structuring elements* $\{S_k\}$. The generating set G_k is a set of four- or eight-connected image points the width of which being equal to unity. The object structuring element S_o defines the object domain which is a subset of the background structuring element in the case of objects located on a background. The background structuring element S_b is larger then the object structuring element $S_o \subset S_b$ and define the background domain. The generating set is a kind of an object skeleton that together with the structuring elements determines the shape and size of image objects. The domain model of a simple local object D_k consists of two distinct sets of points O_k and B_k ($D_k = O_k \cup B_k$; $O_k \cap B_k = \varnothing$) which are formed by using morphological operation of dilation (denoted by $\oplus$) of a single generating set G_k with two structuring elements S_o and S_b:

$$O_k = G_k \oplus S_o \text{ and } B_k = (G_k \oplus S_b) \setminus O_k. \tag{2.1}$$

Fig. 1 shows an example of the formation of a support set D_k using an eight-connected generating set and two square structuring elements. The structuring elements for objects and background are usually symmetric sets of points on the image plane in order to represent isolated objects in a best discrete way. Ideally, the circular shape is used in a continuous case, whereas a discrete square shape is suitable for digital image processing.

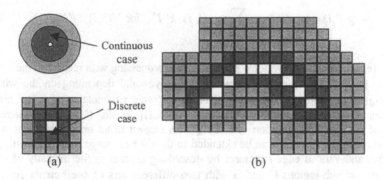

Fig. 1. Examples of structuring elements (a) and formation of a support region (b) for local objects using three generating primitives and two object structuring elements: 2x2 and 3x3.

A *binary primitive* is defined as a subset of support sets $\{D_k\}$ of local objects considered within a window V of local processing which has the property of a regular repetition. Every relevant primitive pattern contains two regions: object region marked by "1" and background region marked by "0".

The presented model has a deficiency of being not able to represent objects with various size and shape at the same time. However, this case with some insignificant restrictions can be implemented by using a multi-scale hierarchical representation of local objects of various sizes and locations. Here, the structuring element of objects at every scale represents the resolution cell on this scale. The corresponding background structuring element represents the object structuring element on the next resolution level. In order to snap to the usual square grid of image definition, let consider, for example at each scale a square structuring element consisting of $3^l \times 3^l$ points for objects and a $3^{l+1} \times 3^{l+1}$ square structuring element for background. The initial level of resolution corresponds to the case $l=0$, i.e. only one point surrounded by eight background points is considered. The use of the size that is multiple by three is due to the constraint of object isolation. The definition of binary primitive patterns is automatically extended to this multi-scale case. Such a hierarchical representation starts from the largest scale of object representation and the objects on each next scale are defined either on the object region or the background region in the previous larger scale.

2.2 Polynomial regression modeling of image intensity

The domain model is restricted to represent possible planar structures of local objects. The intensity changes can be modeled by the polynomial regression model within the considered domain model of local objects [14]. For instance, the polynomial model states that the intensity function g(k,l) can be represented as a polynomial function of order q within a region (window) V(i,j) plus independent noise n(k,l) with a Gaussian distribution N(0;1), i.e.

$$g(k,l) = \sigma \cdot n(k,l) + \sum_{(r+s) \leq q} \rho_{r,s}(i,j) \cdot k^r l^s, \text{ for } \forall (k,l) \in V(i,j), \tag{2.2}$$

where the region V(i,j) is the window of local image processing with respect to the current point (i,j), $\{\rho_{r,s}(i,j)\}$ are the coefficients of the polynomial depending on the window position (i,j) which together with noise variance σ^2 (scale parameter σ of noise) are the model parameters to be estimated. The term $\{\sigma \cdot n(k,l)\}$ in Eq. (2.2) is considered as residuals of polynomial regression of order q with respect to an image fragment within V(i,j). The model by Eq. (2.2) can be extended to the case of image fragments with quite sharp edges and various edge structures by describing separately the intensity of object and background sub-regions O and B with two different sets of coefficients $\{\rho_{r,s}(i,j)\}$. Then, the composite image model is formed by a superposition of local objects on the background:

$$g(i,j) = \varphi(i,j) \cdot o(i,j) + (1 - \varphi(i,j)) \cdot b(i,j), \tag{2.3}$$

where the binary function $\varphi(i,j)$ is the characteristic function of local objects, i.e. $\varphi(i,j)=1$ if $(i,j) \in O$ and $\varphi(i,j)=0$ if $(i,j) \notin O$, $o(i,j)$ is the object's intensity and $b(i,j)$ is the background's intensity which both are modeled by Eq. (2.2) with different coefficients $\{\rho_{r,s}(i,j)\}$.

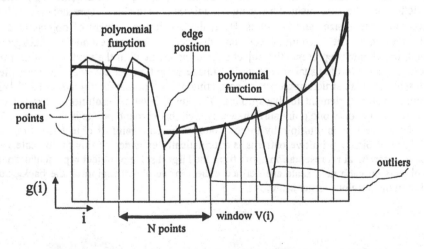

Fig. 2. An illustration in one-dimensional case of the intensity modeling.

A simplification of the model by Eq. (2.3) is the so-called *conformable intensity model* according to which the background intensity follows the object intensity except for the intercept coefficient $\rho_{0,0}(i,j)$ in Eq. (2.2) or vice versa. Usually, the order of dependence is determined by the size of objects. For small objects, the intensity $o(i,j)$ of an object is defined by the object contrast relatively to the background in the object region O:

$$o(i, j) = \alpha \cdot h + b(i, j), for \quad \forall (i, j) \in O, \tag{2.4}$$

where the contrast sign α takes values $\{+1; -1\}$ for bright and dark objects, respectively. It is supposed that the background intensity $b(i,j)$ is modeled by Eq. (2.2). The similar model of intensity as the model by Eq. (2.4) can be used for large objects in which the object intensity is modeled by Eq. (2.2). If the window $V(i,j)$ in Eq. (2.3) has the size equal or less than the size of the object structuring element S_0 then a part of the object or its edges on background will be considered. Fig. 3 illustrates just such an example for the proposed model of intensity function. The introduction of outlier pixels which have other distribution and differ substantially by the amplitude from the inlier Gaussian residuals $\{\sigma \cdot n(k,l)\}$ (see Fig. 2) contributes to adequate representation of the residuals. In the presented approach, the outliers are considered as other present local objects on a finer scale (smaller objects).

3 Learning of Binary Primitives and Structural Description of Local Objects

3.1. Extraction of primitive patterns and their spatial aggregation

In the adopted structural approach, the image analysis consists of a sequential detection of local objects consisting of a spatial aggregation of several structural features termed as primitive patterns. The primitive patterns are determined by their planar shape and pattern attributes, for example, scale (size), contrast, edge smoothness and other possible intensity attributes. The planar shape of a primitive pattern is described by a *binary primitive* obtained in a result of binarization of the considered primitive pattern (with gray-scale representation) within a region of attention. The determination of the regions of attention is based on the maximum finding of a *multi-scale relevance function* and initial hypothesis testing in the point of maximum (see Section 3.3).

The process of object detection is identical to the learning process using the relevance function except for the final stage. Primitive patterns and their spatial aggregations are defined and stored in hierarchical associative structures during the learning process, whereas an object detection proceeds as a structure-driven hypothesis testing of presence of specified in the structure primitive patterns. Learning of primitive patterns and spatial structures means a selection of relevant structural features and spatial (on the image plane) aggregations of these features that allows an unambiguous interpretation of objects.

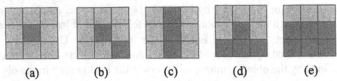

Fig. 3. Examples of binary primitive patterns defined within a 3x3 window that corresponds to the lowest reasonable resolution of pattern representation: (a) an isolated object; (b), (c) line objects; (d), (e) edges.

In the considered application to radiographic image analysis, the differences of intensity attributes, like the contrast and edge smoothness, have been ignored and a single threshold value has been used during the detection. Instead, binary primitives determining planar shape of objects are extracted (learned) for their efficient aggregation in spatial structures. The set of binary primitives to be detected and identified can be given explicitly by the user based on the assumed model (Section 2.1) or generated automatically during the learning phase of primitive patterns and their spatial aggregations. Within the multi-scale concept, the binary primitives have the same size at all scales, instead, the binarization at arbitrary scale is made with a subsequent block averaging and a down-sampling, i.e. with the sampling distance $3^l x 3^l$, where l is the scale number. An example of binary primitive patterns is shown in Fig. 3 for the resolution 3x3 that is the lowest reasonable resolution for their representation.

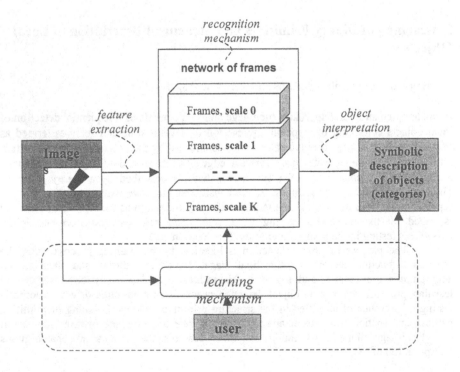

Fig. 4. Detection and automatic learning of primitive patterns in a network of multi-scale frames.

For better efficiency of detection, the automatic learning of primitive patterns and spatial aggregations can be performed through their detection during the learning phase using the relevance function approach. It consists chiefly of determination of the regions of attention by using the relevance function and initial hypothesis testing the outcome of which indicates on the presence of a primitive pattern. Fig. 4 illustrates this approach to detection and learning of primitive patterns and their aggregation in the so-called *frames*, which represent spatial structures of the primitive patterns. Both the learning mechanism and the recognition mechanism in Fig. 4 incorporate the relevance function approach to image analysis.

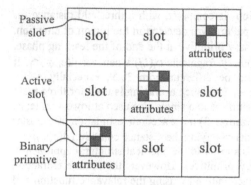

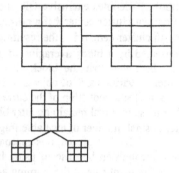

Fig. 5. An example of a 3x3 frame filled by three 3x3 primitive patterns.

Fig. 6. An instance of the association of frames taken at three different scales.

In the case of two-dimensional local structures, the frames represent square tables of a fixed size at all possible scales and consists of *slots* (cells) which are filled by the primitive patterns during the learning stage or derived from the underlying model of local objects. Besides the binary primitive, a slot contains the attribute data indicating on intensity properties and the current scale. For example, a frame consisting of 3x3 slots which represents a local object as a line structure is illustrated in Fig. 5. The frame representation provides natural interpretation of spatial structures of the binary primitives, e.g. "left-below", " right-above" and so on. Frames can be connected in a network of frames where different sub-networks build *associations of frames* with interpretation of particular associations as imaged objects (see Fig. 5 and Fig. 6).

The process of learning of a space structure consists in a filling of slots by the detected primitive patterns if at all. Every slot corresponds to a region of interest in the image. If a primitive pattern is detected within this region, then the corresponding slot is called an active slot and is filled by the correspondent binary primitive and its attributes. Otherwise, the slot is marked as a passive (empty) one and the next region of interest is considered. Such a learning process incorporates the paradigm of an incremental learning because every new slot filling (adding of new information to the object description) occurs after coincidence of structural descriptions by primitive patterns for two local objects with different interpretation.

During the automatic learning, the binary primitives are extracted by using the *clustering* approach as an instance of the unsupervised learning of binary primitives based on a Hamming distance. As a single control parameter, the threshold distance γ is chosen in order to influence on the resulting amount of extracted primitives and hence on the conciseness of object representation. The Hamming distance $d(e_k, \varphi_l)$ between a current cluster center vector $e_k(i,j)$ and the binary fragment $\varphi_l(i,j)$ in a LxL region of attention,

$$d(e_k, \varphi_l) = \sum_{i=1}^{L} \sum_{j=1}^{L} e_k(i,j) \circ \varphi_l(i,j),$$

(symbol "∘" denotes exclusive OR operation) is compared with a threshold distance for each current cluster center k if a primitive pattern was detected in the region of attention. The k-th cluster center, i.e. the resulting binary primitive at the end of the learning phase, is computed by a block averaging of all binary fragments $\varphi_l(i,j)$ whenever $d(e_k, \varphi_l) < \gamma$. It should be noted that the block size could be different from $3^l \times 3^l$, especially, when considering various size of objects of interest. The block averaging is used for three main purposes: 1) size reduction of the current primitive to a single size used at lowest scale; 2) outlier noise removal remaining after binarization; 3) more accurate estimation of a cluster center at small number of available fragments satisfying the distance condition $d(e_k, \varphi_l) < \gamma$.

At the first glance, this approach is similar to the classical structural approach in pattern recognition because of using binary primitives. However, the feature extraction plays a dominant role in the learning and recognition by using the relevance function and binary segmentation because usually few relevant structural features (sufficient for recognition) are extracted during the learning or detection.

3.2 Determination and binarization of regions of attention by using the relevance function

The notion of the relevance function originates from the principle of edge detection by local extrema (or zero crossing) of image derivative operators. Recently, some generalization of this principle has been made toward simulating visual perception in humans and animals. For example, a model for rapid image analysis guided by the local extrema of a saliency map is proposed in Ref. [22, 23]. The approach of relevance function suits also well to the concept of active perception, which is a model-based approach and collects evidence until the object hypothesis attains sufficient confidence.

The relevance function $R\{g(i,j)\}$ is a local image function defined in such a way that it takes larger values at points belonging to an object of interest rather than in background points, $R\{g(i,j)\} \geq R\{g(m,n)\}$ for $\forall$ (i,j)∈O & $\forall$ (m,n)∈B, where O and B are the object region and the background region within a window W, respectively, W=O∪B. This is the first condition the relevance function must obey. The second condition requires that the function $R\{g(i,j)\}$ takes local maximal values at the supposed center location of an object of interest, i.e. they should coincide with the points of the object generating set (see Section 2.1).

The relevance function is defined in two adjacent regions: object region O(i,j) (symmetric structuring element) centered in point (i,j) and background region B(i,j) (background structuring element) be as a ring around it (see Fig. 7). Taking into consideration the structural model of local objects (Section 2.1) and the polynomial regression model of intensity function (Section 2.2), the relevance function $R\{g(i,j)\}$ can be defined as,

$$R\{g(i,j)\} = \frac{1}{|B(i,j)|} \left| \sum_{(m,n)\in B(i,j)} (f(m,n) - g(m,n)) \right| \frac{\delta}{s(i,j)}, \qquad (3.1)$$

where $|B(i,j)|$ denotes the number of points in the background region $B(i,j)$, $f(m,n)$ is the estimated value of intensity function in point (m,n) based on the polynomial coefficients estimated over the region $O(i,j)$, $s(i,j)$ is the local standard deviation in the region $O(i,j)$, δ is a normalizing factor. The use of $s(i,j)$ is aimed at consideration of the object constraint that supposes the polynomial regression modeling of object's intensity (the background's intensity might obey other model) except for a limited amount of outliers. However, in the case when object intensity cannot be modeled by the polynomial regression quite well, the background standard deviation may be considered instead of $s(i,j)$.

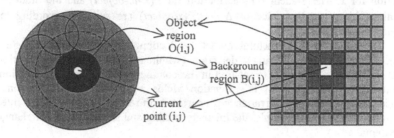

Fig. 7. Two regions O and B in the definition of the relevance function for continuous case (a) and for discrete case (b) with a square 3x3 object structuring element.

The relevance function have to be computed within a region of interest $A(i,j)$ which a square window, the size of which is comparable with the size of structuring element. The point (i_f,j_f) in which the relevance function $R\{g(i,j)\}$ takes maximal value is called a *focus of attention* :

$$(i_f, j_f) = \arg \max_{(m,n)\in A(i,j)} \{R\{g(m,n)\}\} \qquad (3.2)$$

The focus of attention defines a new shifted region of interest, the so-called region of attention $W(i_f,j_f)$ which is centered at this point and the binary segmentation will be performed within this region if at all.

Before the segmentation, the initial hypothesis is generated on a primitive pattern presence (as a part of an object) at the focus of attention. The presence of an object means that the current image fragment is a two-region segment (object's region and background's region) containing an object or its part. If the hypothesis is not true then the next region of interest have to be considered. The normalized local contrast $x=h(i_f,j_f)/s(i_f,j_f)$, where $s(i_f,j_f)$ is the standard deviation, is chosen as a basic feature for initial hypothesis generation and testing with respect to a location (i_f,j_f). The values of $h(i_f,j_f)$ and $s(i_f,j_f)$ are computed by using estimated regression coefficients $\{\rho_{r,s}(i,j)\}$ of the underlying polynomial model of image intensity by Eq. (2.2) [21]. A Bayesian paradigm has been selected for the hypothesis generation using the normalized local contrast because it combines prior available knowledge with new obtained knowledge based on the value of $x = h(i_f, j_f)/s(i_f, j_f)$. A lower bound Δ for the normalized local contrast is supposed to be known. Then, the null hypothesis that no primitive pattern is present in point (i_f, j_f) will be tested against concurrent hypothesis supposing a pattern presence with the normalized contrast Δ. Given the prior probabilities $P(object)$ and $P(no\text{-}object)$ and the confidence level p (as a probability bound for object absence), the decision on the object absence is made upon considering the inequality:

$$\frac{P(x\,/\,no-object)}{P(x\,/\,object)} > \frac{p}{1-p} \cdot \frac{P(object)}{P(no-object)}, \tag{3.3}$$

where $P(x/object)$ and $P(x/no\text{-}object)$ are the respective conditional probabilities. The explicit rule of decision making is obtained after assuming a particular conditional distribution for x. The Student's T-distribution for $P(x/no\text{-}object)$ and the Student's T-distribution shifted on the value of Δ for $P(x/object)$ are suitable according to the underlying image model.

According to the structural model in Section 2.1, the introduced relevance function allows translation-invariant detection (within regions of interest) of primitive patterns and ensures invariance to rotation in the continuous case (Fig. 7a). Additionally, the multi-scale computation of this function yields a scale-invariant detection. The relevance function has useful invariance properties with respect to the assumed intensity model in Section 2.2, for example, the intensity scaling and shifting does not change the local extrema.

The goal of the local binarization is the reduction of store space and time for learning and detection of local objects of interest. Since the image intensity varies significantly within the given structuring element at larger scales, it is reasonable to use a variable threshold, whose variations follow the intensity changes. The optimal threshold for binarization can be derived by the likelihood ratio principle using the described model of a two-region image fragment (see Fig. 2). Assuming the underlying image model and white Gaussian noise according to Eq.(2.2) and Eq.(2.4), the residuals of the polynomial regression for object and background pixels have two Gaussian distributions $N(0, \sigma^2)$ and $N(h, \sigma^2)$, respectively. The likelihood ratio test for binarization in this case is reduced to image intensity comparison with a variable threshold [14],

$$g(i, j) > f(i, j) + \frac{h}{2} + \frac{\sigma^2}{h} \cdot \ln\theta, \tag{3.4}$$

where $f(i,j)$ is the estimated object (or background in the dual case) intensity in the form of a polynomial function, θ is a constant term depending on the prior probabilities of object an background, h is the estimated local contrast as the difference between the object intensity and background intensity. The value of noise variance σ^2 is supposed to be known or already estimated, otherwise it is estimated in the current region of interest. Intensity attributes (e.g., contrast, edge smoothness, intensity flatness, etc.) can be obtained in the result of parameter estimation during the initial hypothesis testing and binarization of a current region of attention. For example, the local contrast h in Eq. (3.4) can be robustly (adaptively) estimated by the maximum likelihood principle considering different edge positions.

4 Experimental Results

The described novel approach to detection of primitive patterns and their spatial aggregation has been tested on synthetic and real radiographic images in industrial and medical imaging. The main purpose of testing on synthetic images was the performance evaluation of the relevance function approach. The quality of binary segmentation of primitive patterns using the relevance function approach has been investigated experimentally by the segmentation error E with respect to signal-to-noise (S/N) ratio for a synthetic image fragment containing one particular primitive pattern corrupted by noise (Fig. 8). The graph in Fig. 9 illustrates the obtained experimental dependence using the normalized Hamming distance as the segmentation error (see Section 3.1). The deterioration of segmentation at present noise with outliers is due to a bias in parameter estimation using the least squares method.

The first group of test images is constituted by radiographic images from non-destructive testing of weld quality, one example of which is shown in Fig. 10. The so-called artificial binary primitives have been defined explicitly using the underlying image model from Section 2.1. In this case study, all primitive patterns have been represented within a 3x3 window at all defined scales providing an additional clustering by reduction of resolution at higher scales. The results of selection and detection of primitive patterns are shown in Fig. 11 for several scales. For instance, the detected patterns on the greatest scale allow detection of such an object of interest as the weld seam. The medium scale local binarization yields detection of some details of the weld seam. In all tested examples, the polynomial regression of zero-order and first-order have been used with square or circle structuring elements $3^l x 3^l$, $l=0,1,...$ The second group of test images is constituted by conventional and tomographic images from chest radiology in medical imaging, one example of which is shown in Fig. 12. The results of primitive pattern detection on this image are shown in Fig. 13 for several scales when using artificial binary primitives. For example, the local binarization at the greatest scale allows the detection of such object of interest as a lesion. The local binarization at medium scale provides detection of the lesion details. The segmentation result for a fragment of real radiographic image in the region of attention with inherent noise using the relevance function approach in shown in Fig. 14.

Fig. 8. A magnified test fragment of synthetic image with added Gaussian noise.

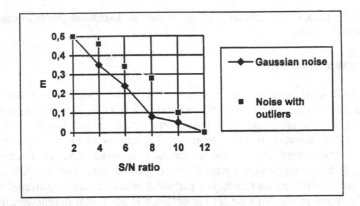

Fig. 9. Error of binary segmentation (E) vs. signal-to-noise (S/N) ratio for the synthetic image fragment in Fig. 10 after application of the segmentation algorithm. The Hamming distance normalized by the total number of pixels has been chosen as the segmentation error.

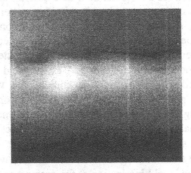

Fig. 10. Initial radiographic image of weld for non-destructive evaluation of weld quality.

Fig. 11. Result of primitive pattern detection on the radiograph shown in Fig. 10 by means of the multi-scale image analysis using relevance function. A set of artificial binary primitives has been used.

Fig. 12. A fragment of a tomographic image used for medical diagnosis.

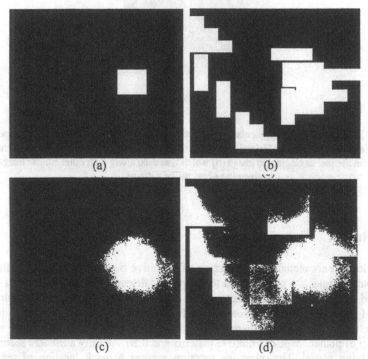

Fig. 13. Result of primitive pattern detection on the image in fig. 12 by means of the multi-scale image analysis using the relevance function approach: (a, b) detected primitive patterns at two coarse scales; (c) binarization results at the coarsest scale; (d) superimposed binarization results at two coarse scales.

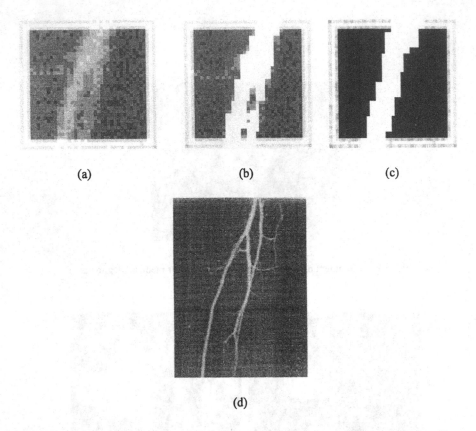

(a)   (b)   (c)

(d)

Fig. 14. Example of binary segmentation (b) of a real image fragment (a) and the corresponding binary primitive (magnified) obtained after the learning process (c). The magnified segment (a) is taken from the real angiographic image (d) which was used along with other similar images for learning of primitive patterns.

5 Conclusion

The developed new method for extraction of primitive patterns as relevant features on radiographic images is a model-based technique for detection of local objects of interest interpreted as flaws or abnormalities (in the case of medical imaging). The introduced concept of image relevance function has the following advantageous features in learning and detection of primitive patterns. It is a feature-based approach with separate description of planar shape of primitive patterns and their intensity attributes according to the underlying model. The relevance function ensures a quick location of regions of attention containing very probably relevant primitive patterns. On the other hand, a meaningful structural description of local objects is achieved in the form of hierarchical (multi-scale) structures as aggregations of primitive patterns. Shape of complex objects can be represented as spatial structures (frames) of binary primitives with corresponding attributes.

The use of the likelihood ratio principle and variable decision threshold contributes to a reliable binarization of primitive patterns and detection for low-contrast objects on noisy background.

The presented method has been tested on synthetic and on real radiographic images in non-destructive testing of weld joints (industrial application) and chest radiology (medical application). The experimental results confirm the model adequacy to real radiographic images and a high performance of the structural feature extraction.

The future work in this context will be directed toward incorporation of a confidence control during object detection into the process of learning of primitives and subsequent learning of structural description of local objects. The computation of relevance function and binary segmentation should be generalized to the case of present outliers.

References

1. A. Kehoe and G. A. Parker. Image processing for industrial radiographic inspection: image inspection, *British Journal of NDT*, Vol. 32, N. 4, pp. 183-190, 1990.
2. M. Sonka *et al.* Adaptive approach to accurate analysis of small-diameter vessels in cineangiograms, *IEEE Trans. on Medical Imaging*, Vol. 16, No. 1, pp. 87-95, 1997.
3. J. J. Heine *et al.* Multiresolution statistical analysis of high-resolution digital mammograms, *IEEE Trans. on Medical Imaging*, Vol. 16, No. 5, pp. 503-515, 1997.
4. A. K. Jain and M.-P. Dubuisson. Segmentation of X-ray and C-scan images of fiber reinforced composite materials, *Pattern Recognition*, Vol. 25, No. 3, pp. 257-270, 1992.
5. T. W. Liao and J. Ni. An automated radiographic NDT system for weld inspection: Part I – Weld extraction, *NDT&E International*, Vol. 29, No. 3, pp. 157-162, 1996.
6. T. W. Liao and Y. Li. An automated radiographic NDT system for weld inspection: Part II – Flaw detection, *NDT&E International*, Vol. 31, No. 3, pp. 183-192, 1998.
7. S. Mallat. A theory for multi-resolution image signal decomposition: the wavelet representation, *IEEE Trans., Vol. PAMI-11*, pp. 674-693, 1989.
8. Ya. Chitti. Detection of small intensity changes in CCD images with non-uniform illumination and large signal dependent noise, *CVGIP: Graph. Models and Image Processing*, Vol. 59, No. 3, pp. 139-148, 1997.
9. C.H. Chen and G.G. Lee. On digital mammogram segmentation and microcalcification detection using multi-resolution wavelet analysis, *CVGIP: Graph. Models and Image Processing*, Vol. 59, No. 5, pp. 348-364, 1997.
10. K. Fukunaga. *Introduction to Statistical Pattern Recognition*, Second Edition, New York: Academic Press, 1990.
11. K. Kanatani. Hypothesizing and testing geometric properties of image data, *CVGIP: Image Understanding* Vol. 54, pp. 349-357, 1992.
12. M. D. Wheeler and K. Ikeuchi. Sensor modeling, probabilistic hypothesis generation, and robust localization for object recognition, *IEEE Trans. Vol. PAMI-17*, No. 3, pp. 252-266, 1995.
13. A. B. Frakt, W.C. Karl and A. S. Willsky. A multiscale hypothesis testing approach to anomaly detection and localization from noisy tomographic data, *IEEE Trans. Image Proc.*, Vol. 7, No. 6, pp. 404-420, 1998.

14. R. M. Palenichka and U. Zscherpel. Detection of flaws in radiographic images by hypothesis generation and testing approach, Proc. Int. Workshop *Advances in Signal Processing for NDE of Materials*, pp. 235-243, 1998.
15. A. Rosenfeld and S. Banerjee. Maximum-likelihood edge detection in digital signals, *CVGIP: Image Understanding*, Vol. 55, No. 1, 1992.
16. L.P. Kaebling and A. W. Moore. Reinforcement learning: a survey, *Journal of Artificial Intelligence Research*, No. 4, pp. 237-285, 1996.
17. P. Perner, T. P. Belikova and N. I. Yashunskaya. Knowledge acquisition by symbolic decision tree induction for interpretation of digital images in radiology, Proc. Int. Workshop *Structural and Syntactic Pattern Recognition*, pp. 208-220, 1996.
18. S. Katsuragawa *et al.* Classification of normal and abnormal lungs with interstatial diseases by rule-based methods and artificial neural networks, *Journal of Digital Imaging*, vol. 10, No. 3, pp. 108-114, 1997.
19. P. Perner. A knowledge-based image inspection system for automatic defect recognition, classification, and process diagnosis, *Machine Vision and Applications*, No. 7, pp. 135-147, 1994.
20. P. Perner and W. Paetzold. An incremental learning system for interpretation of images, Proc. Int. Workshop *Shape, Structure and Pattern Recognition*, pp. 311-319, 1994.
21. R. M. Palenichka *et al.* Structure-adaptive image filtering using order statistics, *Journal of Electronic Imaging*, No. 2, pp. 339-349, 1998.
22. L. Itti, C. Koch, and E. Niebur. A model of saliency-based visual attention for rapid scene analysis, *IEEE Trans.*, Vol. PAMI-20, No. 11, pp. 1254-1259, 1998.
23. T. C. Folsom and R. B. Pinter. Primitive features by steering, quadrature, and scale, *IEEE Trans.*, Vol. PAMI-20, No. 11, pp. 1161-1173, 1998.

Independent Feature Analysis for Image Retrieval

Jing Peng* and Bir Bhanu

Center for Research in Intelligent Systems
University of California, Riverside, CA 92521
Email: {jp,bhanu}@vislab.ucr.edu

Abstract. Content-based image retrieval methods based on the Euclidean metric expect the feature space to be isotropic. They suffer from unequal differential relevance of features in computing the similarity between images in the input feature space. We propose a learning method that attempts to overcome this limitation by capturing local differential relevance of features based on user feedback. This feedback, in the form of accept or reject examples generated in response to a query image, is used to locally estimate the strength of features along each dimension while taking into consideration the correlation between features. This results in local neighborhoods that are constricted along feature dimensions that are most relevant, while enlongated along less relevant ones. In addition to exploring and exploiting local principal information, the system seeks a global space for efficient independent feature analysis by combining such local information. We provide experimental results that demonstrate the efficacy of our technique using real-world data.

1 Introduction

The rapid advance in digital imaging technology makes possible the wide spread use of image libraries and databases. This in turn demands effective means for access to such databases. It has been well documented that simple textual annotations for images are often ambiguous and inadequate for image database search. Thus, retrieval based on image "content" becomes very attractive [2, 5, 6, 8, 9]. Generally, a set of features (color, shape, texture, etc.) are extracted from an image to represent its content. As such, image database retrieval becomes a K nearest neighbor (K-NN) search in a multidimensional space defined by these features under a given similarity metric.

Simple K nearest neighbor search, as an image retrieval procedure, returns the K images closest to the query. Obviously this involves the issue of measuring the closeness or similarity between two images. The most common measure of the similarity between two images, represented by their feature vectors $\mathbf{x}$ and $\mathbf{y}$,

---

* Current address: Computer Science Department, Oklahoma State University, Stillwater, OK 74078. Email: jpeng@cs.okstate.edu is the distance between them. If the Euclidean distance

$$D(\mathbf{x}, \mathbf{y}) = \sqrt{\sum_{i=1}^{q}(x_i - y_i)^2}$$

is used, then the K closest images to the query $\mathbf{x}_Q$ are computed according to

$$\{\mathbf{x}|D(\mathbf{x}, \mathbf{x}_Q) \leq d_K\},$$

where d_K is the Kth order statistic of $\{D(\mathbf{x}_i, \mathbf{x}_Q)\}_1^N$. Here N is the number of images in the database. The major appeal for simple K-NN search methods resides in their ability to produce continuous and overlapping rather than fixed neighborhoods, and to use a different neighborhood for each individual query so that, to the extent possible, all points in the neighborhood are close to the query.

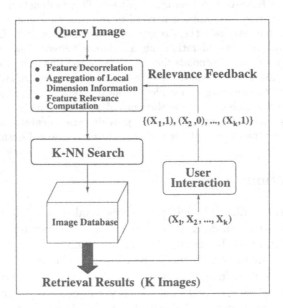

Fig. 1. System for learning feature relevance.

One problem with the Euclidean metric, however, is that it does not take into account the influence of the scale of each feature variable in the distance computation. Changing the scale of a feature dimension in different amountss alters the overall contribution of that dimension to the distance computation, hence its influence in the nearest neighbors retrieved. This is usually considered undesirable. An additional limitation is that the use of the Euclidean distance, while simple computationally, implies that the input space is isotropic. However, isotropy is often invalid and generally undesirable in many practical applications.

In this paper, we propose a novel method that provides a solution to the problems discussed above. With this method image retrieval system is able to learn differential feature relevance in an efficient manner that takes into account the correlation between features, and that is highly adaptive to query locations. In addition, by accumulating experience obtained at each iteration the system is capable of, to the extent possible, continuously improving its retrieval performance.

Figure 1 shows the functional architecture of our system. The user presents a query image to the system. At this time feature relevance weighting is initialized to $1/q$, where q is the dimension of the feature space. The system carries out image retrieval using a K-NN search based on current weightings to compute the similarity between the query and all images in the database, and returns the top K nearest images. The user then marks the retrieved images as positive (class label 1) or negative (class label 0). In practice, only images that are not similar to the query need to be marked. These marked images constitute training data. From the query and the training data, the system performs principal component analysis on images closest to the query to compute the eigenspace of the local scatter matrix. The system then carries out feature relevance (copmutation of weights) within the eigenspace, from which a new round of retrieval begins. The above process repeats until the user is satisfied with the results or the number of iterations exceeds a given threshold.

2 Local Feature Relevance

The performance of retrieval for image databases can be characterized by two key factors. *First*, for a given query image, the relevance of all the features input to the retrieval procedure may not be equal for retrieving similar images. Irrelevant features often hurt retrieval performance. *Second*, feature relevance depends on the location at which the query is made in the feature space. Capturing such relevance information is prerequisite for constructing successful retrieval procedures in image databases. The objective of our approach is to construct retrieval methods that inherit the appealing properties of K-NN search, while at the same time overcoming its limitations by capturing the notion of local feature relevance.

The retrieval problem is opposite to typical classification problems based on regression [1, 3, 4]. While the goal in classification is to predict the class label of an input query from nearby samples, the goal in retrieval is to find samples having the same "label" as that of the query. Moreover, many "lazy" learning techniques in classification lend themselves to the kind of problems retrieval tasks may face.

2.1 Local Relevance Measure

In a two class (1/0) classification problem, the class label $y \in \{0, 1\}$ at query $\mathbf{x}$ is treated as a random variable from a distribution with the probabilities

$\{\Pr(1|\mathbf{x}), \Pr(0|\mathbf{x})\}$. We then have

$$f(\mathbf{x}) \doteq \Pr(y = 1|\mathbf{x}) = E(y|\mathbf{x}), \tag{1}$$

To predict y at $\mathbf{x}$, $f(\mathbf{x})$ is first estimated from a set of training data using techniques based on regression, such as the least-squares estimate. The Bayes classifier can thus be applied to achieve optimal classification performance. In image retrieval, however, the "label" of $\mathbf{x}$ is known, which is 1 (positive image) in terms of the notation given above. All that is required is to exploit differential relevance of the input features to image retrieval. In the absence of any variable assignments, the least-squares estimate for $f(\mathbf{x})$ is

$$E[f] = \int f(\mathbf{x})p(\mathbf{x})dx, \tag{2}$$

where $p(\mathbf{x})$ is the joint density. Now given only that $\mathbf{x}$ is known at dimension $x_i = z_i$. The least-squares estimate becomes

$$E[f|x_i = z_i] = \int f(\mathbf{x})p(\mathbf{x}|x_i = z_i)dx. \tag{3}$$

Here $p(\mathbf{x}|x_i = z_i)$ is the conditional density of the other input variables.

In image retrieval, $f(\mathbf{z}) = 1$, where $\mathbf{z}$ is the query. Then

$$[(f(\mathbf{z}) - 0) - (f(\mathbf{z}) - E[f|x_i = z_i])] = E[f|x_i = z_i] \tag{4}$$

represents a reduction in error between the two predictions. We can now define a measure of feature relevance at query $\mathbf{z}$ as

$$r_i(\mathbf{z}) = E[f|x_i = z_i]. \tag{5}$$

The relative relevance can be used as a weighting scheme. The following exponential weighting scheme

$$w_i(\mathbf{z}) = \exp(Tr_i(\mathbf{z}))/ \sum_{l=1}^{q} \exp(Tr_l(\mathbf{z})) \tag{6}$$

is employed in this paper. Here T is a parameter that can be chosen to maximize (minimize) the influence of r_i on w_i. From (6), we obtain the weighted Euclidean distance

$$D(\mathbf{x}, \mathbf{y}) = \sqrt{\sum_{i=1}^{q} w_i(x_i - y_i)^2}. \tag{7}$$

In order to estimate (6), one must first compute (5). The retrieved images with relevance feedback from the user can be used as training data to obtain estimates for (5), hence (6). Let $\{\mathbf{x}_j, y_j\}_1^K$ be the training data, where $\mathbf{x}_j$ denotes the feature vector representing jth retrieved image, and y_j is either 1 (positive image) or 0 (negative image) marked by the user as the class label associated with x_j. Since there may not be any data at $x_i = z_i$, the data from the vicinity of x_i at z_i are used to estimate $E[y|x_i = z_i]$. Therefore, based on (1), (5) can be estimated according to

$$\hat{E}[y|x_i = z_i] = \frac{\sum_{j=1}^{K} y_j 1(|x_{ji} - z_i| \leq \Omega)}{\sum_{j=1}^{K} 1(|x_{ji} - z_i| \leq \Omega)} \qquad (8)$$

where $1(\cdot)$ is an indicator function. Ω can be chosen so that there are sufficient data for the estimation of (3). In this paper, Ω is chosen such that

$$\sum_{j=1}^{K} 1(|x_{ji} - z_i| \leq \Omega) = C, \qquad (9)$$

where $C \leq K$ is a constant. It represents a trade-off between bias and variance.

3 Feature Decorrelation Using Local Principal Information

In order for Equation (5) to be effective, features must be independent. However, this condition can hardly be met in practice. Often, there is a degree of correlation among the input features. Our goal here is to seek a space into which to project data so that the feature dimensions coincide with the eigenvectors of the space, whereby feature relevance can be estimated at the query along individual dimensions independently. The novelty here is in choosing the space using pooled local principal information.

We begin with linear multivariate analysis. Given a set of q-dimensional data $\{x_j\}_{j=1}^{n}$, the eigenspace is the space spanned by eigenvectors onto which the feature dimensions representing the projected data are statistically uncorrelated. Let $\bar{x}$ denote the mean for the observed data. Then this space corresponds to the eigenspace of the data points $x_j - \bar{x}$, or the local covariance matrix at the query.

In the context of image retrieval, the basic idea is to compute $x_j - \bar{x}$ at a given query using only local information, and then perform the principal component analysis for the local scatter matrix. Specifically, let $\{x_j(i)\}_1^n$ be the set of n nearest neighbors obtained at query i, and $\bar{x}(i)$ be the associated mean vector. Also let

$$S(i) = \frac{1}{n} \sum_{j=0}^{n} (x_j(i) - \bar{x}(i))(x_j(i) - \bar{x}(i))^t \qquad (10)$$

be the scatter matrix at query i, where t denotes transpose. We compute the space spanned by the eigenvectors of $S(i)$ (for query i) onto which the feature relevance analysis of the projected data can be performed independently along each dimension.

The overall algorithm is summarized as follows, where K denotes the number of images returned to the user, and M is an adjustable procedural parameter.

In general, $M \gg K$. We call this algorithm (Figure 2) *adaptive feature relevance estimation* (AFRE). Note that n is the number of data points used to compute the local scatter matrix, whereas M represents the number of data points projected onto the eigenspace within which feature relevance computation is carried out.

---

1. Let i be current query; initialize weight vector **w** to $\{1/q\}_1^q$; training set: $Tset = nil$.
2. Compute $\{x_j\}_1^n$, set of n nearest neighbors using **w**; return the first K nearest neighbors in $\{x_j\}_1^n$ to the user.
3. User marks the K retrieved images as positive (1) or negative (0).
4. Calculate the local scatter matrix $\mathbf{S}(i)$ using $\{x_j\}_1^n$.
5. Project M nearest neighbors onto the eigenspace of $\mathbf{S}(i)$.
6. While *precision* $< \theta$ Do
   (a) $Tset = Tset \cup \{K \ points\}$.
   (b) Update **w** (Eq. (6)) in the transformed space using training data in $Tset$.
   (c) Compute K nearest neighbors using **w** in the transformed space.
   (d) User marks the K points as positive (1) or negative (0).

Fig. 2. The AFRE Algorithm.

The algorithm just described computes the local scatter matrix $\mathbf{S}(i)$ for each given query i. As such, it computes a neighborhood that is highly adaptive to the query location, thereby significantly improving retrieval performance. From a computational viewpoint, however, the amount of computation required for performing principal component analysis might impede its real-time applications. This is particularly true if the feature space has high dimensionality, since a large number of data points may be required to compute the $q \times q$ elements of $\mathbf{S}(i)$ and perform corresponding principal component analysis for each given query. We seek a method here to overcome this limitation by finding a space that is close to the eigenspace of the average local scatter matrices, $\mathbf{S}(i)$s, over all queries.

If we denote by **U** an orthonormal basis for the q dimensional space, we can obtain the space by minimizing the following total residual sum of squares

$$R(\mathbf{U}) = \sum_{i=1}^{N} \sum_{j=1}^{n} (\tilde{\mathbf{x}}_j^t(i)\tilde{\mathbf{x}}_j(i) - \tilde{\mathbf{x}}_j^t(i)\mathbf{U}\mathbf{U}^t\tilde{\mathbf{x}}_j(i)),$$

where $\tilde{\mathbf{x}}_j(i) = (\mathbf{x}_j(i) - \bar{\mathbf{x}}(i))$, n is the number of local retrievals, and N the number of queries. We can obtain the minimum of the above equation by maximizing

$$tr\mathbf{U}^t \{\sum_{i=1}^{N} \mathbf{S}(i)\}\mathbf{U},$$

where tr represents the trace operation of a matrix. This can be solved by finding the eigenvectors of the following matrix

$$\bar{\mathbf{S}} = \sum_{i=1}^{N} \mathbf{S}(i)/N,$$

which is the average scatter matrices over all queries. The main benefit of averaging is that it reduces variance due to skewed local information, thereby improving overall estimation accuracy. The algorithm is summarized in Figure 3, which we call *learning feature relevance estimation* (LFRE).

---

1. Let i be current query; initialize weight vector $\mathbf{w}$ to $\{1/q\}_1^q$; training set: $Tset = nil$; $\bar{\mathbf{S}} = 0$; $l=0$.
2. Compute $\{\mathbf{x}_j\}_1^n$, set of n nearest neighbors using $\mathbf{w}$; return the first K nearest neighbors $\{\mathbf{x}_j\}_1^n$ to the user.
3. User marks the K retrieved images as positive (1) or negative (0).
4. Calculate the local scatter matrix $\mathbf{S}(i)$ using $\{\mathbf{x}_j\}_1^n$.
5. $\bar{\mathbf{S}} = \bar{\mathbf{S}} + (\mathbf{S}(i) - \bar{\mathbf{S}})/(l+1)$; $l = l+1$.
6. Project M nearest neighbors onto the eigenspace of $\bar{\mathbf{S}}$.
7. While *precision* $< \theta$ Do
   (a) $Tset = Tset \cup \{K\ points\}$.
   (b) Update $\mathbf{w}$ (Eq. (6)) in the transformed space using training data in $Tset$.
   (c) Compute K nearest neighbors using $\mathbf{w}$ in the transformed space.
   (d) User marks the K points as positive (1) or negative (0).

Fig. 3. The LFRE Algorithm.

While LFRE demonstrates improvements over AFRE on the problems we examine here, it is still a rather computationally intensive process. We propose to approximate the average scatter matrix without compromising the level of achievable performance. The basic assumption is that $\bar{\mathbf{S}}$ can be reasonably estimated from a few representative local $\mathbf{S}(i)$s. Specifically, we approximate $\bar{\mathbf{S}}$ by incrementally combining the local $\mathbf{S}(i)$'s computed for the queries seen so far, similar to the way it is computed in LFRE. However, the estimation process stops when $\bar{\mathbf{S}}$ becomes sufficiently accurate. Subsequent feature relevance estimates are carried out in the space spanned by the eigenvectors of $\bar{\mathbf{S}}$. In this paper, we measure the accuracy of $\bar{\mathbf{S}}$ using a matrix norm ν. That is, we say that $\bar{\mathbf{S}}$ is accurate if $\nu(\bar{\mathbf{S}}_{t+1} - \bar{\mathbf{S}}_t)$ is sufficiently small. While other measures exist, we do not intend to address this issue further in the rest of this paper.

If we replace lines 4 and 5 in LFRE by the following, we arrive at the *approximate learning feature relevance estimation* (A-LFRE) algorithm (Figure 4), where $\bar{\mathbf{S}}_o$ is initialized to 0.

Here $\nu(\cdot)$ represents the matrix norm operator, and δ is a constant parameter input to the algorithm.

4. If not $(\nu(\bar{S} - \bar{S}_o) < \delta)$ then
   a. $\bar{S}_o = \bar{S}$.
   b. Calculate the local scatter matrix $S(i)$ using the K points.
   c. $\bar{S} = \bar{S} + (S(i) - \bar{S})/(l + 1); l = l + 1$.

Fig. 4. The A-LFRE Algorithm.

4 Empirical Results

In the following we compare three competing retrieval methods using real data.
(a): The probabilistic feature relevance learning (PFRL) algorithm [8], coupled
with the exponential weighting scheme (6). Note that this algorithm, unlike the
ones described above, computes local feature relevance in the original feature
space. It does not perform feature decorrelation. (b): The AFRE algorithm described above. Again, the algorithm is coupled with the exponential weighting
scheme (6). (c): The LFRE algorithm described above. Similar to (a) and (b)
above the algorithm is coupled with the exponential weighting scheme (6). Note
that there is a fourth method, the simple (unweighted) K-NN method, that is
being compared against implicitly. The first retrieval by all the three methods
is based on the unweighted K-NN method. Also, in all the experiments, the
performance is measured using the following average retrieval precision [8, 9].

$$precision = \frac{Positive Retrievals}{Total Retrievals} \times 100\%. \tag{11}$$

In all the experiments the input features are first normalized. The normalization is performed along each feature dimension over the entire data set in
such a way that the normalized feature values lie between 0 and 1. This process
does not in any way provide bias in favor of any particular learning method. It
simply removes some of the artifacts due to different scales of variables that are
generally considered undesirable in the absence of any additional information.
This is particularly true for retrieval procedures whose distance computation is
based on the Euclidean metric.

4.1 The Problems

Database 1. The data, taken from the UCI repository [7], consist of images
that were drawn randomly from a database of 7 outdoor images. The images
were hand segmented by the creators of the database to classify each pixel. Each
image is a region. There are 7 classes: *brickface, sky, foliage, cement, window,
path* and *grass*, each having 330 instances. Thus, there are total 2310 images in
the database. These images are represented by 19 real valued attributes. These
features are basically statistical moments and line counts. For further details,
see [7].

Database 2. The data are obtained from MIT Media Lab at: whitechapel. media.mit.edu/pub/VisTex. There are total 640 images of 128 × 128 in the database with 15 classes. The number of images in each class varies from 16 to 80. The images in this database are represented by 8 Gabor filters (2 scales and 4 orientations). The mean and the standard deviation of the magnitude of the transform coefficients are used as feature components after being normalized by the standard deviations of the respective features over the images in the entire database. Figure 5 shows sample images from the MIT dataset.

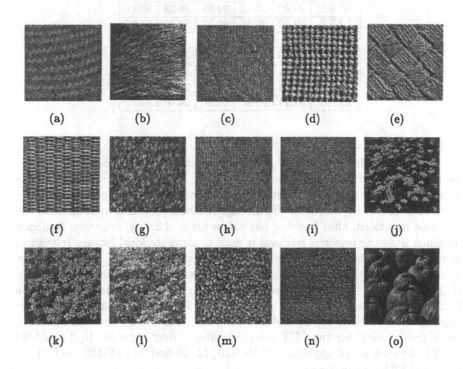

Fig. 5. Sample images from MIT database.

4.2 Results

For both the problems, each image in the database is selected as a query and top 20 (corresponding to parameter K in the algorithms described above) nearest neighbors are returned that provide necessary relevance feedback. Note that only negative images (that are different from the query) need to be marked in practice. Also, M was set to 400 in algorithms AFRE and LFRE (Figures 2 and 3) in these experiments. The average retrieval precision is summarized in

Table 1. There are three rows under each problem in the table, comparing the performance of the three competing methods.

Table 1. Average retrieval precision for real data.

UCI Data Set					
Method	0 (rf)	1 (rf)	2 (rf)	3(rf)	4 (rf)
PFRL	90.90	94.67	95.78	96.49	96.79
AFRE	90.90	93.33	94.89	96.03	96.41
LFRE	90.90	94.36	95.87	97.01	97.32
MIT Data Set					
Method	0 (rf)	1 (rf)	2 (rf)	3 (rf)	4 (rf)
PFRL	81.14	85.30	86.95	88.71	89.46
AFRE	81.14	89.97	91.52	92.91	93.19
LFRE	81.14	88.80	92.36	94.46	94.78

The second column in Table 1 shows the average retrieval precision obtained by the method without any relevance feedback (rf). That is, it is the results of applying the simple K-NN method using unweighted Euclidean metric. The third column and beyond show the average retrieval precision computed, at the specified iterations, after learning has taken place. That is, relevance feedback obtained from the previous retrieval is used to estimate local feature relevance, hence a new weighting. The procedural parameters T (6), C (9) and n (Figures 2 and 3) input to the algorithms under comparison were determined empirically that achieved the best performance. They are by no means exhaustive. For the UCI image database, they were set to 13 and 19 (PFRL, parameter n is not applicable to PFRL), 13, 21 and 200 (AFRE), and 13, 27 and 200 (LFRE), respectively; while for the MIT image database, they were set to 13 and 20 (PFRL, again n is not applicable to PFRL), 15, 19 and 50 (AFRE), and 14, 19 and 70 (LFRE), respectively.

It can be seen from Table 1 that LFRE demonstrates performance improvement across the tasks and over both PFRL and AFRE. However, the improvement is most pronounced on the MIT data set. The reason is that features based on Gabor wavelet filters exhibit a degree of correlation because these filters partially overlap. On the other hand, the features representing the UCI data set are less correlated. Overall, the results show convincingly that feature decorrelation plays important role in improving feature relevance estimates.

An additional experiment was also carried out to examine the performance of the A-LFRE algorithm (Figure 4). In this experiment, 600 images are randomly chosen from the MIT database as query images. We ran both LFRE and A-LFRE on this database and obtained the average retrieval precisions on the query sets. We repeated this process for 10 times, and plotted the average precisions over the 10 runs at iterations 1, 2, 3, 4 and 5 in Figure 6. Note that instead of computing a matrix norm to measure the accuracy of $\bar{S}$, as a first approximation A-LFRE simply computes a fixed number of updates to $\bar{S}$, after which $\bar{S}$ is fixed throughout.

The plots in Figure 6 show that after only a few updates of the average scatter matrix A-LFRE approached the level of performance obtained by LFRE. Furthermore, A-LFRE did so with far less computation than that required by LFRE, thereby demonstrating its computational efficiency and advantage in practical applications. We performed similar experiments on the UCI database, where 2000 images are randomly selected as query images. We omit the details of the experiments except stating that similar results to that of the MIT database were obtained.

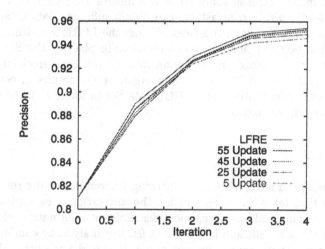

Fig. 6. Performance of the A-LFRE algorithm on the MIT database.

4.3 Discussions

One might contemplate to use a covariance matrix computed from a set of samples to decorrelate the entire database off-line, and then to perform feature relevance estimate in the transformed feature space using the techniques presented in this paper. There may be several reasons against such an idea. the most important reason is when the database is dynamic, as is often the case in practice, such an off-line operation may not be feasible. It is inherently inflexible. Furthermore, such a global process may not be able to sufficiently capture the distinct local structures of the input space. In one experiment the entire UCI data set is used to compute the scatter matrix. We then project the original data into the eigenspace of the matrix. The subsequent feature relevance estimate is carried out in this transformed space. We obtained the following average retrieval precisions at iterations 1, 2, 3, 4 and 5: 91.14, 94.99, 96.07, 96.70 and 96.86, respectively. We ran the same experiment on the MIT database described above and obtained similar results. These results and those obtained earlier (entries under UCI Data Set in Table 1) clearly favor the online techniques proposed in this paper.

Another possibility for feature decorrelation is to project the data into the eigenspace of the between sum-of-squares matrices. That is, we can replace the $S(i)$ matrix with a between sum-of-squares matrix in our algorithms described above. It can be argued that between sum-of-squares matrices carry more discriminant information. However, the computation of such matrices requires sufficient data for each class (1/0), which is difficult to obtain in the context of content-based image retrieval (only 20 or less images are returned to the user for relevance feedback). In contrast, we can obtain sufficient data to accurately estimate within sum-of-squares matrices. We ran the LFRE algorithm with the locally weighted between sum-of-squares matrices in place of the $S(i)$s on the UCI data set, and obtained the following average retrieval precisions: 90.90, 94.43, 95.55, 96.51 and 96.79, respectively. Again, these results in comparison with the earlier results (entries under UCI Data Set in Table 1) favor the techniques presented in this paper.

5 Conclusions

This paper presents a novel method for learning differential feature relevance for a given query that takes into consideration the correlation between features. In addition to exploring and exploiting local discriminant information, the system seeks a global space for efficient independent feature analysis by combining such local information. Furthermore, by accumulating experience obtained at each iteration the system is capable of, to the extent possible, continuously improving its retrieval performance. The experimental results presented demonstrate the potential for substantial improvements over both the technique presented here and simple K-NN search.

Acknowledgements

This work was supported by DARPA/AFOSR grant F49620-97-1-0184. The contents of the information do not necessarily reflect the position or the policy of the U.S. Government.

References

1. R.H. Creecy, B.M. Masand, S.J. Smith, and D.L. Waltz, "Trading Mips and Memory for Knowledge Engineering," *CACM*, 35:48-64, 1992.
2. M. Flickner et al., "Query by Image and Video Content: The QBIC system" *IEEE Computer*, pp. 23-31, September 1995.
3. J.H. Friedman "Flexible Metric Nearest Neighbor Classification," Tech. Report, Dept. of Statistics, Stanford University, 1994.
4. T. Hastie and R. Tibshirani, "Discriminant adaptive nearest neighbor classification," *IEEE Transactions on Pattern Analysis and Machine Intelligence*, Vol. 18 No. 6, pp. 607-616, June 1996.
5. W.Y. Ma and B.S. Manjunath, "Texture features and learning similarity," Proceedings of IEEE Computer Society Conference on Computer Vision and Pattern Recognition, San Francisco, pp. 425-430, June, 1996.
6. T.P. Minka and R.W. Picard, "Interactive Learning with a "Society of Models"", *Pattern Recognition*, vol.30, (no.4):565-81, April 1997.
7. P.M. Murphy and D.W. Aha, UCI repository of machine learning databases. 1995. www.cs.uci.edu/~mlearn/MLRepository.html.
8. J. Peng, B. Bhanu and S. Qing, "Probabilistic Feature Relevance Learning for Content-Based Image Retrieval," *Computer Vision and Image Understanding*, 1999.
9. Y. Rui, T.S. Huang and S. Mehrotra, "Content-based image retrieval with relevance feedback in MARS," Proceedings of IEEE International Conference on Image Processing, pp. 815-818, Santa Barbara, California, October, 1997.

Non-hierarchical Clustering with Rival Penalized Competitive Learning for Information Retrieval *

Irwin King and Tak-Kan Lau

Department of Computer Science & Engineering
The Chinese University of Hong Kong
Shatin, New Territories, Hong Kong
king@cse.cuhk.edu.hk, http://www.cse.cuhk.edu.hk/~king

Abstract. In large content-based image database applications, efficient information retrieval depends heavily on good indexing structures of the extracted features. While indexing techniques for text retrieval are well understood, efficient and robust indexing methodology for image retrieval is still in its infancy. In this paper, we present a non-hierarchical clustering scheme for index generation using the *Rival Penalized Competitive Learning* (RPCL) algorithm. RPCL is a stochastic heuristic clustering method which provides good cluster center approximation and is computationally efficient. Using synthetic data as well as real data, we demonstrate the *recall* and *precision* performance measurement of nearest-neighbor feature retrieval based on the indexing structure generated by RPCL.

1 Introduction

One of the key issues in information retrieval of data in large and voluminous database is the design and implementation of an efficient and effective indexing structure for the data objects in the database.[1] Without a properly designed indexing structure, the retrieval of information may be reduced to a linear exhaustive search. On the other hand, a good indexing structure will make the retrieval accurate and computationally efficient.

The following paragraphs outline the basic feature vector model for nearest-neighbor search. In our framework, we let $DB = \{I_i\}_{i=1}^{N}$ be a set of image objects. Without loss of generality, a feature extraction function $f : I \times \theta \rightarrow \mathcal{R}^d$ extracts from an image I, with a set of parameters $\theta = \{\theta_1, \theta_2, \cdots, \theta_m\}$, a real-valued d-dimensional vector. Hence, we may view the extracted feature vector as a point in a d-dimensional vector space. Furthermore, we may use a random variable X to denote the feature vector extracted from the image set DB and

---

* This work is supported in part by the RGC Grant #CUHK4176/97E. Portions of this manuscript have been presented in [8].
[1] In this paper, data objects and feature vectors are interchangeable unless stated otherwise.

$x_i, i = 1, 2, \cdots, N$ to denote the instance of the feature vector extracted from DB.

Once the feature vectors have been obtained. Similar feature (content-based) search can be performed as a nearest-neighbor search by using a distance function. A typical distance function D is defined as $D : F \times F \to \mathcal{R}$ satisfying: (1) $D(x, y) \geq 0$, (2) $D(x, y) = D(y, x)$, (3) $D(x, y) = 0$ iff $x = y$, and (4) $D(x, y) + D(y, z) \geq D(x, z)$ where x, y, and $z \in F$ and F is a feature vector set. Here, L_2-norm (Euclidean distance) is one of the common distance functions and it is defined as: D as: $D(x, y) = \|x - y\| = (\sum_{i=1}^{d}(x_i - y_i)^2)^{1/2}$.

There are two typical types of query involved in image databases: (1) Range Search and (2) k Nearest-Neighbor Search. Given a set of N features $X = \{x_i\}_{i=1}^{N}$, a *Range Query*, $\hat{x}$, returns the set, P, of features as $P = \{x | x \in X \text{ and } 0 \leq D(x, \hat{x}) \leq \epsilon\}$, where ϵ is a pre-defined positive real number and D is a distance function. As in the k *Nearest-Neighbor Search* case, given a set of N features $X = \{x_i\}_{i=1}^{N}$, a k *Nearest-Neighbor Query*, $\hat{x}$, returns the set $P \subseteq X$ satisfying: (1) $|P| = k$ for $1 \leq k \leq N$ and (2) $D(\hat{x}, x) \leq D(\hat{x}, y)$ for $y \in X - P$ where D is a distance function. In this paper, we will focus on the latter type of query.

Once the features have been extracted and the query model has been defined. The crucial link between the features and user query is the indexing structure (organization). A well-organized indexing structure of the underlying feature vectors support an efficient and effective retrieval of user queries.

Recently, researchers have developed many new indexing methods for content-based retrieval in multimedia databases. For example, rectangle-based indexing as in R-Tree [6], R+-Tree [11], R*-Tree [1], SR-Tree [7]. Partition-based Indexing as in Quad-tree [5], k-d Tree [2], VP-Tree [4, 13], and MVP-tree [3].

However, one major problem of these indexing techniques has been that these methods fail to utilize the underlying data distribution to their advantage in their indexing structure. This results in what is known as the *boundary query problem* where the retrieval *Precision* will degrade when a query is near the boundary of a partition in the indexing structure due to the systematic yet unfavorable partitioning of some indexing techniques. To overcome this, we will present a non-hierarchical clustering algorithm based on Rival Penalized Competitive Learning (RPCL) heuristic and demonstrate its effectiveness in generating indexing structure for large image databases.

In Section 2 we will present more details on RPCL and the associated non-hierarchical indexing. Experimental results of the proposed method are presented in Section 3. We will discuss some issues associated with the proposed method and conclude in Section 4.

2 Non-hierarchical Clustering with RPCL

There are two main goals in our proposed solution: (1) find a quick way to partition the input feature set into partitions and (2) impose an indexing structure over these partitions so that the nearest-neighbor information retrieval can be made effectively.

Rival Penalized Competitive Learning (RPCL) clustering [12] can be regarded as an unsupervised extension of Kohonen's supervised learning vector quantization algorithm LVQ2 [9]. It can also be regarded as a variation to the more typical Competitive Learning (CL) algorithms [10]. RPCL is a stochastic clustering algorithm that is able to perform adaptive clustering efficiently and quickly leading to an approximation of clusters that are statistically adequate.

The proposed solution is to use RPCL to find hierarchical clusters such that the indexing structure can be created based on a natural partition of the feature vector distribution. Although this may not result in a balanced tree structure, this indexing structure will be able to answer nearest-neighbor queries more effectively.

The main advantages of RPCL are: (1) the heuristic is computationally efficient, (3) it is no worse than other methods when high dimensional features, and (3) RPCL can be implemented in a distributed environment achieving even greater speed-up in generating indexing structure of feature vectors.

2.1 The RPCL Algorithm

Step 0: **Initialization** Randomly pick $c_i, i = 1, 2, \cdots, k$ as the initial cluster centers.

Step 1: **Winner-Take-All Rule** Randomly take a feature vector x from the feature sample set X, and for $i = 1, 2, \cdot, k$, we let

$$u_i = \begin{cases} 1, & \text{if } i = w \text{ such that} \\ & \quad \gamma_w \|x - c_w\|^2 = \min_j \gamma_j \|x - c_j\|^2, \\ -1, & \text{if } i = r \text{ such that} \\ & \quad \gamma_r \|x - c_r\|^2 = \min_j \gamma_j \|x - c_j\|^2, \\ 0, & \text{otherwise} \end{cases} \quad (1)$$

where w is the winner index, r is the second winner (rival) index, $\gamma_j = n_j / \sum_{i=1}^{k} n_i$ and n_i is the cumulative number of the occurrences of $u_i = 1$. This term is added to ensure that every cluster center will eventually become the winner during the updating process.

Step 2: **Updating Cluster Centers** Update the cluster center vector c_i by

$$\Delta c_i = \begin{cases} \alpha_w (x - c_i), & \text{if } u_i = 1, \\ -\alpha_r (x - c_i), & \text{if } u_i = -1, \\ 0, & \text{otherwise.} \end{cases} \quad (2)$$

where $0 \leq \alpha_w, \alpha_r \leq 1$ are the learning rates for the winner and rival unit, respectively.

Assuming there are k cluster centers, the basic idea behind RPCL is that in each iteration, the cluster center for the winner's unit is accentuated where as the weight for the second winner, or the rival, is attenuated. The remaining $k - 2$ centers are unaffected. The winner is defined as the cluster center that is closest to the randomly selected feature vector. Instead of k can be of any value, in our application we use the special version of the RPCL clustering algorithm when $k = 2^i, i = 1, 2, 3, \cdots$ so that a systematic index tree can be formed.

Let k, c_w and c_r to denote the number of clusters, cluster center points for the winner and rival clusters respectively. The algorithm is illustrated in the boxed region above.

Step 1 and 2 are iterated until one of the following criteria is satisfied: (1) the iteration converges, (2) $\alpha_w \rightarrow \epsilon$ for a time decaying learning rate of α_w with a pre-specified threshold of ϵ, or (3) the number of iterations reaches a pre-specified value.

2.2 Non-hierarchical RPCL Indexing

There are two ways to perform the clustering. One is the non-hierarchical approach and the other is the hierarchical approach. In this paper, we will only focus on the former approach.

The non-hierarchical indexing approach considers the whole feature vector space each time for clustering by RPCL. We use an example here to explain its basic idea. Given a set of feature vectors, our method clusters the set into 2 clusters at the first time (see Fig. 1 (a)). If four partitions are required at the next time, our method will consider the whole space again and clusters the set into 4 clusters (see Fig. 1 (b)). In the non-hierarchical clustering, clusters at a subsequent stage may not be nested into clusters from a previous stage, but this method ensures to obtain the correct natural clusters at each stage.

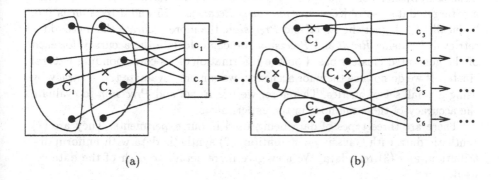

(a)   (b)

Fig. 1. (a) Two and (b) Four cluster partitions generated by the non-hierarchical approach. The dots are the database objects whereas the crosses are the centers. An inverted file (the right one) is used for indexing.

3 Experimental Results

We conducted four different sets of experiments for the four methods: RPCL, k-means, Competitive Learning (CL) clustering, and VP-tree to test their accuracy and efficiency for indexing and retrieval. All of the experiments were conducted on an Ultra Sparc 1 machine running Matlab V4.2c. Here we assume that a cluster of feature vectors is often retrieved as the result of a query for nearest-neighbor search. An indexing method which can locate natural clusters from the input feature vector set accurately and quickly will make nearest-neighbor search more effective and efficient. Therefore, in these experiments, we restrict to retrieve the first visited feature vector cluster or leaf node as the result of a nearest-neighbor query so that, based on the result, we can show that how accurate and efficient the tested methods are to locate natural clusters for indexing and retrieval.

We used two performance measurements: *Recall* and *Precision* in the experiments to measure the accuracy of the tested methods. Given a set of user-specified target database objects, *Recall* and *Precision* performance measurements are defined as:

$$Recall = \frac{\text{Number of target database objects retrieved}}{\text{Number of target database objects}}, \tag{3}$$

$$Precision = \frac{\text{Number of target database objects retrieved}}{\text{Number of database objects retrieved}}, \tag{4}$$

where $0 \leq Recall, Precision \leq 1$. *Recall* shows the ratio of target database objects are actually retrieved out of all the expected target database objects whereas *Precision* indicates the ratio of target database objects in the retrieved set. For example, there are 10 database objects and 4 of them are pre-specified as target database objects. For a query, 5 database objects are retrieved and 3 of them are target database objects. In this case, *Recall* is 0.75 and *Precision* is 0.6. Typically, the higher the *Recall* and *Precision*, the more accurate the method for retrieval. By using *Recall* and *Precision*, we can calculate the accuracy for each of the generated clusters based on the information of its corresponding natural cluster. If we do not use them for accuracy, we can only evaluate the accuracy by using a small set of queries. Therefore, we use *Recall* and *Precision* to evaluate the accuracy of these methods in the experiments.

There are three types of data being used in our experiments. They are (1) synthetic data with Gaussian distribution, (2) synthetic data with uniform distribution, and (3) real data. We now give more details to each of the data set used.

1 Synthetic Data in Gaussian Distribution:

We test our method with synthetic data sets in Gaussian distribution. It is because many distributions can be approximated by using Gaussian distribution. Let $\mu = (\mu_1, \mu_2, \ldots, \mu_n)$ and $\sigma = (\sigma_1, \sigma_2, \ldots, \sigma_n)$, we generated the input distribution of the feature vectors from the mixture of n

Gaussian distributions $N(\mu, \sigma^2)$ with the generating function defined as $g(x) = 1/(\sigma\sqrt{2\pi})\exp[-[(x - \mu)^2/2\sigma^2]]$, $-\infty < x < \infty$. In our experiments, we used a constant 0.05 for σ. Moreover, we let $n = 2, 4, 8, 16$, and 32. Finally, for each input distribution, different numbers of cluster partitions are generated for the input feature vectors for testing.

2 Synthetic Data in Uniform Distribution:

We also use synthetic data sets in uniform distribution with no clear bias toward any cluster centers.

3 Real Data:

Apart from the two synthetic data sets, we also use real data in the experiments to test our method in a real world situation. For our experiments, the real data features are the feature vectors extracted from real images. Basically, we firstly find some real images from different kinds of catalogs. By considering the global color information of each image, we calculate an 8-bucket color histogram form the image and transform it into a feature vector. All of the output feature vectors form the real data set for testing.

We have devised four experiments to test out various aspects of the proposed indexing scheme. The first experiment tests the *Recall*, *Precision*, and the pre-processing speed performance of RPCL, CL, k-means, and VP-tree. Once the favorable results from RPCL has been established. The second experiment focuses on RPCL's performance under different sizes of input data set. The third experiment measures the RPCL performance with different numbers of dimensions. The last experiment compares the RPCL indexing scheme against actual nearest-neighbor results.

3.1 Experiment 1: Test for *Recall* and *Precision* Performance

In the first experiment, we evaluate the accuracy and efficiency of the four tested methods: RPCL, CL, k-means, and VP-tree to build indexing structures for retrieval. We measure the *Recall* and *Precision* performance of these methods for accuracy. Moreover, we also kept the time used for pre-processing which includes clustering and indexing of the feature vectors for efficiency. The main aim of this experiment is to find out which tested method has the best overall performance for locating natural clusters for indexing and retrieval.

We used three different kinds of data sets in this experiment: (1) synthetic data in Gaussian distribution, (2) synthetic data in uniform distribution, and (3) real data. Each of the data sets consists of 2048 8-dimensional feature vectors. In addition, we used 8-D feature vectors in our experiment. Moreover, for each input data set, different numbers of cluster partitions were generated for the input feature vectors by the four tested methods respectively. We conducted 20 trails with different initial starting points of the centers of the to-be generated cluster partitions for these methods to calculate their average *Recall* and *Precision* performance measurement and the average time used for building indexing structure.

The results are presented as follows. For the data sets in Gaussian distribution with different mixture groups, Tables 1 and 2 show the *Recall* and *Precision* results. For the data set in uniform distribution and the real data set, we can simply use Figures 2 and 3 to present their results respectively. Moreover, Tables 3, 4, and 5 show the main observations of this experiment.

#MG	No. of Generated Clusters (RPCL, CL, k-means, VP-tree)				
	2	4	8	16	32
2	1.0, 1.0, 1.0, 1.0	.51, .45, .66, .50	.27, .25, .57, .25	.15, .14, .53, .13	.22, .09, .51, .06
4	1.0, 1.0, 1.0, 1.0	1.0, 1.0, 1.0, 1.0	.52, .58, .80, .50	.39, .43, .77, .25	.53, .31, .76, .13
8	1.0, .91, 1.0, .87	1.0, 1.0, 1.0, .71	1.0, 1.0, .94, .56	.75, 1.0, .89, .31	.73, .56, .88, .17
16	.96, .95, 1.0, .90	1.0, .99, 1.0, .86	1.0, 1.0, 1.0, .76	.99, .98, .96, .65	.93, .83, .94, .41
32	.96, .98, .99, .93	.98, .96, 1.0, .86	.97, .87, .99, .80	.98, .87, 1.0, .69	.98, .87, .94, .63

Table 1. *Recall* table for the data sets in Gaussian distributions in Experiment 1. #*MG* is the number of Gaussian mixture groups.

#MG	No. of Generated Clusters (RPCL, CL, k-means, VP-tree)				
	2	4	8	16	32
2	1.0, 1.0, 1.0, 1.0	1.0, 1.0, 1.0, 1.0	1.0, 1.0, 1.0, 1.0	1.0, 1.0, 1.0, 1.0	1.0, 1.0, 1.0, 1.0
4	.50, .50, .50, .50	1.0, 1.0, 1.0, 1.0	1.0, 1.0, 1.0, 1.0	1.0, 1.0, 1.0, 1.0	1.0, 1.0, 1.0, 1.0
8	.25, .23, .25, .15	.46, .50, .50, .20	1.0, 1.0, .93, .36	1.0, 1.0, .97, .63	1.0, 1.0, 1.0, .79
16	.11, .12, .13, .10	.26, .24, .27, .16	.54, .54, .61, .21	.97, .93, .88, .39	.98, .85, .97, .68
32	.06, .05, .06, .05	.11, .11, .14, .08	.25, .18, .26, .13	.51, .39, .56, .21	.94, .71, .87, .41

Table 2. *Precision* table for the data sets in Gaussian distributions in Experiment 1. #*MG* is the number of Gaussian mixture groups.

Measures	RPCL	CL	k-means	VP-tree
Recall	high	middle	highest	lowest
Precision	high	middle	highest	lowest
Preprocessing Speed	highest	high	lowest	middle

Table 3. Comparison of the average performance of the four methods for indexing and retrieval with data sets in Gaussian distributions.

3.2 Experiment 2: Test for Different Sizes of Input Data Sets

In this experiment, we test the accuracy and efficiency of RPCL for indexing and retrieval with different sizes of input feature vector sets. We measure the *Recall*

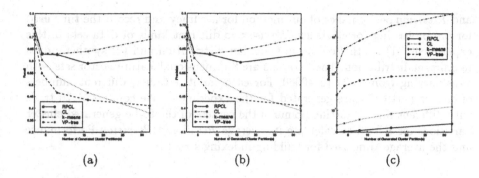

(a)   (b)   (c)

Fig. 2. Results for the uniform data set in Experiment 1. (a) The *Recall* results. (b) The *Precision* results. (c) The pre-processing time.

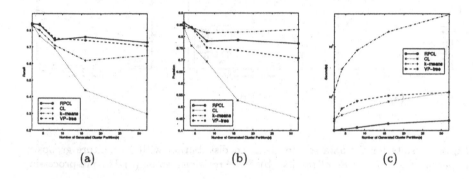

(a)   (b)   (c)

Fig. 3. Results for the real data set in Experiment 1. (a) The *Recall* results. (b) The *Precision* results. (c) The pre-processing time.

Measures	RPCL	CL	k-means	VP-tree
Recall	high	low	highest	low
Precision	high	low	highest	low
Preprocessing Speed	highest	high	lowest	middle

Table 4. Comparison of the average performance of the four methods for indexing and retrieval with the uniform data set.

Measures	RPCL	CL	k-means	VP-tree
Recall	high	low	high	high
Precision	high	low	high	high
Preprocessing Speed	highest	middle	lowest	middle

Table 5. Comparison of the average performance of the four methods for indexing and retrieval with a given real data set.

and *Precision* performance of our method for accuracy and record the time used for pre-processing for efficiency. We use two different kinds of data sets in this experiment: (1) synthetic data in Gaussian distribution and (2) synthetic data in uniform distribution. The data sets are 8-dimensional feature vector sets with sizes varying from 1024 to 40960. For each input data set, different numbers of cluster partitions are generated for the experiment. We conducted 20 trails with different initial starting points of the centers of the to-be generated cluster partitions for RPCL to calculate its average *Recall* and *Precision* Performance and the average time used for building indexing structure.

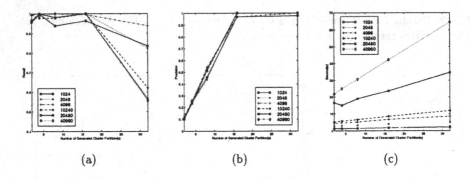

(a) (b) (c)

Fig. 4. Results for the data sets in Gaussian distribution with 16 mixture groups in Experiment 2. (a) The *Recall* results. (b) The *Precision* results. (c) The pre-processing time.

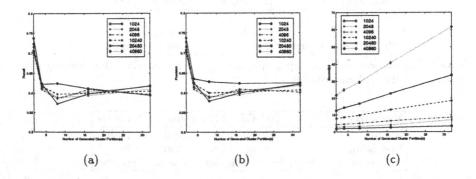

(a) (b) (c)

Fig. 5. Results for the uniform data sets in Experiment 2. (a) The *Recall* results. (b) The *Precision* results. (c) The pre-processing time.

#MG	No. of Generated Clusters				
	2	4	8	16	32
2	1.0	.47	.28	.23	.17
	1.0	.47	.28	.12	.06
	1.0	.51	.26	.11	.11
	1.0	.47	.30	.12	.06
	1.0	.47	.29	.14	.06
	1.0	.53	.29	.14	.06
4	1.0	1.0	.54	.67	.57
	1.0	1.0	.50	.37	.43
	1.0	1.0	.64	.25	.14
	1.0	1.0	.62	.25	.15
	1.0	1.0	.64	.25	.12
	1.0	1.0	.65	.26	.13
8	1.0	1.0	1.0	1.0	.79
	.99	1.0	1.0	.78	.64
	1.0	.92	1.0	.53	.56
	1.0	1.0	1.0	.57	.31
	1.0	1.0	1.0	.62	.27
	1.0	1.0	1.0	.57	.27
16	.96	1.0	.94	.96	.84
	.97	1.0	.98	1.0	.82
	1.0	1.0	1.0	1.0	.94
	.99	.98	.98	1.0	.62
	.96	1.0	.98	1.0	.56
	.96	.99	1.0	1.0	.56
32	.97	.96	.97	.95	.95
	.98	.95	.97	.98	1.0
	.98	.90	.96	.96	1.0
	.97	.98	.98	.99	1.0
	.99	1.0	.97	1.0	.99
	.99	.98	1.0	.99	1.0

(a)

#MG	No. of Generated Clusters				
	2	4	8	16	32
2	1.0	1.0	1.0	1.0	1.0
	1.0	1.0	1.0	1.0	1.0
	1.0	1.0	1.0	1.0	1.0
	1.0	1.0	1.0	1.0	1.0
	1.0	1.0	1.0	1.0	1.0
	1.0	1.0	1.0	1.0	1.0
4	.50	1.0	1.0	1.0	1.0
	.50	1.0	1.0	1.0	1.0
	.50	1.0	1.0	1.0	1.0
	.50	1.0	1.0	1.0	1.0
	.50	1.0	1.0	1.0	1.0
	.50	1.0	1.0	1.0	1.0
8	.27	.58	1.0	1.0	1.0
	.23	.58	1.0	1.0	1.0
	.27	.46	1.0	1.0	1.0
	.27	.50	1.0	.97	1.0
	.25	.50	1.0	1.0	1.0
	.25	.58	1.0	1.0	1.0
16	.10	.25	.46	.97	.98
	.11	.24	.44	1.0	1.0
	.13	.25	.54	.97	1.0
	.11	.24	.51	1.0	1.0
	.11	.23	.52	1.0	1.0
	.11	.26	.52	1.0	1.0
32	.06	.10	.20	.44	.83
	.06	.09	.23	.50	.97
	.05	.10	.19	.46	.97
	.05	.11	.23	.42	.97
	.05	.11	.19	.46	.97
	.05	.10	.20	.47	.98

(b)

Table 6. Results for the data sets in Gaussian distributions in Experiment 2. (a) The *Recall* table. (b) The *Precision* table. Each entry of the tables is a column of 6 values for 6 different sizes of the data sets: 1024, 2048, 4096, 10240, 20480, and 40960. $\#MG$ is the number of Gaussian mixture groups.

Size of Data Set	# Generated Clusters				
	2	4	8	16	32
1024	.73	.62	.62	.61	.59
2048	.70	.61	.59	.59	.61
4096	.70	.61	.59	.61	.60
10240	.72	.62	.60	.60	.61
20480	.71	.62	.57	.60	.62
40960	.72	.61	.59	.60	.62

(a)

Size of Data Set	# Generated Clusters				
	2	4	8	16	32
1024	.74	.64	.63	.62	.63
2048	.70	.61	.59	.60	.62
4096	.70	.61	.59	.61	.60
10240	.72	.62	.60	.60	.61
20480	.71	.63	.58	.60	.62
40960	.73	.61	.59	.61	.62

(b)

Table 7. Results for the data sets in uniform distribution in Experiment 2. (a) The *Recall* table. (b) The *Precision* table.

#MG	No. of Generated Clusters (DIM = 4, 8, 16, 32)				
	2	4	8	16	32
2	1.0, 1.0, 1.0, 1.0	.51, .49, .53, .55	.25, .25, .26, .28	.13, .12, .14, .11	.07, .07, .06, .06
4	1.0, 1.0, 1.0, 1.0	1.0, 1.0, 1.0, 1.0	.61, .48, .62, .62	.27, .27, .27, .26	.14, .14, .13, .12
8	1.0, 1.0, 1.0, 1.0	1.0, 1.0, 1.0, 1.0	1.0, 1.0, 1.0, 1.0	.50, .49, .54, .64	.32, .24, .27, .28
16	1.0, .96, .98, 1.0	1.0, 1.0, 1.0, 1.0	.98, 1.0, 1.0, 1.0	.98, 1.0, 1.0, 1.0	.58, .57, .57, .57
32	.94, .99, .99, .98	.93, .97, .99, .99	.93, .95, 1.0, .98	.96, .97, 1.0, 1.0	.97, 1.0, 1.0, 1.0

Table 8. The *Recall* table for the data sets in Gaussian distributions in Experiment 3.

3.3 Experiment 3: Test for Different Numbers of Dimensions

Apart from different sizes of data sets, we also test the performance of RPCL for indexing with feature vectors having different numbers of dimensions in terms of *Recall* and *Precision* for accuracy and the pre-processing time for efficiency. Two different kinds of data sets are used in this experiment: (1) synthetic data in Gaussian distribution and (2) synthetic data in uniform distribution. All the data sets are fixed to have 10240 feature vectors with different numbers of dimensions such as 4, 8, 16, and 32. We fixed the size of each data set to 10240 as it is not too large or too small for testing and we do not use data more than 32-D because it is not so efficient for our method to work with such high dimensional data. Moreover, for each input data set, different numbers of cluster partitions are generated for the experiment. We conducted 20 trails with different initial starting points of the centers of the to-be generated cluster partitions for RPCL to calculate its average *Recall* and *Precision* Performance and the average time used for building indexing structure.

By increasing the number of dimensions, the experimental results show that the accuracy is not affected for the data sets in Gaussian distributions, but it may be lowered for the data sets in uniform distribution. The relatively lower *Recall* and *Precision* results found for uniform data because there are no explicit

127

#MG	No. of Generated Clusters (DIM = 4, 8, 16, 32)				
	2	**4**	**8**	**16**	**32**
2	1.0, 1.0, 1.0, 1.0	1.0, 1.0, 1.0, 1.0	1.0, 1.0, 1.0, 1.0	1.0, 1.0, 1.0, 1.0	1.0, 1.0, 1.0, 1.0
4	.50, .50, .50, .50	1.0, 1.0, 1.0, 1.0	1.0, 1.0, 1.0, 1.0	1.0, 1.0, 1.0, 1.0	1.0, 1.0, 1.0, 1.0
8	.23, .27, .25, .57	.67, .58, .54, .80	1.0, 1.0, 1.0, 1.0	1.0, 1.0, 1.0, 1.0	1.0, 1.0, 1.0, 1.0
16	.11, .09, .12, .21	.23, .20, .22, .25	.48, .48, .50, .54	.80, 1.0, 1.0, 1.0	.92, 1.0, 1.0, 1.0
32	.05, .05, .07, .06	.08, .11, .11, .11	.15, .20, .25, .32	.39, .51, .53, .54	.72, 1.0, 1.0, 1.0

Table 9. The *Precision* table for the data sets in Gaussian distributions in Experiment 3.

DIM	# Generated Clusters				
	2	**4**	**8**	**16**	**32**
4	.80	.74	.78	.83	.78
8	.71	.60	.59	.58	.62
16	.69	.55	.47	.45	.45
32	.65	.49	.41	.36	.34

DIM	# Generated Clusters				
	2	**4**	**8**	**16**	**32**
4	.80	.74	.78	.83	.78
8	.72	.60	.59	.58	.63
16	.69	.55	.47	.45	.45
32	.65	.49	.41	.36	.34

(a)   (b)

Table 10. Results for the uniform data sets in Experiment 3. (a) The *Recall* table. (b) The *Precision* table.

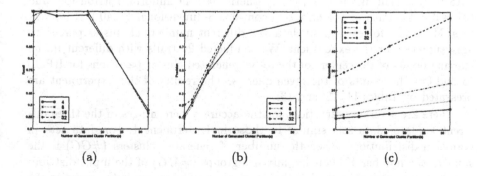

(a)   (b)   (c)

Fig. 6. Results for the data sets in Gaussian distribution with 16 mixture groups in Experiment 3. (a) The *Recall* results. (b) The *Precision* results. (c) The pre-processing time.

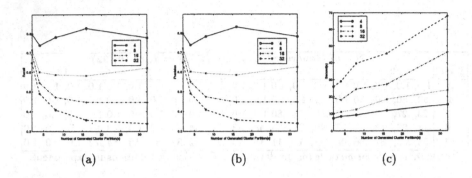

(a)   (b)   (c)

Fig. 7. Results for the uniform data sets in Experiment 3. (a) The *Recall* results. (b) The *Precision* results. (c) The pre-processing time.

natural clusters for RPCL to locate. Therefore, we can conclude that our method is more suitable for data sets with distributions similar to Gaussian distribution.

3.4 Experiment 4: Compare with Actual Nearest-Neighbor Results

In this experiment, we compare the results given by our method with the actual nearest-neighbor results in order to check the actual accuracy of our method. In the first three sets of experiments, we mainly evaluate the *Recall* and *Precision* performance of the tested methods. We want to find out the (accuracy) percentage of the database objects retrieved by our method can also be found in the actual nearest-neighbor results in the experiment for accuracy.

We use three different kinds of data sets in this experiment: (1) synthetic data in Gaussian distribution, (2) synthetic data in uniform distribution, and (3) real data. Each of the data sets contains 8-dimensional 10240 feature vectors. Moreover, for each input data set, different numbers of cluster partitions are generated for the experiment. We conducted 20 trails with different initial starting points of the centers of the to-be generated cluster partitions for RPCL to find out the results of the given queries. The results of this experiment are presented by Tables 11, 12, and 13.

There are several observations for the accuracy percentages of the three different kinds of data sets similar to those in Experiment 1. For data sets in Gaussian distributions, when the number of generated clusters ($\#GC$) is the same as the number of Gaussian mixture groups ($\#MG$) of the input distribution, the percentages are higher than the others. The reason is the same as the one in Experiment 1. Another observation with the same reason as the one in Experiment 1 is that the percentages for the uniform data set are the lowest and those for the real data set are in the middle. These same observations show that *Recall* and *Precision* are good measurements for accuracy.

#MG	No. of Generated Clusters				
	2	4	8	16	32
2	88.14	56.14	40.72	33.40	29.55
4	73.42	84.34	56.58	40.85	29.30
8	65.40	60.97	79.10	54.41	39.58
16	62.14	54.14	57.22	75.34	45.04
32	64.05	49.82	49.42	49.88	73.08

Table 11. Accuracy percentages for the data sets in Gaussian distributions in Experiment 4. $\#MG$ is the number of Gaussian mixture groups.

No. of Generated Clusters				
2	4	8	16	32
59.67	42.43	35.09	32.08	28.91

Table 12. Accuracy percentages for the uniform data set in Experiment 4.

From the experimental results, the accuracy percentages (for first cluster retrieval) are relatively high (73%-88%) for the data sets in Gaussian distribution when $\#GC = \#MG$, but we find that the larger the number of generated cluster partitions, the lower the accuracy percentage. It is because the chance of the occurrence of the boundary problem is higher when there are many generated clusters. It shows that our method can lessen the boundary problem, but it still cannot solve it completely.

4 Discussion and Conclusion

From Experiment 1, we find that although k-means is the most accurate way for clustering, it is also the slowest and most inefficient. RPCL turns out to be a good compromise when accuracy and efficiency are both taken into account. RPCL's accuracy is unaffected by the input size in general in Experiment 2. The results in Experiment 3 suggests that RPCL's accuracy depends on the underlying data distribution when the feature vector has high dimensions since the accuracy is lower in the uniform distribution case than the Gaussian distribution case. In the last experiment, the result correlates well with Experiment 1. Hence we may conclude that RPCL is most effective when the underlying data has a Gaussian distribution.

In summary, we propose a novel way to use RPCL algorithm to produce non-hierarchical cluster partitions for generating indexing structures. From the experimental results, we show that our RPCL indexing method gives good searching

No. of Generated Clusters				
2	4	8	16	32
67.72	56.97	48.39	44.76	37.51

Table 13. Accuracy percentages for the real data set in Experiment 4.

performance and it is the fastest method to build an indexing structure among the tested methods.

Our method using the non-hierarchical approach for indexing seems to be a good method, but there are still some limitations. First, it is not so efficient to perform insertion and deletion in our indexing method. Since our method uses a non-hierarchical indexing structure, there is no relationship in between two different levels' nodes. We have to find the target node at each level individually for insertion and deletion. Second, we find that our method still cannot solve the boundary problem completely. It does not give 100% nearest-neighbor result for a query in general. One possible extension of the proposed method is to add the branch-and-bound search technique to the indexing structure for better results.

References

1. N. Beckmann, H. P. Kriegel, R. Schneider, and B. Seeger. "The R*-tree: an efficient and robust access method for points and rectangles". *ACM SIGMOD Record*, 19(2):322–331, 1990.
2. J. L. Bentley. "Multidimensional Binary Search Trees Used for Associative Searching". *Communications of the ACM*, 18(9):509–517, 1975.
3. Tolga Bozkaya and Meral Ozsoyoglu. "Distance-Based Indexing for High-dimensional Metric Spaces". *SIGMOD Record*, 26(2):357–368, June 1997.
4. T. C. Chiueh. "Content-Based Image Indexing". In *Proceedings of the 20th VLDB Conference*, pages 582–593, September 1994.
5. R. A. Finkel and J. L. Bentley. "Quad Trees: A Data Structure for Retrieval on Composite Keys". *Acta Informatica*, 4(1):1–9, 1974.
6. A. Guttman. "R-trees: A Dynamic Index Structure for Spatial Searching". *ACM SIGMOD*, 14(2):47–57, June 1984.
7. Norio Katayama and Shinichi Satoh. "The SR-tree: an index structure for high-dimensional nearest neighbor queries". *SIGMOD Record*, 26(2):369–380, June 1997.
8. I. King, L. Xu, and L.W. Chan. Using rival penalized competitive clustering for feature indexing in Hong Kong's textile and fashion image database. In *Proceedings to the International Joint Conference on Neural Networks (IJCNN'98)*, pages 237–240. IEEE Computer Press, May 4-9, 1998.
9. T. Kohonen. The self-organizing map. *Proc. IEEE*, 78:1464–1480, 1990.
10. R. Rosenblatt. *Principles of Neurodynamics*. Spartan Books, New York, 1959. neural networks.
11. T. Sellis, N. Roussopoulos, and C. Faloutsos. "The R+-tree: a dynamic index for multidimensional objects". In *Proceedings of the 13th VLDB Conference*, pages 507–518, 1987.
12. Lei Xu, Adam Krzyżak, and Erkki Oja. Rival penalized competitive learning for clustering analysis, RBF net, and curve detection. *IEEE Trans. on Neural Networks*, 4(4):636–649, 1993.
13. P. N. Yianilos. "Data structures and algorithms for nearest neighbor search in general metric spaces". In *Proc. of the 4th Annual ACM-SIAM Symp. on Discrete Algorithms*, pages 311–321, 1993.

Automatic Design of Multiple Classifier Systems by Unsupervised Learning

Giorgio Giacinto and Fabio Roli

Department of Electrical and Electronic Engineering, University of Cagliari, Italy
Piazza D'Armi, 09123, Cagliari, Italy
Phone: +39-070-6755874 Fax: +39-070-6755900
{giacinto,roli}@diee.unica.it

Abstract. In the field of pattern recognition, multiple classifier systems based on the combination of the outputs of a set of different classifiers have been proposed as a method for the development of high performance classification systems. Previous work clearly showed that multiple classifier systems are effective only if the classifiers forming them make independent errors. This achievement pointed out the fundamental need for methods aimed to design ensembles of "independent" classifiers. However, the most of the recent work focused on the development of combination methods. In this paper, an approach to the automatic design of multiple classifier systems based on unsupervised learning is proposed. Given an initial set of classifiers, such approach is aimed to identify the largest subset of "independent" classifiers. A proof of the optimality of the proposed approach is given. Reported results on the classification of remote sensing images show that this approach allows one to design effective multiple classifier systems.

1. Introduction

In the field of pattern recognition, multiple classifier systems (MCSs) based on the combination of the outputs of a set of different classifiers have been proposed as a method for the development of high performance classification systems. Typically, the combination is based on voting rules, belief functions, statistical techniques, Dempster-Shafer evidence theory, and other integration schemes [1, 2]. The most of such combination methods assume that the classifiers forming the MCS make independent classification errors. This assumption is necessary to guarantee an increase of classification accuracy with respect to the accuracies provided by classifiers forming the MCS. As an example, Hansen and Salamon showed that a MCS based on a simple "majority" combination rule can provide very good increases of accuracy if classifiers make independent errors [3]. Tumer and Ghosh pointed out that accuracy increases depend on error uncorrelation much more that on the particular combination method adopted [4].

The above-mentioned achievements pointed out the fundamental need for methods aimed to design ensembles of independent classifiers. However, in the pattern recognition field, the most of the work focused on the development of combination methods. Some papers addressing the problem of the design of an ensemble of independent nets appeared in the neural networks literature [5]. However, the results of such work can be exploited only in part for the MCSs formed by different classifiers (e.g., statistical and neural classifiers). An overview of the work related to the design of MCSs is given in Section 2.

In this paper, an approach to the automatic design of MCSs formed by different classification algorithms is proposed (Section 3). Instead of attempting to design a set of "independent" classifiers directly, a large set, usually containing independent but also correlated classifiers, is initially created (Section 3.1). Given such a set, our approach is aimed to identify the largest subset of independent classifiers by an unsupervised learning algorithm (Section 3.2). We also point out the rationale behind the proposed approach and prove the optimality of our design method (Section 3.3). Experimental results and comparisons are reported in Section 4. Conclusions are drawn in Section 5.

2. Related Work

In the pattern recognition literature, to the best of our knowledge, no work directly addressed the problem of designing ensembles of independent classifiers. Some papers indirectly addressed it by proposing combination methods that that do not need of the assumption of independent classifiers [6-8]. It is easy to see that such methods exhibit advantages from the viewpoint of the design of the MCSs. However, the related combination functions are much more complex than the ones based on the "independence" assumption. In addition, the theory developed for ensembles of independent classifiers cannot be exploited to evaluate the performances of the MCSs based on these methods. As an example, it is not possible to assume that the error rate is monotonically decreasing in the number of the combined classifiers [3].

Research work addressing the problem of designing an ensemble of "independent" nets has been carried out in the neural networks field. Earlier studies investigated the effectiveness of different "design parameters" for creating independent neural nets [5]. In particular, Partridge quantified the relative impact of the major parameters used in the design of a neural network and he found the following "ordering": "net type", "training set structure", "training set elements", "number of hidden units", and "weight seed" [9]. Recently, it seems to the authors that two main strategies for designing an ensemble of independent nets emerged from the neural networks literature [5]. One, that can be named "overproduce and choose" strategy, is based on the creation of an initial large set of nets and a subsequent choice of an "optimal" subset of independent nets. The other strategy attempts to generate a set of independent nets directly. Partridge and Yates described a design method for neural network ensembles based on the "overproduce and choose" strategy [10]. They introduced some interesting "diversity" measures that can be used for choosing an "optimal" subset of independent classifiers. However, they did not propose a systematic method for choosing such a set. Only an experimental investigation of three possible techniques is described. In addition, the problem of the optimality of such "choose" techniques is not addressed. Opitz and Shavlik presented and algorithm called ADDEMUP that uses genetic algorithms to search actively for a set of independent neural networks [11]. Rosen described a method that allows one to train individual networks by backpropagation not only to reproduce a desired output, but also to have their errors linearly decorrelated with the other networks [12]. Individual networks so trained are then linearly combined.

However, the results of the above research work can be exploited only in part for MCSs formed by different classifiers (e.g., statistical and neural classifiers). As an example, the "diversity" measures proposed by Partridge and Yates can be exploited in general, while the work of Rosen is tailored to neural network ensembles. In addition, to the best of our knowledge, no work addressed the problem of the optimality of the design method proposed.

3. Automatic Design of MCSs by Unsupervised Learning

3.1 Background and Basic Concepts of the Proposed Approach

First of all, let us formulate briefly the task of the design of a MCS. In general, such task can be subdivided into two subtasks: the design of the "members" of the MCS, and the design of the combination function.

It is worth remarking that, in this paper, we address the problem of the design for MCSs based on combination functions that assume the independence of classifiers. Therefore, the design task basically consists of finding a set of independent classifiers as large as possible. Given such a set, a simple majority rule is sufficient to design an effective MCS. (Hansen and Salamon showed that the error rate of such a MCS goes to zero in the limit of infinite set size [3]).

Among the two main design strategies recently defined in the neural networks literature, our approach follows the so called "overproduce and choose" strategy (see Section 2). The rationale behind this choice is that we think that the direct design of only independent classifiers is a very difficult problem that is beyond the current state of the theory of MCSs. In addition, the overproduce and choose strategy seems to fit well with the novel paradigm of "weak" classifiers (i.e., the creation of very large sets of classifiers which can do a little better than making random guesses [13]). Also the interesting paradigm of "reusable" classifiers recently introduced by Bollacker and Ghosh might be exploited for the creation of large sets of classifiers [14]. Finally, the overproduce and choose strategy is successfully used in other fields (e.g., in the field of the software engineering [15].).

With regard to the overproduction phase, we basically extended to MCSs the conclusions of Partridge concerning the design parameters that maximize the independence for neural network ensembles [9]. In particular, we basically create the initial set of classifiers using different classification algorithms, as the "classifier type" is the best design parameter according to Partridge.

Concerning the choose phase, first of all, let C be the set of the N classifiers generated by the overproduction phase:

$$C = \{c_1, c_2, ..., c_N\}. \tag{1}$$

The rationale behind our approach is based on the following assumptions on such set C (equations 2, 3, and 4).

Let us assume that C is formed by the following union of M subsets C_i:

$$C = \bigcup_{i=1}^{M} C_i \tag{2}$$

where the subsets C_i meet the following assumption:

$$\forall i, j \; i \neq j \; C_i \cap C_j = \varnothing \tag{3}$$

and the classifiers forming the above subsets satisfy the following requirements:

$$\forall c_l, c_m \in C_i, \forall c_n \in C_j, \forall i, j \; i \neq j \; prob(c_l \; fails, \; c_m \; fails) > prob(c_l \; fails, \; c_n \; fails). \tag{4}$$

In the above equation, the terms $prob(c_l$ fails, c_m fails) and $prob(c_l$ fails, c_n fails) state for the compound error probabilities of the related classifier couples. Such error probabilities can be estimated by the number of coincident errors made by the couples of classifiers on a validation set.

Equation 4 simply states that the compound error probability between any two classifiers belonging to the same subset is higher than the one between any two classifiers belonging to different subsets. Consequently, theoretically speaking, the M subsets forming C can be identified by any "clustering" algorithm grouping the classifiers on the basis of the compound error probability [16].

After the identification of the subsets C_i, i=1...M, our approach takes one classifier from each subset in order to create the largest subset $C^* = \{c^*_1, c^*_2, ..., c^*_M\}$ containing only independent classifiers. (Or the subset C^* of the most independent classifiers, if the complete independence cannot be obtained).

It can be seen that the creation of the "optimal" subset C^* is as much difficult as the number of the possible subsets to be considered is large. (In Section 3.3, some additional hypotheses that allows one to guarantee the creation of the optimal subset C^* are given).

According to the above hypotheses, the subset C^* is the best solution for our design task, as it contains the largest subset of independent classifiers, or the subset of the most independent classifiers, contained into the initial set C.

Finally, it is worth doing the following remarks on the proposed approach:

- The above hypotheses on the set C are in agreement with real cases related to the "production" of classifier ensembles. As an example, a neural network ensemble obtained by trainings with different weight seeds is likely to meet the assumptions of equations 1-4 due to the common problem of "local minima". (We can assume that the subsets C_i are formed by nets related to the different local minima);

- The rationale behind the "clustering-based" approach to the identification of the set C^* is analogous to the one behind the "region-based" approach to image segmentation. It can be convenient to group "similar" pixels in order to identify the most "independent" ones (i.e., the edge pixels);

- The identification of classifier "clusters" allows one to highlight cases of "unbalanced" ensembles where, for example, there is a majority of "correlated" classifiers that negatively influences the ensemble performances.

3.2 The Proposed Approach

As described in the previous section, the proposed approach is constituted by two main phases: the overproduction and the choose phases. In this section, we give further details on the choose phase. With regard to the overproduction phase, let us assume that the set C has been generated according to the strategy outlined in Section 3.1.

The choose phase is subdivided into the following main stages:
- Unsupervised learning for identifying the subsets C_i, i=1...M
- Creation of the subset C*

Unsupervised Learning for Subsets Identification

This stage is implemented by an unsupervised learning algorithm that, according to equation 4, basically groups the classifiers belonging to the set C on the basis of the compound error probability. In particular, a hierarchical agglomerative clustering algorithm is used [16]. Such algorithm starts assigning each of the N classifiers to an individual cluster. Then, two or more of these trivial clusters are merged, thus nesting the trivial clustering into a second partition. The process is repeated to form a sequence of nested clusters. The stop criterion is based on the analysis of the so called "dendogram". The reader interested in more details about hierarchical agglomerative clustering is referred to [16].

In order to understand better this stage of our approach, it is worth remarking the analogy with the well known problem of "data clustering" [16]. The classifiers belonging to the set C play the roles of the "data" and the subsets C_i represent the data "clusters". Analogously, the compound error probability among couples of classifiers plays the role of the distance measure used in data clustering. In particular, in order to perform such a clustering of classifiers, it is easy to see that two "distance" measures are necessary: a distance measure between two classifiers and a distance measure between two clusters of classifiers. We defined the first measure on the basis of the compound error probability:

$$\forall \, c_s, c_t \in C \quad d(c_s, c_t) = 1 - prob(c_s \text{ fails}, c_t \text{ fails}). \tag{5}$$

According to equation 5, two classifiers are as more distant as more they do not make coincident errors. Therefore, the above distance measure groups classifiers that make coincident errors and assigns independent classifiers to different clusters.

The "distance" between two clusters was defined as the maximum "distance" between two classifiers belonging to such clusters:

$$\forall \, C_i, C_j \, i = 1...M, j = 1...M \, i \neq j \quad d(C_i, C_j) = \max_{c_s \in C_i, \, c_t \in C_j} \{d(c_s, c_t)\}. \tag{6}$$

The rationale behind equation 6 can be seen by observing that two clusters containing two independent classifiers must not be merged (even if the other classifiers belonging to such clusters are very correlated), as the subset C* is formed by extracting one classifiers from each cluster. (It is worth also noticing that the same kind of distance measure is also used for data clustering purposes [16]).

It is easy to see that equation 6 can be used also for measuring the distance between a classifier and a cluster previously formed.

Finally, it is worth also noticing that our method computes all the above distance measures with respect to a validation set in order to avoid "overfitting" problems.

Creation of the Subset C*

The subset C* is created by taking one classifier from each cluster C_i. In particular, for each classifier of a given cluster, the average distance from all the other clusters is computed. The classifier characterized by the maximum distance is chosen. The set C* is formed by repeating this procedure for each subset C_i.

3.3 Optimality of the Proposed Approach

Given the above defined set C, let us assume that:

$$\forall c_i \in C,\ i = 1...N,\ \text{prob}(c_i \text{ fails}) = p, \quad p < 0.5 \tag{7}$$

$$\forall C_i, i = 1...M,\ C_i = \{c_{i1}, c_{i2}, ..., c_{in_i}\}, n_i < N \quad \text{prob}(c_{i1} \text{ fails}, c_{i2} \text{ fails}, ..., c_{in_i} \text{ fails}) = p \tag{8}$$

$$\forall c_1 \in C_1,\ \forall c_2 \in C_2, ..., \forall c_M \in C_M \ \text{prob}(c_1 \text{ fails},\ c_2 \text{ fails}, ..., c_M \text{ fails}) = p^M. \tag{9}$$

Equation 7 assumes that all the classifiers belonging to the set C exhibit the same error probability. Equations 8 implies that the classifiers belonging to a given subset make exactly the same errors (i.e., they are completely correlated with respect to the classification errors). According to equation 9, classifiers belonging to different subsets are independent.

Given the above hypotheses, we can prove that the following equation is satisfied:

$$\forall S \subseteq C, S \neq C^*\ p(MCS(S) \text{ fails}) \geq p(MCS(C^*) \text{ fails}) \tag{10}$$

where p(MCS(S) fails) and p(MCS(C*) fails) state for the error probabilities of the MCSs based on the sets S and C*, respectively. C* is the subset of C extracted by our design approach, that is, the set formed by one classifier for each subset C_i (Section 3.2). The majority rule combination function is assumed for such MCSs. (Hereafter the majority rule is always assumed).

The optimality of our design method is proved by equation 10, as such equation states that any subset of C different from C* exhibits a higher error probability. Consequently, C* is the largest subset of independent classifiers contained into the set C.

Proof of Equation 10

Without loosing in generality, we can assume that the subset S mentioned in equation 10 is formed according to one of the following ways:

- by subtracting some classifiers from C*;
- by adding to C* some classifiers taken from the set (C - C*);
- by using both of the two previous ways.

(It is worth noticing that any subset S can be formed according to the above strategy).

Firstly, let us consider the case that the subset S is formed by subtracting some classifiers from the set C*. In this case, the proof comes directly from the following achievement of Hansen and Salamon: the error rate of a MCS based on the majority rule is monotonically decreasing in the number of the independent classifiers combined [3]. Consequently, as the set C* is formed by a number of independent classifiers, subtracting some classifiers from C* surely increases the error rate.

Secondly, let us consider the case that the subset S is formed by adding to C* some classifiers taken from the set (C - C*).

First of all, let us point out that, according to Hansen and Salamon, the error probability of the MCS based on the set C* can be computed as follows:

$$p(MCS(C^*)\,fails) = \sum_{K>\frac{M}{2}}^{M} \binom{M}{K} p^K (1-p)^{M-K}. \tag{11}$$

Without loosing in generality, let us assume to add some classifiers to the set C* so that the cardinality of the set S is "m", $M<m\leq N$.

It should be remarked that the classifiers added to the set C* necessarily belong to the subsets C_i. Consequently, the set S can be regarded as formed by M clusters. It is worth noticing that the set C* can be also regarded as formed by M clusters. The basic difference with respect to the set S is that such clusters can contain only one classifier. It should be also remarked that equation 8 still holds for the clusters of the set S obtained from C* by adding classifiers.

In order to compute the value of the p(MCS(S) fails), we can still use equation 11 by observing that the set S is constituted by M clusters of classifiers completely correlated. This implies that, from the viewpoint of the error probability, any cluster can be regarded as a single classifier with a value of the error probability equal to "p". On the other hand, different clusters are independent according to equation 9. However, with respect to equation 11, it should be noticed that not all the combinations of M/2 clusters belonging to the set S contain a number of classifiers higher than m/2. In particular, the "majority", that is, m/2, can be obtained by numbers of clusters lower and higher than M/2.

Consequently, the value of the p(MCS(S) fails) can be computed as follows:

$$p(MCS(S)\,fails) = \sum_{K>\frac{M}{2}}^{M} \left(\binom{M}{K} - \alpha_K \right) p^K (1-p)^{M-K} + \sum_{K>\frac{M}{2}}^{M} \alpha_K p^{M-K} (1-p)^K \tag{12}$$

where the terms α_K state for the number of the combinations of "K" clusters that do not contain a number of classifiers higher than m/2 (i.e., they do not contain a "majority").

It is easy to see that, for any combination of K clusters that do not contain a "majority", the remaining M-K clusters forming the set S necessarily contain a "majority". This is the reason for the term $\sum_{K>\frac{M}{2}}^{M} \alpha_K p^{M-K}(1-p)^K$ in equation 12.

Equation 12 can be rewritten as follows:

$$p(MCS(S) fails) = \sum_{K>\frac{M}{2}}^{M} \binom{M}{K} p^K (1-p)^{M-K} +$$

$$+ \sum_{K>\frac{M}{2}}^{M} \alpha_K p^{M-K}(1-p)^{M-K} \left((1-p)^{2K-M} - p^{2K-M}\right). \tag{13}$$

As p<0.5, then p<1-p. In addition, 2K-M>0, as K>M/2. Consequently, the error probability in equation 12 is higher, or equal, than the one in equation 10.

Finally, let us consider the last possible way of forming the set S. The proof of equation 10 for this case is straightforward. We have already proved that the p(MCS(S) fails) increases by subtracting classifiers from C*. According to equation 13, it is also proved that such error probability further increases if classifiers taken from the set (C - C*) are then added.

This completes the proof of equation 10.

It is worth noticing that the assumptions of equations 7-9 are likely to be completely or partially met in many real cases of classifier ensembles. As an example, in neural network ensembles obtained by trainings with different weight seeds (see the remarks at the end of Section 3.1). The same holds for the ensembles of k-nearest neighbour classifiers, as subsets of very correlated classifiers are related to different ranges of the "k" parameter.

4. Experimental Results

4.1 The Data Set

The data set used for our experiments consists of a set of multisensor remote-sensing images related to an agricultural area near the village of Feltwell (UK). The images (each of 250 x 350 pixels) were acquired by two imaging sensors installed on an airplane: a multi-band optical sensor (an Airborne Thematic Mapper sensor) and a multi-channel radar sensor (a Synthetic Aperture Radar). More details about the selected data set can be found in [17, 18]. For our experiments, six bands of the optical sensors and nine channels of the radar sensor were selected. Therefore, we used a set of fifteen images. As the image classification process was carried out on a "pixel basis", each pixel was characterised by a fifteen-element "feature vector" containing the brightness values in the six optical bands and over the nine radar channels considered. For our experiments, we selected 10944 pixels belonging to five agricultural classes (i.e., sugar beets, stubble, bare soil, potatoes, carrots) and randomly subdivided them into a training set (5124 pixels), a validation set (582 pixels), and a test set (5238 pixels). We used a small validation set in order to simulate real cases where validation data are difficult to be obtained. (Validation data are extracted from the training sets. Consequently, strong reductions of training sets are necessary to obtain large validation sets).

4.2 Experimentation Planning

Our experiments were mainly aimed to:
- evaluate the effectiveness of the proposed design approach;
- compare our approach with other design approaches proposed in the literature.

Concerning the first aim, we performed different "overproduction" phases, so creating different sets C. Such sets were formed using the following classification algorithms: a k-nearest neighbour (k-nn) classifier, a multilayer perceptron (MLP) neural network, a Radial Basis Functions (RBF) neural network, and a Probabilistic Neural Network (PNN). For each algorithm, a set of classifiers was created by varying the related design parameters (e.g., the network architecture, the "weight seed", the value of the "k" parameter for the k-nn classifier, and so on). In the following, for the sake of brevity, we report the results related to some of such sets C (here referred as C^1, C^2, C^3, and C^4):
- the set C^1 was formed by fifty MLPs. Five architectures with one or two hidden layers and various numbers of neurons per layer were used. For each architecture, ten trainings with different weight seeds were performed. All the networks had fifteen input units and five output units as the numbers of input features and data classes, respectively (Section 4.1);
- the set C^2 was formed by the same MLPs belonging to C^1 and by fourteen k-nn classifiers. The k-nn classifiers were obtained by varying the value of the "k" parameter in the following two ranges: (15, 17, 19, 21, 23, 25, 27) and (75, 77, 79, 81, 83, 85, 87);
- the set C^3 was formed by nineteen MLPS and one PNN. Two different architectures were used for the MLPSs (15-7-7-5 and 15-30-15-5). For the PNN, an a priori fixed value of the smoothing parameter equal to 0.1 was selected [19].
- the set C^4 was formed by the same MLPs belonging to C^3, three RBF neural networks, and one PNN.

With regard to the second aim of our experimentation, we compared our design method with two methods proposed by Partridge and Yates [10]. One is the "choose the best" method that, given an a priori fixed size of the set C*, choose the classifiers with the highest accuracies in order to form C*. The other is the so called "choose from subspaces" method that, for each classification algorithm, choose the classifier with the highest accuracy. (The term "subspace" is therefore referred to the subset of classifiers related to a given classification algorithm).

4.3 Results and Comparisons

Experimentation with the Set C^1

The main aim of this experiment was to evaluate the effectiveness of our approach for the design of neural network ensembles formed by a single kind of net. It is worth noticing that this is a difficult design task, as nets of the same type are poorly independent according to the Partridge results [9]. Our algorithm created a set C^* formed by 7 MLPs belonging to three different architectures. This is a not obvious result, as the most obvious set C^* should be formed by taking one net from each of the five architectures. Table 1 reports the performances of the MCS based on the set C^* designed by our algorithm. For comparison purposes, the performances of the MCSs based on the initial set C^1 and on the other two design methods are also reported. A size of the set C^* equal to five was fixed for the "choose the best" method. The performances are measured in terms of the percentage of classification accuracy, the rejection percentage, and the difference between accuracy and rejection. All the values are referred to the test set. The performances of all the three design methods are similar. (Our method is slightly better, but the difference is very small). This can be seen by observing that the initial set C^1 also provides similar performances. This means that the set C^1 does not contain classifiers very "uncorrelated" that can be extracted by a design method in order to improve performances.

Table 1. Results provided by different design methods applied to the set C^1.

MCS based on	%Accuracy	%Rejection	%(Accuracy-Rejection)
Our design method	90.52	0.82	89.70
C^1	89.83	1.20	88.63
Choose the best	90.10	0.49	89.60
Choose from subspaces	89.98	0.49	89.48

Experimentation with the Set C^2

Our algorithm extracted a set C^* formed by 5 MLPs and two k-nn classifiers. The five MLPs belonged to the same three architectures of the previous experiment. The two k-nn classifiers corresponded to values of the "k" parameter equal to 21 and 77, respectively. It is worth noticing that such values are quite distant. (This result is in agreement with the expected correlation of the k-nn classifiers for close values of the "k" parameter). Table 2 reports the performances of the MCS based on the set C^* designed by our algorithm. For comparison purposes, the performances of the MCSs based on the initial set C^2 and on the other two design methods are also reported. All the values are referred to the test set. A size of the set C^* equal to seven was fixed for the "choose the best" method. The performances of all the three design methods are similar. Therefore, conclusions similar to the ones of the previous experiment can be drawn.

Table 2. Results provided by different design methods applied to the set C^2.

MCS based on	%Accuracy	%Rejection	%(Accuracy-Rejection)
Our design method	91.59	1.14	90.45
C^2	90.49	1.01	89.48
Choose the best	90.27	0.11	90.16
Choose from subspaces	91.32	0.97	90.35

Experimentation with the Set C^3

This experiment was aimed to evaluate the capability of our design method of exploiting the "uncorrelation" of a set of "weak" classifiers in order to improve the performances of the initial set C^3. Therefore, we created a set of nineteen MLPs whose performances were not good (ranging from 80.41% to 85.05%). However, such MLPs were based on two different architectures and different weight seeds in order to assure a reasonable degree of error uncorrelation. In addition, we used a PNN that can be expected to be "independent" from the MLPs. Our algorithm extracted a set C* formed by two MLPs, characterized by two different architectures, and the PNN.

Table 3 reports the performances of the MCSs based on the different classifier sets. All the values are referred to the test set. A size of the set C* equal to three was fixed for the "choose the best" method. The results show that our design method is able to choose classifiers more independent than the ones selected by the other methods. This achievement can be explained by observing that a detailed analysis of error uncorrelation is necessary in order to choose effective classifiers from a set of weak classifiers. This kind of analysis is not carried out by the other methods.

Table 3. Results provided by different design methods applied to the set C^3.

MCS based on	%Accuracy	%Rejection	%(Accuracy-Rejection)
Our design method	91.31	2.20	89.11
C^3	87.87	2.37	85.50
Choose the best	88.78	1.65	87.13
Choose from subspaces	89.35	1.57	87.78

Experimentation with the Set C^4

The aim of this experiment is basically similar to the previous one. Our algorithm extracted a set C* formed by one MLPs, one RBF neural network, and the PNN. Table 4 reports the performances of the MCSs based on the different classifier sets. All the values are referred to the test set. A size of the set C* equal to three was fixed for the "choose the best" method. It is easy to see that conclusions similar to the ones of the previous experiment can be drawn.

Table 4. Results provided by different design methods applied to the set C^4.

MCS based on	%Accuracy	%Rejection	%(Accuracy-Rejection)
Our design method	94.83	4.71	90.11
C^4	90.46	3.05	87.41
Choose the best	88.78	1.65	87.13
Choose from subspaces	89.35	1.57	87.78

5. Conclusions

In this paper, an approach to the automatic design of MCSs formed by different classification algorithms has been described. To the best of our knowledge, in the pattern recognition field, no previous work directly addressed such a problem. Some work was carried out by neural network researchers. However, the results of such research work can be exploited only in part for MCSs formed by different classifiers. The experimental results reported in this paper showed the effectiveness of the proposed design approach. In addition, a proof of the optimality of our approach has been provided. It is worth noticing that the assumptions required by such proof are completely or partially met in many real cases of classifier ensembles.

References

1. L. Xu, A. Krzyzak, and C.Y. Suen, "Methods for combining multiple classifiers and their applications to handwriting recognition", IEEE Trans. on Systems, Man, and Cyb., Vol. 22, No. 3, May/June 1992, pp. 418-435
2. J. Kittler, M. Hatef, R.P.W. Duin and J. Matas "On Combining Classifiers", IEEE Trans. on Pattern Analysis and Machine Intelligence, Vol.20, No.3, March 1998, pp. 226-239
3. L. K. Hansen, and P. Salamon, "Neural network ensembles", IEEE Trans. on Pattern Analysis and Machine Intelligence, Vol. 12, No. 10, October 1990, pp. 993-1001
4. K. Tumer and J. Ghosh, "Error correlation and error reduction in ensemble classifiers", Connection Science 8, December 1996, pp. 385-404
5. A. J. C. Sharkey (Ed.), Special Issue: Combining Artificial Neural Nets: Ensemble Approaches. Connection Science Vol. 8, No. 3 & 4, Dec. 1996
6. Y.S. Huang, and C.Y. Suen, "A method of combining multiple experts for the recognition of unconstrained handwritten numerals", IEEE Trans. on on Pattern Analysis and Machine Intelligence, Vol.17, No.1, January 1995, pp.90-94
7. Y.S. Huang, K. Liu and C. Y. Suen,, "The combination of multiple classifiers by a neural network approach", Int. Journal of Pattern Recognition and Artificial Intelligence, Vol. 9, no.3, 1995, pp.579-597
8. G. Giacinto and F. Roli, "Ensembles of Neural Networks for Soft Classification of Remote Sensing Images", Proc. of the European Symposium on Intelligent Techniques, Bari, Italy, pp. 166-170
9. D.Partridge, "Network generalization differences quantified", Neural Networks, Vol.9, No.2, 1996, pp.263-271

10. D.Partridge and W.B.Yates, "Engineering multiversion neural-net systems", Neural Computation, 8, 1996, pp. 869-893
11. D.W.Opitz and J.W.Shavlik, "Actively searching for an effective neural network ensemble", Connection Science Vol. 8, No. 3 & 4, Dec. 1996, pp. 337-353
12. B.E.Rosen, "Ensemble learning using decorrelated neural networks", Connection Science Vol. 8, No. 3 & 4, Dec. 1996, pp. 373-383
13. C.Ji and S.Ma, "Combination of weak classifiers", IEEE Trans. On Neural Networks, Vol.8, No.1, Jan. 1997, pp. 32-42
14. K.D.Bollacker, and J.Ghosh, "Knowledge reuse in multiple classifier systems", Pattern Recognition Letters, 18, 1997, pp. 1385-1390
15. B.Littlewood and D.R.Miller, "Conceptual modelling of coincident failures in multiversion software", IEEE Trans. On Software Engineering, 15(12), 1989, pp; 1569-1614
16. A.K.Jain and R.C.Dubes, Algorithms for clustering data, Prentice Hall, 1988
17. F. Roli, "Multisensor image recognition by neural networks with understandable behaviour" International Journal of Pattern Recognition and Artificial Intelligence Vol. 10, No. 8, 1996, pp. 887-917
18. S. B. Serpico, and F. Roli, "Classification of multi-sensor remote-sensing images by structured neural networks", IEEE Trans. Geoscience Remote Sensing 33, 1995, pp. 562-578.
19. S.B.Serpico., L. Bruzzone and F.Roli, "An experimental comparison of neural and statistical non-parametric algorithms for supervised classification of remote-sensing images" Pattern Recognition Letters 17, 1996, 1331-1341.

A Comparison between Neural Networks and Decision Trees

Carsten Jacobsen, Uwe Zscherpel and Petra Perner[*]

Bundesanstalt für Materialforschung und -prüfung, Unter den Eichen 87, 12205 Berlin
[*]Institute of Computer Vision and Applied Computer Sciences Leipzig
Arno-Nitzsche-Str. 45, 04277 Leipzig, Germany
ibaiperner@aol.com, uwez@bam.de

Abstract. In the paper, we empirical compare the performance of neural nets and decision trees based on a data set for the detection of defects in welding seams. The data set was created by image feature extraction procedures working on x-ray images. We consider our data set as highly complex and containing imprecise and uncertain data's. We explain how the data set was created and what kinds of features were extracted from the images. Then, we explain what kind of neural nets and induction of decision trees were used for classification.
We introduce a framework for distinguishing classification methods. We observed that the performance of neural nets is not significant better than the performance of decision trees if we are only looking for the overall error rate. We found that more detailed analysis of the error rate is necessary in order to judge the performance of the learning and classification method. However, the error rate can not be the only criteria for the comparison between the different learning methods. It is a more complex selection process that involves more criteria's that we describe in the paper.

1 Introduction

The development of an image interpretation system is comprised of the two tasks: selection of the right features and construction of the classifier.

The selection of the right method for the classification is not easy and often depends on the preference of the system developer. The paper describes a first step towards a methodology for the selection of the appropriate classification method. Our investigation hasn't been done on a standard academic data set where the data's are usually nicely cleaned up. The basis for our investigation is an image database that contains x-ray images from welding seams. An image is decomposed into region of interest and for each region of interest are calculated 36 features by image processing procedure. A detailed description of this process is given in Section 2. In the resulting database each entry describes a region of interest by its 36 feature values and a class entry determined by a skilled operator. The task is to classify the regions of interest automatically into background or into defects like crack and undercut.

Based on the data set we learnt two different types of classifiers: neural nets and decision trees. The different kind of neural nets and decision trees are described in Section 3. Since the class is given we deal with supervised learning. The design and test data set is described in Section 4.

We introduce a framework for distinguishing learning and classification methods in Section 5. A detailed description of the performance analysis is given in Section 6. We observed that the performance of neural nets is not significant better than the performance of decision trees if we are only looking for the overall error rate. In opposition to most other work on performance analysis [Statlog], we found that a more detailed analysis of the error rate is necessary in order to judge the performance of the learning and classification method. However, the error rate can not be the only criteria for the comparison between the different learning methods. It is a more complex selection process that involves more criteria's like explanation capability, number of features involved in classification etc. Finally, we give conclusions in Section 7.

2 The Application

2.1 The Inspected Welds

The subject of this investigation is a set of austenitic welds. The flaws in the austenitic welds are due to intergranular stress corrosion cracking at the inner side of the tube. The inspected tubes have a wall thickness between 5 mm and 15 mm and a diameter of 80-250 mm. They were penetrated by a x-ray tube with 120 kV or 160 kV.

2.2 Feature Extraction by Digital Image Processing

The schematic representation of the processing chain is shown in Figure 1. The radiographs of the welds are digitized by a CCD-line scanner, type "Image Master", manufactured by DBA Systems, U.S.A. The scanner provides an optical density resolution of $\Delta D < 0{,}02$ within an optical density range from 0 to 4.5. The radiographs are digitized with a spatial resolution of 70µm and a gray level resolution of 16 bit per pixel. Afterwards they are stored and decomposed into various Regions of Interest ROIs) of 50x50 pixel size. The essential info at the ROIs is described by a set of features, which is calculated from various image-processing methods.

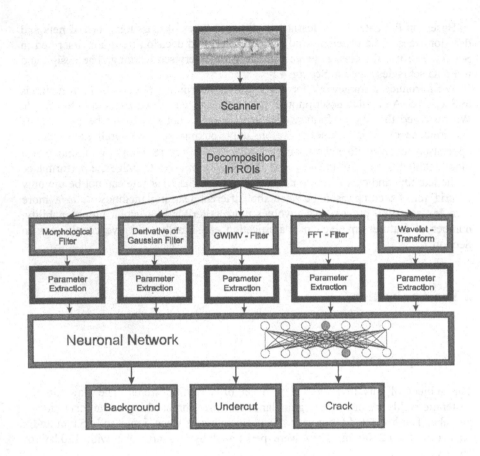

Fig. 1. Schematic representation of the processing chain

The image processing procedures are based on the assumption that the crack is roughly parallel to the direction of the weld. This assumption is reasonable because of material and welding technique. It allows the definition of a marked preferential direction. Because of this the images are digitized and rotated in a way that the weld direction is positioned in the image in an approximate horizontal direction. It is now feasible to search for features in gray level profiles perpendicular to the weld direction in the image. In Figure 2 the ROIs of a crack, an undercut and of no disturbance are shown with the corresponding cross sections and profile plots.

Edge detection operators were developed originally to detect object borders and - edges in images. The principle of many of these methods is based on the detection of local gray value discontinuities. Flaws in welds imaged in a radiograph behave in this manner. Thus it is reasonable to apply the Morphological Edge Finding Operator, the Derivative of Gaussian Operator and the Gaussian Weighted Image Moment Vector - Operator.

The Morphological Edge Detection Operator, which is introduced in [2], consists of a combination of the morphological operators Dilation and Erosion, which move the gray value edges in an image in different directions. The difference-images

$$dilation(g(p))\text{-}g(p) \ and \ g(p)\text{-}erosion(g(p))$$

result in respective shifted edge-images (g(p) is the original image). After a final minimum operation on both images the steepest edges remain in the resulting image as maxima.

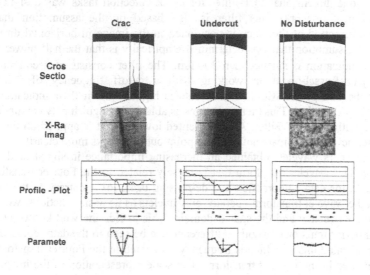

Fig. 2. ROI of a crack, of an undercut and of a region without disturbance with corresponding crossections and profile plots.

The Derivative of Gaussian Filter is described in [3] and is based on a combination of a Gaussian smoothing with a following partial derivation of the image in x- and y-direction. The result of the filter is chosen as the maximum of the derivatives.

Another filter, which was designed especially for flaw detection in radiographs of welds, is introduced in [4]. This method uses the vector representation of the image and calculates, analogous to the model known from mechanics, the image moment:

$$\vec{M}(i,j) = \sum_{\substack{(x,y)\in N \\ (x,y)\neq(i,j)}} \vec{r}(x,y) \times \vec{P}(x,y) \tag{1}$$

In equation (1) M represents the Image Moment Vector while r defines the distance between the points (x,y) and (i,j). The vector P is defined as follows:

$$\vec{P}(x,y) = P(x,y) \cdot \vec{n} \cdot \qquad (2)$$

In (2) P(x,y) represents the respective image gray value and n represents the normal vector of the image plane. The respective components of the cross product in equation (1) represent a convolution of the image, which disappears in the background regions and has a response unequal to zero in case of an edge in the image region. Pixels located at a greater distance from the observed center have to be weighted less strongly than pixel closer to the center. Weighting the results with a Gaussian function compensates this effect. The filter is called Gaussian Weighted Image Moment Vector-Operator (GWIMV).

In [5] a one-dimensional FFT-Filter for crack detection tasks was designed and considered in this work. This filter is also based on the assumption that the preferential direction of the crack is positioned in the image in horizontal direction. The second assumption that was determined empirically is that the half power width of a crack indication is smaller than 300 μm. The filter consists of a column wise FFT-Highpass-Bessel-operation working with a cutoff frequency of 2 LP/mm. Normally the half-power width of undercuts is bigger so that their indications are suppressed by this filter. This means that one is able to distinguish between undercuts and cracks with this FFT-Filter. A row-oriented lowpass that is applied on the result of this filter helps to eliminate noise and to point out the cracks more clearly.

In recent years wavelets obtained an increasing importance in signal- and image processing. The wavelet transform that is closely related to the Fourier transform is very suitable for data compression and de-noising tasks [6]. Contrary to the Fourier transform the wavelet transform operates on wavelets as its basis functions, which are finite in the frequency and the spatial domain. This avoids the well-known artifacts from the Fourier transform. Another difference can be seen in the data representation of the transformed image, which is frequency orientated in the Fourier transform and scale orientated in the wavelet transform. The scale representation of the image after the wavelet transform makes it possible to suppress the noise in the image with a simple threshold operation without loosing significant parts of the content of the image. The noise in the image is an interference of film- and scanner noise and irregularities caused by the material of the weld.

The features, which describe the content of the ROIs and are used to train the neuronal networks, are extracted from profile plots, which run through the ROI perpendicular to the weld. The principle is shown in figure 3.

In a single profile plot the position of a local minimum is detected, which is surrounded by two as large as possible maxima. This definition varies a little depending on the respective image processing routine. A template, which is adapted to the current profile of the signal, allows the calculation of various features (S1, S2, L1, L2). Moreover the half-power width and the respective gradients between the local extrema are calculated. To avoid statistical calculation errors the calculation of the template features is averaged over all columns along a ROI. This procedure leads to a number of 36 parameters.

For a more detailed description of the application, we refer the interested reader to [7].

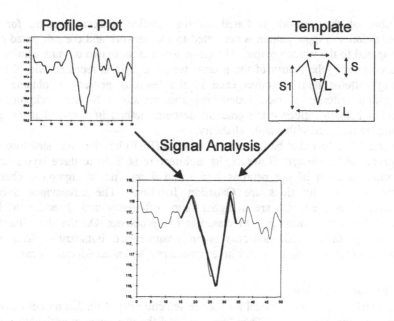

Fig. 3. Schematic representation of the feature calculation from the profile plots with a template.

3 Methods

3.1 Neural Nets

Neural networks, which are motivated in their structure by the human brain, are often applied in classification and controlling tasks [8]. In this paper a neuronal network is used to classify the ROIs according to the applied features into three categories (no disturbance, undercut and crack).

Two types of neuronal networks are used here: A Backpropagation Network and a Radial Basis Function Network (RBF), which are similar in structure and processing behavior.

The elementary entity of a neuronal network is a neuron. A simple neuron principally operates like an adding machine with weighted inputs. Moreover, a neuron produces an output only if the sum from the adding process exceeds a certain threshold. This is called: "The neuron fires". If the neuron fires, the calculated sum is weighted with a so-called activation function, which is of sigmoidal character in the case of a backpropagation network. A layer-wise connection of many neurons is called a neuronal network. The backpropagation network consists of several (at least two) layers of neurons which are connected to each other completely. Connections that skip a layer are forbidden in the backpropagation and RBF structure. The learning algorithm of the network is based on the gradient descent method for error minimization. An input pattern is presented to the network and the calculated output is compared to the wanted output. The error between these two outputs is minimized by reconfiguring the matrix of the neuron weights. This is repeated with the other training patterns until a convergence in the learning process is obtained or a termination criterion is met. Extensions and variations of the backpropagation algorithm help to influence the gradient descent method in a way that the global minima are obtained with a high reliability.

In principle, the radial basis function network (RBF) has the same structure as the backpropagation network. However, its architecture is fixed to three layers and the activation function of the neurons has a radial and not a sigmoidal character. Frequently these functions are Gaussian functions. The advantages over the backpropagation networks are a higher learn efficiency and detection of better decision boundaries according to classification problems. On the other hand, the disadvantage of the RBF-networks is an unsupervised initializing phase at the beginning of the learning process where important discriminate decisions can get lost.

3.1.1 Feature Selection

First, we tried the wrapper model for feature selection [9]. With that model we did not obtain any significant result. Therefore, we used the parameter significance analysis by a neural network [10] for feature selection.

By that model we can reduce the parameter to a number of 7 significant parameters. The significance of a parameter can be determined by changing the value of a parameter that is applied to a neuronal net. Small changes of the parameter value are processed and the changes at the output of the network are inspected. A significant feature shows a large change at the output, although there is a relatively small change at the input. The parameters that were evaluated as the most significant are the following:

- the variable S1 and the gradient of the morphologic edge finding operator,
- the variable S2 of the Derivative of Gaussian Filter,
- the half-power L3 width of the indication after de-noising by wavelets,
- the half-power width L3 and the contrast S1 of the indication after the FFT-Highpass and
- the variable S2 of the GWIMV-filter.

3.2 Induction of Decision Trees

3.2.1 Decision Trees

Decision trees partition decision space recursively into subregions based on the sample set. By doing so they break down recursively the complexity of the decision space. The representation form that comes out is a format, which naturally covers the cognitive statregy for humans decision making process.

A decision tree consists of nodes and branches. Each node represents a single test or decision. In the case of a binary tree, the decision is either true or false.

Geometrically, the test describes a partition orthogonal to one of the coordinates of the decision space. The starting node is usually referred to as the root node. Depending on whether the result of a test is true or false, the tree will branch right or left to another node. Finally, a terminal node is reached (sometimes refereed as leaf), and a decision is made on the class assignment. All paths in a tree are mutually exclusive. For any new case, one and only one path in the tree has always have to be satisfied. Nonbinary decision trees are also widely used. In these trees, more than two branches may leave a node, but again only one branch may enter a node. In this type of tree, a test performed at a node result in a partition of two or more disjoint sets that cover every possibility, i.e., any new case must fall into one of the disjoint subsets. For any tree, all paths lead to a terminal node corresponding to a decision rule that is a conjunction (AND) of various tests. If there are multiple paths for a given class, then the paths represent disjunction's (ORs) [11].

Attribute selection and splitting into subregion is done automatically during decision tree learning.

The most used criteria for automatic splitting of the sample set [12][13], which is simple to calculate and performs well, is the Shannon entropy:

$$I = - \sum_i p_i \, log_2 \, p_i \tag{3}$$

Note that I has a maximum value when the entire p_i 's are equal; that is, the classes are uniformly distributed throughout the set. This means that there is still a lot of information in this set. I is minimized to zero if one of the p_i 's is unity and the others are zero: In this case all examples belong to one class, and there is no more information in the set.

Now if we subdivide the subset according to the values of an attribute, we shall have a number of subsets. For each of these subsets we can compute the information value. Let the information value of subset n be i_n, then the new information value is given by

$$I_i = \sum q_n \, i_n \tag{4}$$

where q_n is the portion of examples having attribute values n. I_i will be smaller than I, and the difference $(I - I_i)$ is a measure of how well the attribute has discriminated between different classes. The attribute that maximizes this difference will be selected.

The recursive partitioning method of constructing decision trees will continue to sub-divide the set of training cases until each subset in the partition contains cases of single class, or until no test offers any improvement. For this tree based on the sample cases the error rate is calculated, which is:

$$E = S_m / N, \tag{5}$$

where S_m is the number of samples that were misclassified and N is the whole number of samples.

The result is often a very complex tree that "overfits the data" by inferring more structure than is justified by the training cases. Therefore, pruning techniques are used which simplify the tree by discarding one or more subtrees and replacing them with leaves. We use reduced-error pruning technique [14], which accesses the error rates of the tree and its components directly on the set of cases. The predicted error rate is calculated

$$E_{pred} = \sum_i N_i \, U_{CF} \, (\, E_i, \, N_i), \tag{6}$$

where N_i is the number of sample cases covered by the leave, E_i is the number of misclassified sample cases covered by the leave, $U_{CF}(E_i, N_i)$ is the upper limit on the probability for a chosen confidence value CF for the binomial distribution and i is the number of leaves. This implies that a tree with fewer leaves will have a lower error rate than a tree with more leaves.

While the above-described method will only induce binary decision trees, the method described in [15] can also produce n-ary decision trees.

For our experiment, we use the software tool *DECISION MASTER* [16].

3.2.1 Feature Selection

Since only relevant attributes are chosen for decision rule, decision tree induction can also be considered as a method for attribute selection. The attribute that maximizes the difference $(I - I_j)$ will be selected during the tree construction process.

However, the selection criteria can not sort out correlated attributes. Two linear correlated attributes would bring nearly the same result but only the first appearing attribute that might not be the truly relevant attribute is chosen for the next node. The second attribute, which has not been chosen for the node, is not sorted out; it is still left in the sample set and gets still processed during tree building process.

In case, there are two attributes having the same value for the attribute selection criteria, the first appearing attribute will be chosen. That means the attribute selection process is sensitive to the order of the attributes.

4 Data Set

For the learning data set of the neuronal networks and the decision tree ROIs from background, crack and undercut regions of the images were extracted from the films and their features were calculated. The learning data set for the austenitic welds consists of altogether 1924 ROIs. 1024 are extracted from regions of no disturbance, 465 from regions with cracks and 435 from regions with undercuts. Additional to the learning data set a test data set is arranged of 390 patterns (208 background, 102 crack and 80 undercuts).

For the evaluation of the error rate we use test and train method. Decision Master is also able to do cross validation but we are not able to evaluate the neural nets in the same manner.

5 Evaluation Criteria

The most used evaluation criteria for a classifier is the error rate $f_r = N_f/N$ with N_f the number of false classified samples and N the whole number of samples. In addition to that we use a contingency table in order to show the qualities of a classifier, see Table 1. In the field of the table are inputted the actual and the real class distribution as well as the marginal distribution c_{ij}. The main diagonal is the number of correct classified samples. The last row shows the number of samples assigned to the class shown in row 1 and the last line shows the real class distribution. From this table, we can calculate parameters that assess the quality of the classifier.

		Real Class Index				
		1	i	...	m	Sum
	1	c_{11}	...	...	c_{1m}	
Assigned	j	...	c_{ji}	...	...	
Class	...	...	...	...	...	
Index	m	c_{m1}	...	...	c_{mm}	
	Sum					

Table 1. Contingency Table

The *correctness p* that is number of correct classified samples according to the number of samples:

$$p = \frac{\sum_{i=1}^{m} c_{ii}}{\sum_{i=1}^{m}\sum_{j=1}^{m} c_{ij}} \qquad (7).$$

For the investigation of the classification quality we measure the classification quality p_{ki} according to a particular class i and the number of correct classified samples for one class p_t:

$$p_{ki} = \frac{c_{ii}}{\sum_{j=1}^{m} c_{ji}} \qquad p_{ti} = \frac{c_{ii}}{\sum_{i=1}^{m} c_{ij}} \qquad (8).$$

In addition to that we use other criteria's shown in Table 2.

One of these criteria's is the cost for classification expressed by the number of features and the number of decisions used during classification. The other criteria is the time needed for learning. We also consider the explanation capability of the classifier as another quality criteria. It is also important to know if classification method can learn the classification function (the mapping of the attributes to the classes) correct based on the training data set. Therefore, we not only consider the error rate based on the test set we also consider the error rate based on the training data set.

Generalization Capability of the Classifier	Error Rate based on the Test Data Set
Representation of the Classifier	Error Rate based on the Design Data Set
Classification Costs	• Number of Features used for Classification • Number of Nodes or Neurons
Explanation Capability	Can a human understand the decision
Learning Performance	Learning Time
	Sensitivity to Class Distribution in the Sample Set

Table 2. Criteria`s for Comparison of learned Classifiers

6 Results

The error rate for the design data set and the test data set is shown in Table 3. The unprunend decision tree shows the best error rate for the design data set. This tree represents best the data. However, if we look for the error rate calculated based on the test data set then we note that the RBF neural Net and the Backpropagation network can do better. Their performance show not such a big difference in the two error rates like for the decision tree. The representation and generalization ability is more balanced in case of the neural networks whereas the unprunend decision tree gets overfitted to the data. This is a typical characteristic of decision tree induction. Pruning techniques should reduce this behavior. The representation and generalization ability of the pruned tree shows a more balanced behavior but it can not outperform the results of the neural nets.

The behavior of the neural nets according to the representation and generalization ability is controlled during the learning process. The training phase has been regular interrupted and the error rate was determined based on the training set. If the error rate decreases after a maximum value then the net has been reached the maximal generalization ability.

It is interesting to note that the Fuzzy-ARTMAP-Net and the LVQ have the same behavior in the representation and generalization ability as the decision trees.

The observation for the decision tree suggests another methodology for using decision trees. In data mining, where we mine a large database for the underlying knowledge it might be more appropriate to use decision tree induction since it can represent the data well.

The performance of the RBF expressed by the error rate is 4% better than it is for the decision tree. The question is: How to judge that? Is 4 % a significant difference? We believe it is not. Nevertheless, the decision must be made based on the application. In some cases it might be necessary to have a 4% better error rate whereas in other cases it might not have a significant influence.

Name of Classifier		Error Rate on Design Data Set in %	Error Rate on the Test Data Set in %
Binary Decision Tree	unpruned	1,6632	9,8
	pruned	4,6065	9,5
n-ary Decision Tree	unpruned	8,627	12,32
	pruned	8,627	12,32
Backpropagation Network		3	6
Radial Basis Function Neural Net		5,00	5
Fuzzy-ARTMAP-Net		0,0	9
LVQ		1,0	9

Table 3. Error Rate for Design Data Set and Test Data Set

					Real Class Index
		Background	Crack	Undercut	Sum
Classification	Background	196	2	1	199
Result	Crack	12	99	22	132
	Undercut	0	1	58	59
	Sum	208	102	80	390
	p_k	0,94	0,97	0,725	
	p_t	0,98	0,744	0,98	
				p=0,901	k=0,85

Table 4. Contingency Table of the Classification Result for the Decision Tree

					Real Class Index
		Background	Crack	Undercut	Sum
Classification	Background	194	5	1	200
Result	Crack	1	97	3	100
	Undercut	13	0	76	90
	Sum	208	102	80	390
	p_k	0,93	0,95	0,95	
	p_t	0,97	0,96	0,85	
				p=0,94	k=0,90

Table 5. Contingency Table of the Classification Result for the Backpropagation Net

A more clear picture of the performance of the various methods we obtain if we look for the classification quality p_k and the class-specific error rate p_t, see Table 4 to Table 8. In case of the decision tree, we observe that the class specific error rate for class "undercut" is very good and can outperform the error rate obtained by neural nets. In opposition to that, the classification quality for decision trees is worse. Samples from the class "crack" are false classified into class "undercut". That results in a low classification quality of the class "crack". In opposition to that, the neural nets show a difference in class specific recognition. Mostly, the class specific error for class "crack" is worse. However, the value difference is not so significant as in case of the decision trees. Since a defect "crack" is more important than a defect "undercut" it would be good to have a better class specific error for "crack".

				Real Class Index	
		Background	Crack	Undercut	Sum
Classification	Background	198	2	1	201
Result	Crack	1	100	7	108
	Undercut	9	0	72	81
	Sum	208	102	80	390
	p_k	0,95	0,98	0,90	
	p_t	0,99	0,93	0,89	
					p=0,95 k=0,92

Table 6. Contingency Table of the Classification Result for the Radial Basis Function Net

				Real Class Index	
		Background	Crack	Undercut	Sum
Classification	Background	183	2	0	185
Result	Crack	7	100	7	114
	Undercut	18	0	73	91
	Sum	208	102	80	390
	p_k	0,88	0,98	0,91	
	p_t	0,99	0,87	0,80	
					p=0,91 k=0,86

Table 7. Contingency Table of the Classification Result for the LVQ

				Real Class Index	
		Background	Crack	Undercut	Sum
Classification	Background	191	5	1	197
Result	Crack	10	96	10	116
	Undercut	7	1	69	77
	Sum	208	102	80	390
	p_k	0,92	0,94	0,86	
	p_t	0,97	0,83	0,90	
					p=0,91 k=0,86

Table 8. Contingency Table of the Classification Result for the Fuzzy-ARTMAP Net

Our decision tree produces decision surfaces that are axis parallel to the feature axis. This method should be able to approximate a non-linear decision surface with of course a certain approximation error which will lead to a higher error rate in classification. Therefore, we are not surprised that there are more features involved in the classification, see Table 9. The unpruned tree uses 14 features and the pruned tree 10 features. The learned decision tree is a very big and bushy tree with 450 nodes. The pruned tree gets reduced to 250 nodes but still remains as very big and bushy tree.

Name of Classifier		Number of Features	Number of Nodes
Decision Tree	Unpruned	14	450
	Pruned	10	250
Backpropagation Net		7	72 neurons
RBF Net		7	
LVQ		7	51 neurons
Fuzzy ARTMAP Net		7	

Table 9. Number of Features and Number of Nodes

The neural nets work only on 7 features and e.g. for the backpropagation net we have 72 neurons. That reduces the effort for feature extraction drastically.

One of the advantages of induction of decision trees is its easy use. Feature selection and tree construction is done automatically without any human interaction. For the used data set of 1924 samples and on a PC 486 it takes only a few seconds until the decision tree has been learned. In opposition to that, neural network learning can not be handled so easy. The learning time for the neural nets was on a workstation type INDY Silicon Graphics (R4400-Processor, 150 MHz) with the neural network simulator NeuralWorks Professional II/Plus version 5.0   15 minutes for the backpropagation net by 60 000 learning steps, 18 minutes for RBF net, 20 minutes for LVQ net, and 45 minutes for the Fuzzy-ARTMAP-net.

A disadvantage of neural nets is that the feature selection is a pre-step before learning. In our case it had been done with a backpropagation net. The parameter significance is determined based on the contribution analysis method (see Section 3).

Although, the class distribution in the design data set was not uniform, both methods neural net-based learning and decision tree learning did well on the data set. It might be that in case of decision trees the worse class specific error rate for "crack" results from the non-uniform sample distribution. But that is not proved yet it will be proven as soon as new samples are available.

One of big advantages of decision trees is their explanation capability. A human can understand the rules and can control the decision making process. Neural nets can not do this.

7 Conclusion

We have compared decision trees to neural nets. For our empirical evaluation, we used a data set of x-ray images that were taken from welding seams. 36 features described the defects contained in the welding seams. Image feature extraction were used to create the final data set for our experiment.

We found that special types of neural nets have slightly better performance than decision trees. In addition to that, there are not so much features involved for classification that is especially for image interpretation tasks a good argument. Image processing and feature extraction is mostly time-consuming and requires for real time use special purpose hardware for the computation. But the explanation capability that exists for trees producing axis-parallel decision surfaces is an important advantage over neural nets. Moreover, the learning process is not so time-consuming and it is easy to handle in case of decision trees.

All that shows that the decision what kind of method should be used is not only a question of the resulting error rate. It is more complex selection process that can only be decided based on the constraints of the application.

References

1. D. Michie, D.J. Spiegelhalter, and C.C. Taylor, Machine Leaning, Neural Nets and Statistical Classsification, Ellis Horwood Series in Artificial Intelligence, 1994
2. R. Klette and P. Zamperoni, Handbuch der Operatoren für die Bildbearbeitung, Vieweg Verlagsgesellschaft, 1992
3. K.W. Pratt, Digital Image Processing, John Wiley & Sons, Inc. New York Chichester Brisbane Toronto Singapore, 1991
4. N. Eua-Anant, I. Elshafiey, Upda, L., Gray, J. N.: A Novel Image Processing Algorithm for Enhancing the Probability of Detection of Flaws in X-Ray Images, Review of Progress in Quantitative Nondestructive Evaluation, Vol. 15, Plenum Press, New York, 1996, pp.: 903-910
5. Zscherpel, U., Nockemann C., Mattis A., Heinrich W.: Neue Entwicklungen bei der Filmdigitalisierung, DGZfP-Jahrestagung in Aachen, Tagungsband, 1995
6. Strang, G.: Wavelets and Dilation Equations: A Brief Introduction, Sam Review 31, 1989, pp.: 613-627
7. C. Jacobsen, Verbesserung der bildverarbeitungsgestützen Rißdetektion an Schweißnahtradiographien mit neuronalen Netzen, Thesis Kiel, 1999
8. Zell, A.: Simulation Neuronaler Netze, Addison Wesley, Bonn, Paris, 1994
9. Huan Lui and Hiroshi Motoda, Feature Selection for Knowledge Discovery and Data Mining, Kluwer Academic Publishers 1998
10. Egmont-Petersen et a., Contribution Analysis of multi-layer Perceptrons. Estimation of the Input Sources Importance for the Classification, Pattern Recognition in Practice IV, Proceedings International Workshop, Vlieland, The Netherlands, 1994, p. 347-357.
11. S.M. Weiss and C.A. Kulikowski, Computer Systems that learn, Morgan Kaufmann, 1991
12. J.R. Quinlain, Induction of Decision Trees, Machine Learning 1 (1996): 81-106
13. P. Vanroose, Luc Van Gool, and Andre Oosterlinck, Buca: A new pattern classificaiton algorithm, In Proc. 12th Prague conference on Infomation Theoretical Decision Functions and Random Processes, August 29-Sept 1, 1994
14. J.R. Quinlain, „Simplifying decision trees," Intern. Journal on Man-Machine Studies, 27 (1987): 221-234.
15. P. Perner and S. Trautzsch, On Feature Partioning for Decision Tree Induction, A. Amin and P. Pudil (Eds.), SSPR98 and SPR98, Springer Verlag 1998
16. P. Perner, Decision Master, http://www.ibai-solutions.de/

Symbolic Learning Techniques in Paper Document Processing

Oronzo Altamura   Floriana Esposito   Francesca A. Lisi   Donato Malerba

Dipartimento di Informatica, Università degli Studi di Bari
via Orabona 4, 70126 Bari, Italy
{ altamura I esposito I lisi I malerba } @di.uniba.it

Abstract. WISDOM++ is an intelligent document processing system that transforms a paper document into HTML/XML format. The main design requirement is adaptivity, which is realized through the application of machine learning methods. This paper illustrates the application of symbolic learning algorithms to the first three steps of document processing, namely document analysis, document classification and document understanding. Machine learning issues related to the application are: Efficient incremental induction of decision trees from numeric data, handling of both numeric and symbolic data in first-order rule learning, learning mutually dependent concepts. Experimental results obtained on a set of real-world documents are illustrated and commented.

1. Introduction

In the past decade studies on document analysis and recognition (DAR) have received increasing attention within the pattern recognition community because of the need for tools that are able to transform the great amount of data still available on paper into an electronic web-accessible format [20, 13]. The DAR process typically consists of the following steps: 1) document image acquisition by means of a scanner; 2) preprocessing, separation of text from graphics and extraction of the layout structure (*document analysis*); 3) extraction of logical relationships between layout components (*document understanding*); 4) optical character recognition (OCR) of textual components. Esposito *et al.* [7] introduced an additional intermediate step for the recognition of the type or class of the document (*document classification*), under the assumption that processed documents can be grouped into a finite set of classes with their own layout conventions. The output of all these steps can be subsequently exploited to transform the original paper document into a web-accessible format.

Flexible document processing systems require a large amount of knowledge at each step (see Fig. 1). For instance, the segmentation of the document image can be based on the layout conventions (or layout structure) of specific classes, while the separation of text from graphics requires knowledge on how text blocks can be discriminated from non-text blocks. The important role of knowledge management in document processing has led some authors to define document analysis and understanding as a branch of artificial intelligence [25]. Although this point of view can be criticized, the relevance of problems related to knowledge representation and

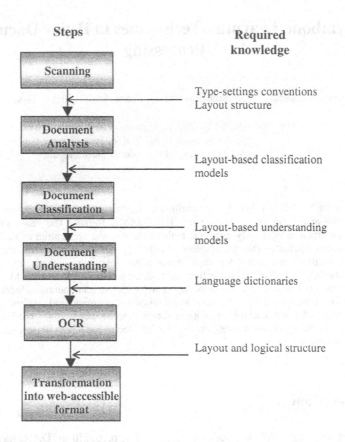

Fig. 1. Different steps for intelligent document processing and required knowledge.

acquisition is unquestionable for the development of "intelligent" document processing systems. In many applications presented in the literature, a great effort is made to hand-code the necessary knowledge according to some formalism (e.g., block grammars [19], geometric trees [5], frames [3]). In this work, we propose different machine learning algorithms in order to solve the knowledge acquisition problem. In particular, we advocate the application of *symbolic* inductive learning techniques, since they generate human-comprehensible hypotheses of the underlying patterns. Indeed, comprehensibility is a key factor for the validation of the acquired knowledge: Logic-style descriptions of the discovered patterns make relationships and properties of the layout components explicit and easily verifiable.

The symbolic learning techniques considered in this study are two: Induction of decision trees and induction of first-order rules from a set of training examples. The former is applied to the block classification problem, which is raised during the document analysis step, while the latter is applied to the document classification and understanding problems. It is worthwhile to observe that the application of the learning techniques is not straightforward. A first requirement is related to the problem of automatically acquiring knowledge from examples and revising it whenever new training examples are available: This leads to the adoption of *incremental* learning techniques. In this work, attention has been focused on the incremental decision tree induction, which exhibits high predictive accuracy but shows space inefficiency in the case of numerical features as those used for the block classification problem. Another issue is the choice of a suitable representation language capable to capture the relevant characteristics of the blocks as well as of the page layout. Indeed, the choice of the set of attributes and relations is crucial for the success of the application. In the paper, experiments with first-order representations of the page layout are reported. They confirm Connel and Brady's [4] observation that both numeric and symbolic descriptions are essential to generate models of visual objects, since the former increase the sensitivity while the latter increase the stability of the internal representation of visual objects. In this paper, the results obtained using purely symbolic descriptions and mixed symbolic-numeric descriptions are compared. Finally, the application of first-order rule induction to the document understanding problem raises the issue of learning multiple dependent concepts. Actually, the induction of rules to recognize the logical components of a document from their spatial displacement corresponds to a new learning problem where the concepts to be learned are the logical components which may be related (e.g., the title is written above the authors). Some consideration concerning the concept dependencies is reported in this work.

This pervasive application of inductive learning techniques to the DAR process has led to the development of an intelligent document processing system, named WISDOM++[1], which operates in five steps: Document analysis, document classification, document understanding, text recognition with an OCR, and transformation of the document image into HTML/XML format. The main functions performed by WISDOM++ are illustrated in the next section. In Section 3, the decision tree induction for the classification of blocks is discussed, while Section 4 is devoted to the problems of document classification and understanding. Experimental results obtained on a set of real-world documents processed by WISDOM++ are also reported.

2. The system WISDOM++

WISDOM++ is an intelligent document analysis system that can transform paper documents into HTML format. One of its distinguishing features is the use of a knowledge based-system capable of supplying assistance to the user during the first three steps of the DAR process. The knowledge base, declaratively expressed in the form of a decision tree or of a set of production rules, is automatically built from a set of training documents using symbolic machine learning tools and techniques, which make the system highly *adaptive*. *Real-time* user interaction is another relevant feature that characterizes WISDOM++, which has been designed as a multi-user system, in the sense that each authorized user has his/her own rule base. Another

---

[1] WISDOM++ is a newer version of the system WISDOM (Windows Interface System for DOcument Management), originally written in C [14] and used to feed up a digital library [11]. WISDOM++ has been designed according to an object-oriented analysis and design methodology and implemented in Microsoft Visual C++.

important characteristic is the capability of managing *multi-page* documents, each of which is a *sequence* of pages. The definition of the right sequence is responsibility of the user, since the optical scan function is able to work on a single page at a time. Pages of multi-page documents are processed independently of each other in all steps. Initially, each page is scanned with a resolution of 300 dpi and thresholded into a binary image. The bitmap of an A4-sized page takes 2,496×3,500=1,092,000 bytes and is stored in TIFF format. The *document analysis* process is performed in four main steps:

1. *Preprocessing*. This involves the evaluation of the skew angle, the rotation of the document, and the computation of a spread factor. Following Baird's definition [2], the skew angle of a document image I is the orientation angle θ of its text baselines: It is positive when the image is rotated counter-clockwise, otherwise it is negative. In WISDOM++ the estimation of the actual skew angle θ is obtained as composition of two functions: $S(I)$, which returns a *sample region R* of the document image I, and $E(R)$, which returns the *estimation* of the skew angle in the sample region R. The selection of a sample region is necessary to reduce the computational cost of the estimation step. Once the sample region R has been selected, $E(R)$ is computed. Let H_θ be the horizontal projection profile of R after a virtual rotation of an angle θ. The histogram H_θ shows sharply rising peaks with base equal to the character height when text lines span horizontally. In the presence of a large skew angle, smooth slopes and lower peaks characterize H_θ. This observation is mathematically captured by a real-valued function, $A(\theta)$, which has a global maximum at the correct skew angle. Thus finding the actual skew angle is cast as the problem of locating the global maximum value of $A(\theta)$. Since this measure is not smooth enough to apply gradient techniques, the system adopts some peak-finding heuristics. Details on the selection of the sample region and the peak-find heuristics can be found in [1]. WISDOM++ uses the estimated skew angle when the user asks the system to *rotate* the document. Another parameter computed during the preprocessing phase is the *spread factor* of the document image. It is defined as the ratio of the average distance between the regions R_i (*avdist*) and the average height of the same regions (*avheight*). In quite simple documents with few sparse regions, this ratio is greater than 1.0, while in complex documents with closely written text regions the ratio is lower than the unit. The spread factor is used to define some parameters of the segmentation algorithm.

2. *Segmentation*. The segmentation of the document image into rectangular *blocks* enclosing content portions is performed by means of a variant of the Run Length Smoothing Algorithm (RLSA) [29]. Such an algorithm applies four operators to the document image:

- Horizontal smoothing with a threshold C_h
- Vertical smoothing with a threshold C_v
- Logical AND of the two smoothed images
- Additional horizontal smoothing with another threshold C_a.

Although conceptually simple, this algorithm requires scanning the image four times. WISDOM++ implements a variant that scans the image only twice with no additional cost [24]. Another novelty of WISDOM++ is that the smoothing parameters C_v and C_a are adaptively defined on the ground of the spread factor.

Finally, in order to speed up RLSA, the segmentation is performed on a document image with a resolution of 75 dpi (*reduced* document image).

3. *Blocks classification.* In order to separate text from graphics it is necessary to classify blocks returned by the segmentation process. Which classifiers are used for this task and how they are automatically built from training examples is explained in the next section.

4. *Layout analysis.* This term denotes the process of perceptual organization that aims at detecting structures among *blocks*. The result is a hierarchy of abstract representations of the document image, called the *layout structure* of the document. The leaves of the layout tree are the blocks, while the root represents the set of pages of the whole document. A page may include several layout components, called *frames*, which are rectangular areas corresponding to groups of blocks. The various approaches to the extraction of the layout structure can be classified along two distinct dimensions: 1) Direction of construction of the layout tree (top-down or bottom-up), and 2) amount of explicit knowledge used during the layout analysis. In LEX [9] a knowledge-based, bottom-up approach has been adopted. Generic knowledge on typesetting conventions is considered in order to group basic blocks together into frames. Knowledge is represented as Prolog rules and is independent of the particular class of processed documents. The layout analysis is performed in two steps:

- A *global* analysis of the document image in order to determine possible areas containing paragraphs, sections, columns, figures and tables. This step is based on an iterative process in which the vertical and horizontal histograms of text blocks are alternatively analyzed in order to detect columns and sections/paragraphs, respectively.

- A *local analysis* of the document aiming at grouping together blocks which possibly fall within the same area. Three perceptual criteria are considered in this step: *Proximity* (e.g., adjacent components belonging to the same column/area are equally spaced), *continuity* (e.g., overlapping components) and *similarity* (e.g., components of the same type with an almost equal height). Pairs of layout components that satisfy some of these criteria may be grouped together. Each layout component is associated with one of the following types: Text, horizontal line, vertical line, picture, graphic and mixed. When the constituent blocks of a logical component are homogeneous, the same type is inherited by the logical component, otherwise the associated type is set to *mixed*.

The first version of LEX was implemented in Prolog [17], which allows a simple representation and manipulation of declarative knowledge. In order to reduce the execution time, a more recent C++ version has been implemented and embedded in WISDOM++. In Fig. 2, the various steps of the layout analysis process performed by WISDOM++ are shown.

Fig. 2. The five levels of the hierarchical layout structure extracted by WISDOM++: basic blocks, lines, set of lines, frame1 and frame2.

While the layout structure associates the content of a document with a hierarchy of layout objects, such as blocks, frames and pages, the *logical structure* of the document associates the content with a hierarchy of *logical objects*, such as sender/receiver of a business letter, title/authors of a scientific article, and so on. The problem of finding the logical structure of a document can be cast as the problem of defining a *mapping* from the layout structure into the logical one. In WISDOM++, this mapping is limited to the association of a page with a document class (document classification) and the association of page layout components with basic logical components (document understanding). The mapping is built by *matching* the document description against both *models* of classes of documents and models of the *logical components* of interest for that class. How models are represented and automatically built from some training examples is explained in Section 4.

WISDOM++ allows the user to set up the text extraction process by selecting the logical components to which an OCR has to be applied. Then the system generates an HTML/XML version of the original document: It contains both text returned by the OCR and pictures extracted from the original bitmap and converted into the GIF format. Text and images are spatially arranged so that the HTML/XML reconstruction of the document is as faithful as possible to the original bitmap. Moreover the XML format maintains information extracted during the document understanding phase, since the Document Type Definition (DTD) is specialized for each class of documents in order to represent the specific logical structure.

3. Inducing decision trees for block classification

Blocks determined by the RLSA enclose different types of content. In order to separate text from graphics the type of content has to be recognized. Wong *et al.* [29] proposed to classify blocks into four classes (text, graphic/halftone image, horizontal line, and vertical line) on the basis of four geometric features (or attributes): 1) the height of a block, 2) the eccentricity of the block, 3) the mean horizontal length of the black runs of the original data within each block, and 4) the ratio of the number of black pixels to the area of the surrounding rectangle. Wang and Srihari [28] considered five classes (halftones, text with large letters, text with medium-sized letters, text with small letters, and graphics) and three additional textural features: F1) short run emphasis, F2) long run emphasis, and F3) extra long run emphasis. In both works linear discriminant functions are used as block classifiers, whereas a rule-based classification method is proposed in Fisher *et al.*'s work [12]. A common aspect of all these studies is that classifiers are hand-coded for some specific classes of documents.

As already pointed out, in WISDOM++ block classifiers are automatically built by means of inductive learning techniques, namely decision tree induction. The choice of a tree-based method instead of the most common generalized linear models is due to its inherent flexibility, since decision trees can handle complicated interactions among features and give results that can be easily interpreted. WISDOM++ discriminates between *text blocks, horizontal lines, vertical lines, pictures* (i.e., halftone images) and *graphics* (e.g., line drawings). Each block is represented by a set of numeric attribute-value couples:
1. *Height*: Height of the reduced block image.
2. *Length*: Length of the reduced block image.
3. *Area*: Area of the reduced block image (*height*length*).
4. *Eccen*: Eccentricity of the reduced block image (*length/height*).
5. *Blackpix*: Total number of black pixels in the reduced block image.
6. *Bw_trans*: Total number of black-white transitions in all rows of the reduced block image.
7. *Pblack*: Percentage of black pixels in the reduced block image (*blackpix/area*).
8. *Mean_tr*: Average number of black pixels per black-white transition (*blackpix/ bw_trans*).
9. *F1*: Short run emphasis.
10.*F2*: Long run emphasis.
11.*F3*: Extra long run emphasis.

In a preliminary study, a decision tree was induced using a set of 5473 examples of pre-classified blocks obtained from 53 documents of various kinds.[2] The system used for this learning task is an extension of C4.5 [22]. Interesting results were obtained with an average accuracy above 97% [10].

However, C4.5 operates in *batch* mode: It is not possible to revise the decision tree when some blocks are misclassified, unless a new tree is generated from scratch using an extended training set. In order to give the user the possibility of training WISDOM++ on-line, we considered several *incremental* decision tree learning systems presented in the literature, namely ID4 [23], ID5R [26], and ITI [27].

---

[2] The data set is available in the UCI ML Repository (www.ics.uci.edu/~mlearn/MLRepository.html).

Nevertheless, only the latter can handle numerical attributes as those used to describe the blocks.

ITI can operate in three different ways. In the *batch* mode, it works as C4.5. In the *normal* operation mode, it first updates the frequency counts associated to each node of the tree as soon as a new instance is received. Then it restructures the decision tree according to the updated frequency counts. In the *error-correction* mode, frequency counts are updated only in case of misclassification of the new instance. The main difference between the two incremental modes is that the normal operation mode guarantees to build the same decision tree independently of the order in which examples are presented, while the error-correction mode does not.

In order to test the performance of the block classifier, a set of 112 real, single-page documents have been considered as input data. Documents are distributed as follows: Thirty are the first page of articles appeared on the proceedings of the International Symposium on Methodologies for Intelligent Systems (*ISMIS94*),[3] twenty-eight are the first page of articles published on the proceedings of the 12th International Conference on Machine Learning (*ICML95*), thirty-four are the first page of articles published in the IEEE Transactions on Pattern Analysis and Machine Intelligence (*TPAMI*),[4] and twenty documents of different type or published on other proceedings, transactions and journals (*Reject*). The set of documents has been split into training set (70%) and test set (30%) according to a stratified random sampling. The number of training blocks is 9,429 while the number of test blocks is 3,176. Three experiments have been organized. ITI has been trained in the batch mode in the first experiment, in the pure error-correction mode in the second, and in a mixed incremental/error-correction mode in the third (incremental mode for the first 4,545 examples and error-correction mode for the remaining 4,884).

The main characteristics of the learned trees are reported in Table 1. The fourth column shows the features selected in the first two levels of the tree, likely the most relevant features, while the last column refers to the number of examples stored in the nodes of the induced trees.

Table 1. Characteristics of the learned decision trees.

	Size Kb	No. Nodes	No. leaves	Selected Features	No. incorporated examples
Batch	24,320	229	114	cccen / F1 F1	9,429
Pure Error-correction	982	159	79	area / cccen p. black	277
Mixed	13,150	235	117	height / cccen cccen	4,545+125

[3] Published by Springer Verlag in the series "Lecture Notes in Artificial Intelligence," Vol. 869.
[4] Period January-June, 1996.

The decision tree built in the batch mode takes more than 24Mb, since all instances have to be stored, while the decision tree obtained in the error-correction mode requires 982Kb. Nevertheless, this difference in tree size does not correspond to a significant difference in predictive accuracy estimated on the independent test set (see Table 2). Indeed, the difference between the predictive accuracy in the batch mode and in the error correction mode is less then 0.2%. This justifies the use of the decision tree developed according to the error-correction operation mode in many practical situations.

Table 2. Predictive accuracy of the learned decision trees.

	ISMIS94	ICML95	TPAMI	Reject	Total
Batch	95.78	97.74	98.26	97.00	97.48
Pure Error-correction	97.05	98.39	98.01	95.06	97.45
Mixed	95.99	97.63	98.18	97.35	97.51

The learned trees are not shown in the paper because of their large size. We limit ourselves to report that the set of features actually used in the decision tree built by the pure error-correction procedure does not contain two features, namely width of a block and F3. The latter exclusion is due to the fact that documents considered in this experiment have few occurrences of large text blocks, while F3 characterizes extra-long runs of black pixels.

4. Inducing first-order rules for document classification and understanding

In many real applications, documents to be processed can be grouped into classes such that documents in the same class have a similar layout structure. For instance, results reported in the previous section concerned the first page of articles appeared on different proceedings and journals. These documents were actually used to feed up a digital library [11] and can be naturally grouped into four classes (ICML95, ISMIS94, TPAMI, Reject), each of which with a different layout structure. In particular, papers in ISMIS94 are single-columned, while ICML95 and TPAMI papers are organized in two columns. Moreover, the layout structures of ICML95 and TPAMI documents present several distinguishing characteristics (e.g., absence/presence of a running head). Therefore, it is reasonable to perform a classification of documents of these three classes basing upon the within-class similarities and between-class differences of their layout structures. On the contrary, documents of the class Reject have no homogeneous layout, therefore no layout-based classification rule can be built. When learning rules for document classification, reject documents will be used as negative examples only.

In order to apply machine learning techniques to induce rules for layout-based document classification, it is important to define a suitable representation of the layout structure of training documents. In this work, we confine ourselves to representing the most abstract level of the layout structure (frame2), and we deliberately ignore other levels as well as their composition hierarchy. Nevertheless, description of the frame2 layout level is not a trivial task, since the layout components are spatially related and the feature-vector representation adopted for the block classification problem cannot capture these relations. Indeed, Eshera and Fu [6] recognized that the classical decision-theory approach based on feature-vector representations is often unable to solve pattern recognition problems when underlying patterns are characterized by some kind of relationship. For this reason they resorted to syntactic grammars and graph-based representations and studied related pattern recognition problems. Since such representations are encompassed by first-order logic formalisms, which have been extensively investigated in artificial intelligence, we preferred to describe both documents and rules by means of a first-order language. In this language, unary function symbols, called *attributes*, are used to describe properties of a single layout component (e.g., height and length), while binary predicate and function symbols, called *relations*, are used to express spatial relationships among layout components (e.g., part-of and on-top). The semantics of both attributes and relations is reported in [8]. An example of page layout description automatically generated by WISDOM++ is reported in Fig. 3.

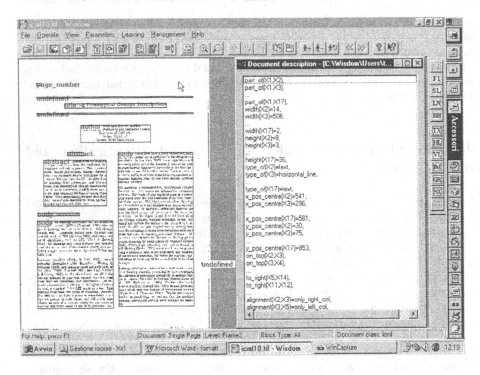

Fig. 3. Frame2 layout level of a document processed by WISDOM++ (left). The document has been classified as an ICML95 paper (bottom-right hand corner) and its logical structure has been understood (see labels associated to the layout components). First-order logical description of the page layout (right). Distinct constants (X2, ..., X17) denote distinct layout components. The constant X1 denotes the whole page.

In a previous work [7], a first-order learning system was applied to the document classification task. The system returned encouraging results, but some degree of improvement was still possible. One of the main issues seemed to be the purely symbolic representation adopted for the page layout. All attributes and relations took values in a discrete range (e.g., {very-small, small, medium, ...}), since the numeric attributes height, width and position of a block were discretized a priori, that is *off-line* with respect to the learning process. The explanation of this choice is that the first-order learning system used to automatically learn classification rules was not able to perform an *on-line*, autonomous discretization of numerical descriptors.

These considerations prompted the investigation of an extension of our first-order learning algorithm in order to handle numerical descriptors as well. On-line discretization of numerical descriptors is performed by a specialization operator, which can specialize a first-order rule by adding literals of the type $f(X_1, ..., X_n) \in [a..b]$, where [a..b] is a closed interval. An information-theoretic heuristic is used to choose among different intervals. It has been proven that this heuristic satisfies a property that can be exploited in order to improve the efficiency of the interval selection. Details on the specialization operator are reported in [15]. Rules generated by the extended first-order learning system, called INDUBI/CSL, are used by WISDOM++ for both document classification and understanding. The output of the system is a set of production rules formulated as follows:

$$H \leftarrow L_1, L_2, .., L_m$$

where the conclusion part H (called *head*) represents either a document class or a logical component, while the premise part $L_1, L_2, .., L_m$ (called *body*) is a conjunction of conditions involving either attribute or relation. Two examples of rules learned by the embedded system are reported below. It is worthwhile to observe that such rules capture some spatial relationships between layout components, thus confirming the importance of adopting a first-order representation for document classification and understanding.

class(X) = icml ←   part_of(X,Y), on_top(W,Z), on_top(Y,U), to_right(Y,V),
                      alignment(Z,U)=only_left_col, alignment(V,Y)=only_middle_col
class(X) = icml ←   part_of(X,Y), x_pos_centre(Y)∈[301 .. 557],
                      y_pos_centre(Y)∈[25 ..190], on_top(V,Y), on_top(Z,V), on_top(W,Y)

In order to test the efficiency and the effectiveness of the proposed operator, an experiment has been organized on the same set of document images used for the block classification problem. The experimental procedure followed is ten-fold cross validation. At each trial three statistics are collected: Number of errors on the test cases, number of generated clauses, and learning time. Results are reported in Table 3, The entries labeled "mixed" refer to symbolic/numeric representation and on-line discretization.

Table 3. Experimental results for document classification.

class	Av. Number of Errors		Number of Clauses		Av. Learning Time	
	symbolic	mixed	symbolic	mixed	symbolic	mixed
ICML'95	1.4	0.8	4.8	2.0	4:42	9:54
ISMIS'94	1.3	0.2	5.7	1.0	5:30	9:18
TPAMI	1.0	0.7	4.4	1.9	5:06	10:06
TOTAL	3.7	1.7	14.9	4.9	15:36	29:30

In the document classification problem, the average number of errors for mixed data is significantly lower than the average number of errors for symbolic data. Indeed, the p-value returned by the non-parametric Wilcoxon signed-ranks test [21] is 0.0144. Moreover, the introduction of numerical descriptors simplifies the classification rules, although the learning time is doubled (time is in prime minutes and refers to a workstation SUN 10, since INDUBI/CSL operates off-line and WISDOM++ runs under Windows 95).

A similar experiment has been performed for document understanding. In this case the learning problems are three, one for each class. For ICML95 pages, we are interested to find five logical components, namely *page number, title, author, abstract*, and *body* of the paper. For ISMIS94 papers we considered the following logical components: Title, authors, abstract and body (of the paper). Finally, for TPAMI papers we defined five logical components, namely running head, page number, title, abstract, and (body of the) paper. Obviously, for the Reject class no learning problem is defined, since it is not possible to define a homogeneous set of logical components. The set of rules learned by INDUBI/CSL for the ICML95 documents in one experiment are reported below:

logic_type(X)=page_number ← width(X) ∈ [8 ..16], height (X) ∈ [7.. 8]
logic_type(X)=title ← height(X) ∈ [13 .. 31], x_pos_centre(X) ∈ [280 .. 348]
logic_type(X)=author ← height(X) ∈ [42..79], y_pos_centre(X) ∈ [173 .. 279]
logic_type(X)=abstract ← y_pos_centre(X) ∈ [256 .. 526], on_top(Y,X), to_right(X,Z)
logic_type(X)=abstract ← x_pos_centre(X) ∈ [147.. 218], on_top(X,Y), to_right(Y,Z)
logic_type(X)=body ← width(X) ∈ [242..255], type_of(X)=text
logic_type(X)=body ← x_pos_centre(X) ∈ [368..477], on_top(Z,X), to_right(Y,Z)
logic_type(X)=body ← width(X) ∈ [78 .. 136], type_of(X)=text, on_top(X,Y), to_right(Y,Z)
logic_type(X)=body ← width(X) ∈ [237.. 255], alignment(Y,X)=only_right_col
logic_type(X)=body ← height(X) ∈ [422 .. 519]

Experimental results are reported in Table 4. The choice of the representation language for the page layout seems to be much more critical for document understanding than for document classification. In fact, satisfactory error rates are obtained only with numeric/symbolic representations. For all classes the average number of errors for mixed data is significantly lower than the average number of errors for symbolic data (the worst p-value of the Wilcoxon test is 0.0072). Once again, the introduction of numerical descriptors simplifies significantly the classification rules and decreases the learning time for two classes.

Table 4. Experimental results for document understanding.

class	Av. Number of Errors		Number of Clauses		Av. Learning Time	
	symbolic	mixed	symbolic	mixed	symbolic	mixed
ICML'95	6.6	3.2	31.6	8.4	44:30	26:00
ISMIS'94	6.3	3.2	43.8	10.8	50:36	25:24
TPAMI	9.2	2.0	39.5	9.0	30:24	32:00

Actually, learning rules for document understanding is more difficult than learning rules for document classification, since logical components refer to a part of the document rather than to the whole document. Logical components may be related to each other, as in the case of standard scientific papers, where the author's affiliation is above the abstract and under the title. Thus, it would be more appropriate to learn rules that reflect these dependencies among logical components. For instance, for ICML95 documents the following rule:

logic_type(X) = body ← to_right(Y,X), logic_type(Y) = abstract

captures the fact that a layout component to the right of an abstract is a body (see Fig. 3). INDUBI/CSL has also been extended in order to learn multiple dependent concepts provided that the user defines a graph of possible dependencies between logical components. Experimental results obtained in a previous study confirm that by taking into account concept dependencies it is possible to improve the predictive accuracy for the document understanding problem [18].

5. Conclusions and future work

Empirical results presented above prove the applicability of symbolic machine learning techniques to the problem of automating the capture of data contained in a document image. Three research issues have been discussed in the paper. Firstly, the space inefficiency of incremental decision tree learning systems when examples are described by many numerical features. This problem will be investigated in the future work. Secondly, the importance of first-order symbolic/numeric descriptions for both document classification and document understanding. Experimental results obtained by extending the system WISDOM++ have confirmed that such descriptions significantly improve predictive accuracy in all learning problems as well as the learning time for some document understanding problems. Thirdly, document understanding rules that take into account dependencies between logical components can lead to higher predictive accuracy. Current experimental results have been obtained by defining *a priori* possible concept dependencies. For the future, we plan to use the multiple predicate learning system ATRE [16], which is able to autonomously discover the concept dependencies.

Acknowledgments

The authors would like to thank Francesco De Tommaso, Dario Gerbino, Ignazio Sardella, Giacomo Sidella, Rosa Maria Spadavecchia, and Silvana Spagnoletta for their contribution to the development of WISDOM++. Thanks also to the authors of the systems C4.5 and ITI.

References

[1] O. Altamura, F. Esposito & D. Malerba (1999). WISDOM++: An Interactive and Adaptive Document Analysis System. To appear in *Proc. of the 5th Int. Conf. on Document Analysis and Recognition*, IEEE Computer Society Press: Los Alamitos.

[2] H.S. Baird (1987). The Skew Angle of Printed Documents. *Proc. Conf. Of the Society of Photographic Scientists and Engineers*, 14-21 (also in R.K.L. O'Gorman (ed.), *Document Image Analysis*, 204-208, IEEE Computer Society: Los Alamitos, CA, 1995).

[3] T. Bayer, U. Bohnacher, & H. Mogg-Schneider (1994). InforPortLab: An Experimental Document Analysis System. *Proc. of the IAPR Workshop on Document Analysis Systems*, Kaiserslautern, Germany.

[4] J.H. Connell & M. Brady. Generating and Generalizing Models of Visual Objects. *Artificial Intelligence*, 31, 2, 159-183, 1987.

[5] A. Dengel & G. Barth. ANASTASIL: A Hybrid Knowledge-based System for Document Layout Analysis. *Proc. of the 6th Int. Joint Conf. on Artificial Intelligence*, 1249-1254, 1989.

[6] M.A. Eshera, & K.S. Fu (1986). An Image Understanding System using Attributed Symbolic Representation and Inexact Graph-matching. *IEEE Transactions on Pattern Analysis and Machine Intelligence*, 8, 604-618.

[7] F. Esposito, D. Malerba, G. Semeraro, E. Annese, & G. Scafuro (1990). An Experimental Page Layout Recognition System for Office Document Automatic Classification: An Integrated Approach for Inductive Generalization. *Proceedings of the 10th International Conference on Pattern Recognition*, IEEE Computer Society Press: Los Alamitos, CA, 557-562.

[8] F. Esposito, D. Malerba, & G. Semeraro (1994). Multistrategy Learning for Document Recognition. *Applied Artificial Intelligence*, 8, 1, 33-84.

[9] F. Esposito, D. Malerba, and G. Semeraro (1995). A Knowledge-based Approach to the Layout Analysis. *Proc. of the 3rd Int. Conf. on Document Analysis and Recognition*, IEEE Computer Society: Los Alamitos, CA, 466-471.

[10] F. Esposito, D. Malerba, & G. Semeraro (1997). A Comparative Analysis of Methods for Pruning Decision Trees. *IEEE Transactions on Pattern Analysis and Machine Intelligence*, 19, 5, 476-491.

[11] F. Esposito, D. Malerba, G. Semeraro, N. Fanizzi, & S. Ferilli (1998). Adding Machine Learning and Knowledge Intensive Techniques to a Digital Library Service. *International Journal on Digital Libraries*, 2, 1, 3-19.

[12] J.L. Fisher, S.C. Hinds, & D. P. D'Amato (1990). A Rule-based System for Document Image Segmentation. *Proc. of the 10th Int. Conf. on Pattern Recognition*, IEEE Computer Society Press: Los Alamitos, CA, 567-572.

[13] T. Hong, & S. N. Srihari (1997). Representing OCRed Documents in HTML. *Proc. of the 4th Int. Conf. on Document Analysis and Recognition*, IEEE Computer Society Press: Los Alamitos, CA, 831-834.

[14] D. Malerba, F. Esposito, G. Semeraro, & L. De Filippis (1997). Processing Paper Documents with WISDOM. In M. Lenzerini (Ed.), *AI*IA 97: Advances in Artificial Intelligence*, Lecture Notes in Artificial Intelligence, Springer: Berlin, 1321, 439-442.

[15] D. Malerba, F. Esposito, G. Semeraro, & S. Caggese (1997). Handling Continuous Data in Top-down Induction of First-order Rules. In M. Lenzerini (Ed.), *AI*IA 97: Advances in Artificial Intelligence*, Lecture Notes in Artificial Intelligence, Springer: Berlin, 1321, 24-35.

[16] D. Malerba, F. Esposito, & F. A. Lisi (1998). Learning Recursive Theories with ATRE. In H. Prade (Ed.), *Proc. of the 13th European Conf. on Artificial Intelligence*, John Wiley & Sons: Chichester, UK, 435-439.

[17] D. Malerba, G. Semeraro, & E. Bellisari (1995). LEX: A Knowledge-Based System for the Layout Analysis. *Proc. of the 3rd Int. Conf. on the Practical Application of Prolog*, 429-443.

[18] D. Malerba, G. Semeraro, & F. Esposito (1997). A Multistrategy Approach to Learning Multiple Dependent Concepts. Chapter 4 in C., Taylor & R., Nakhaeizadeh (Eds.), *Machine Learning and Statistics: The Interface*, Wiley: London, United Kingdom, 87-106.

[19] G. Nagy, S. Seth & M. Viswanathan (1992). A Prototype Document Image Analysis System for Technical Journals. *IEEE Computer*, 25, 7, 10-22.

[20] L. O'Gorman (1992). Image and Document Processing Techniques for the RightPages Electronic Library System. *Proc. of the 11th Int. Conf. on Pattern Recognition*, 260-263.

[21] M. Orkin & R. Drogin (1990). *Vital Statistics*, McGraw Hill: New York.

[22] J. R. Quinlan (1993). *C4.5: Programs for induction*. Morgan Kaufmann: San Mateo, CA.

[23] J. C. Schlimmer, & D. Fisher (1986). A Case Study of Incremental Concept Induction. *Proc. of the 5th Nat. Conf. on Artificial Intelligence*, Morgan Kaufmann: Philadelphia, 496-501.

[24] F. Y. Shih, & S.-S. Chen (1996). Adaptive Document Block Segmentation and Classification. *IEEE Trans. on Systems, Man, and Cybernetics - Part B*, 26, 5, 797-802.

[25] Y. Y. Tang, C. De Yan & C. Y. Suen. Document Processing for Automatic Knowledge Acquisition. *IEEE Trans. on Knowledge and Data Engineering*, 6(1) (1994) 3-21.

[26] P. E. Utgoff (1989). Incremental Induction of Decision Trees. *Machine Learning*, 4, 2, 161-186.

[27] P. E. Utgoff (1994). An Improved Algorithm for Incremental Induction of Decision Trees. *Proc. of the 11th Int. Conf. on Machine Learning*, Morgan Kaufmann: San Francisco, CA.

[28] D. Wang & R.N. Srihari (1989). Classification of Newspaper Image Blocks Using Texture Analysis. *Computer Vision, Graphics, and Image Processing*, 47, 327-352.

[29] K. Y. Wong, R.G. Casey, & F. M. Wahl (1982). Document Analysis System. *IBM Journal of Research Development*, 26, 6, 647-656.

Recognition of Printed Music Score

Tomáš Beran and Tomáš Macek

Department of Computer Science and Engineering, Faculty of Electrical Engineering,
Czech Technical University, Karlovo namesti 13, 121 35 Praha 2 Czech Republic

Abstract. This article describes our implementation of the Optical Music Recognition System (OMR). The system implemented in our project is based on the binary neural network ADAM. ADAM has been used for recognition of music symbols. Preprocessing was implemented by conventional techniques. We decomposed the OMR process into several phases. The results of these phases are summarized.

1 Introduction

We describe in this article an implementation of the Optical Music Recognition System. The system implemented in our project is based on the binary neural network ADAM (Advanced Distributed Associative Memory).

The aim of the OMR system is to save time in converting hardcopy of the music score into an electronic version. The result of the conversion is a file, which can be directly interpreted by MIDI instruments and can be edited, reprinted, transposed, or converted to other formats.

Input to the OMR system is a bitmap file containing a scanned music score. OMR recognizes music elements and tries to understand the content of the music score. The output is the file, which contains recognized music symbols (e.g. in MIDI format).

We describe our draft in Section 2. Sections 3, 4 and 6 describe phases of OMR. In Section 5 we briefly summarize the structure and behaviour of the neural network ADAM.

2 Draft of Solution OMR

In this section we describe the draft we used in this project. The OMR problem is rather difficult. It can decompose into several subsequent phases. We decomposed the problem into five phases.

1. **Scanning and importing the music score into memory**. The music score is represented as a binary or grayscale bitmap in memory.
2. **Preprocessing**. This phase includes thresholding, skew correction, getting the scale and rescaling.
3. **Finding and erasing staffs**.
4. **Recognition of music symbols**. The neural network ADAM recognizes most of the music symbols. Some symbols are recognized by another technique.
5. **Writing the results into an output file**.

3 Preprocessing

We describe the preprocessing phase in this section. This phase makes the recognition task easier. The output of this phase is a binary image with horizontal staff lines. Music symbols are in the standard size.

3.1 Thresholding

The thresholding technique transforms the input grayscale image to a binary one. The binary representation of the image is used by all techniques of OMR except rotation and rescaling.

First, the grayscale histogram of the input image is created in order to find the threshold. The threshold is found in this histogram by the iterative method of Ridler and Calvard [10]. The average brightness of background is also obtained from this histogram. This value is later used for filling "empty" places made by rotation.

3.2 Skew correction

Most segmentation techniques in OMR require that the music score is not skewed. The most sensitive technique to skewing the input image is horizontal projection, which is used for finding staff lines. Therefore, we correct the skew of the input music score in this phase. This operation includes two steps. First we determine the skew angle, then we rotate the image.

The skew angle of the music score is determined by finding the skew angle of the staff lines. We used the technique described in [8]. This technique is a modification of Martin and Bellissant's technique [7].

We implemented two techniques for de-skewing the image: rotation and double sharing. We tested them for both binary and grayscale image. It is better to use the grayscale image than the thresholded binary image for rotation. Results are significantly better.

The double sharing technique for binary images gives slightly better results than the rotation technique and it is also faster. Both techniques give the same results for grayscale image and they also take the same amount of time.

3.3 Getting the scale

The scale of a music score is the most important parameter for the recognition phase. The scale expresses the average distance between two neighboring staff lines. In this article we call this parameter α. Figure 1 shows how we get this parameter. First we compute frequencies of white and black vertical segments. The most frequent black segment is the average thickness of staff line α_l. The most frequent white segment is the average space between two neighboring staff lines, α_h. The sum of these value is the scale of music score α. This technique is described e.g. in [11]. It gives very precise results and it is also very quick.

After determining the α parameter we can rescale the score into the required size. This value is also used for many thresholds in the recognition phase (e.g. it is used in horizontal projection for finding staffs).

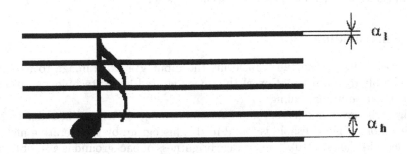

Fig. 1. The scale of music score $\alpha = \alpha_h + \alpha_l$.

3.4 Rescaling

We used the neural network ADAM, which learned the specific size of music symbols. Therefore, we rescaled the music score in order to have both learned symbols and symbols for recalling, be the same size. Input to the rescaling technique is the original grayscale image (if it is available).

4 Finding and erasing music staffs

The first music symbols looked for are staffs. After finding staffs their positions are remembered and they are erased from the image. Erasing staffs makes it easier to recognize of other music symbols.

In order to find staffs we compute a histogram of horizontal projection. We find five equally spaced (by the approximate value of parameter α) local maxims in this histogram. The y co-ordinate of staffs from the histogram are called rough positions of staffs. They are called rough positions because staff lines are not always straight. In this case one y co-ordinate for a whole staff line can be insufficient. So each staff line are explored to determine next y co-ordinates which depend on the x co-ordinate. The erasing technique is very similar to the exploration technique. Both techniques are described in [8]. Erasing of staff lines is sensitive to symbols which lie on the staff line. This technique often disturbs the shape of small symbols.

5 Neural network ADAM

This section describes the binary (weightless) neural network ADAM. We used ADAM for recognition of music symbols in the image. The ADAM recognition technique is based on the Generalised Hough Transformation (GHT). More details can be found in [5].

5.1 Structure of neural network ADAM

Figure 2 shows the structure of the neural network ADAM. ADAM consists of two binary correlation matrices. The output of the first correlation matrix is connected to the input of second correlation matrix. The first matrix recognizes features of learned objects. The second matrix associates recognized features with pair objects – centers of object, which belong to features. One feature can belong to one object a number of times or can belong to one or more objects.

The basic GHT method detects edges in the image and it finds objects by these edges. On the other hand ADAM detects features. Features are small parts of objects (parts of an image, e.g. 16x16 pixels).

Detection of features is done by the first correlation matrix. Association of the feature with the pair object–center is done by the second correlation matrix (it is similar to the R-table in GHT). ADAM can recognize more then one object at the same time. This is the advantage of ADAM compared with the basic GHT.

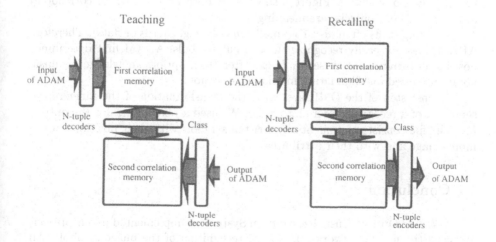

Fig. 2. Structure of neural network ADAM.

In our work we modified the neural network ADAM. We used a table instead of the second correlation matrix. This modification makes the recognition process more precise and quick.

The output from the recognition process by neural network ADAM is the set of counter grids. Each learned object has one counter grid. The size of the counter grid is the same as the size of the searched area of the image. Each counter in the grid corresponds to one pixel in the input image. The value of the counter gives the likehood that the center of a learned object lies at the corresponding pixel. An example of the counter grid is shown in the Fig. 3.

6   Recognition

In this chapter we describe recognition of music symbols. The neural network ADAM recognizes most of the symbols. Some symbols are difficult to recognize by this technique. Therefore, we used another technique of recognition for these symbols.

Symbols are not searched in the whole image. They are searched only in some areas around staffs that have been found. This approach improves the speed of recognition.

We used apriori knowledge of size and position for each symbol. For example, the treble clef lies at the beginning of each staff at a precise vertical position. The height of note heads can't be larger then the value of $\alpha + \alpha_1$. Using this knowledge we can recognize misclassified symbols.

Figure 3 shows two counter grids for treble and bass clef. The counter grid is the result of the recognition technique based on ADAM. The value of the counter is expressed by the brightness of pixel in this figure. Darker pixels represent higher values of counters. Figure 3 shows that both maxims, which correspond to centers of both objects, are meaningful.

Removing staffs often disturbs small symbols (e.g. sharps or flats). Therefore ADAM does not easily recognize these small symbols. ADAM first determines possible occurrences of these symbols. After that, apriori knowledge of music notation is used for eliminating misclassified symbols.

The last step of the OMR system is the transformation of the inner representation of a recognized score into a file. We used a text format for the output file. The file consists of sequentially written symbols with their positions in the input image and with their attributes.

7   Conclusion

We presented Optical Music Recognition System we implemented in our project. We used the neural network ADAM for recognition of the music symbols. All preprocessing techniques give very good results. The results are better in the case of grayscale input image. Our experiments show that using the neural network ADAM is suitable for the OMR problem.

Fig. 3. Counter grids for treble and bass clef.

References

1. T. Beran, Optical Music Recognition (in Czech), MSc report Department of Computer Science and Engineering Czech Technical University in Prague (1999)
2. J. E. Bresenham: Algorithm for Computer Control of a Digital Plotter. IBM Systems Journal 4 (1965) 25–30
3. J. Gomes and L. Velho: Image Processing for Computer Graphics. (1997) Springer-Verlag New York
4. V. Hlaváč and M. Šonka: Computer vision (in Czech). (1992) Grada Prague
5. S. E. M. O'Keefe and J. Austin: Application of an Associative Memory to the Analysis of Document Fax Images. Br. Machine Vision Conference (1994) 315-326
6. D. E. Lloyd: Automatic Target Classification Using Moment Invariants of Image Shapes. Technical Report RAE IDN AW126. (1978) Farnborough U.K.
7. P. Martin and C. Bellissant: Low-level analysis of music drawing images. First International Conference Document Analysis and Recognition (1991) 417-425
8. K. C. Ng and R. D. Boyle: Segmentation of Music Primitives. Br. Machine Vision Conference (1990) 345–347
9. K. C. Ng and R. D. Boyle: Recognition and Reconstruction of Primitives in Music Scores. Image and Vision Computing 14 (1996) 39–46
10. T. W. Ridler and S. Calvard: Picture thresholding using an iterative selection method. IEEE Transaction SMC 8 (1978) 630–632,
11. M. Roth: An Approach To Recognition Of Printed Music. Eidgenössische Technische Hochschule Zrich, MSc Report (1994)
12. M. Šonka, V. Hlaváč and R. Boyle: Image processing, Analysis, and Computer Vision. Chapman & Hall Computing London (1993)

Reproductive Process-Oriented Data Mining from Interactions between Human and Complex Artifact System

Tetsuo Sawaragi
Dept. of Precision Eng., Graduate School of Eng.,
Kyoto University
Yoshida Honmachi, Sakyo, Kyoto 606-8501, Japan.
sawaragi@prec.kyoto-u.ac.jp

Abstract

This paper presents a method for concept formation of a personal learning apprentice (PLA) system that attempts to capture users' internal conceptual structure by observing interactions between user and system. Current hot topics on techniques of data mining may potentially contribute to the above purpose, but different from the conventional approaches of data mining, we have to consider more about the aspects in which how the mined knowledge should be used by the human in the consequent processes, not only about what knowledge should be extracted. In this paper we propose such a process-oriented data mining method based upon an idea of soft systems methodologies proposed by P.B. Checkland in 1980's, and we propose an algorithm for its implementation using evolutional computing.

1 Introduction

Recently, due to the improvement of information infrastructures such as information networks and multimedia communication, the amount of information that requires processing is immense. Accordingly, the interface system should be designed to provide information that is coherent with the cognitive processes, and must be *human-friendly* in that the information presented to a human operator must be deliberately selected to avoid information overloading the user with information. Related to this research area, the idea of *interface agents* [9], which are semi-intelligent computer programs that employ machine learning techniques to provide assistance to human operators dealing with a particular computer application. Such systems are called *learning apprentice* systems, which learn by continuously "looking over the shoulder" of the user during operation. The interface agent monitors the actions of the user over long periods of time, determines recurrent patterns, infers the concepts of the user, and offers to automate them [8], [4].

As for a learning methodology for an interface agent, many learning methods have been proposed, and application of ID3, a decision tree learning algorithm, has been adopted for this purpose. The bottleneck of this approach is limitation of adaptation to a large variability of ways of interactions between system and user. Those learning methods have been developed for a product-oriented goal of extracting some fixed and sound knowledge implied within an accumulation of human-system interaction data. However, human-system interaction data are sometimes too complex and often apt to change, so such an product-oriented approach cannot successfully extract regular knowledge. We have to to change our view on the learning towards more process-oriented one, in which a systematicity is sought for within a process of data mining, rather than within the data isolated from the mining algorithm.

Here we introduce an idea of soft system methodologies (SSM) that was originally proposed by P.B. Checkland in 1980's [2], [17]. Checkland has distinguished this approach from the conventional hard systems approaches putting an emphasis on its process-oriented systematicity. Although this idea is very conceptual and just provides with a framework of general problem solving activity, we implement this idea as a learning algorithm of an interface agent as a living system that can coexist with, and be adaptive to, a human operator; the interface agent has to be capable of simulating a human operator's mental activities of organizing experiences when encountering previous analogous situations at the most appropriate level of abstraction.

In this paper, as a method of interface learning we propose the use of an inductive and unsupervised learning technique called *concept formation*; also called *conceptual clustering* and *learning from observations*, to construct the operator's conceptual structures and to infer their behavior under particular problem solving situations. To make an interface agent a proactive learner, we have revised a conventional concept formation technique (*i.e.*, COBWEB) by adding novel feature-selection and feature-discovery capabilities.

2 Checkland's Soft Systems Methodologies

Checkland's idea of SSM provided a drastic paradigmatic shift from the conventional systems approaches in the following points. The first issue concerns with the identification between a model builder and a model user. In the conventional systems approach, those two different model-related activities are separated clearly and are attributed to two different actors. Second, SSM focuses on the appearance of the world (i.e., a subjective view on the messy, complex world) rather than on mirroring an objectively true world. From this view, a systematicity does not exists within the actual reality, but only within the ways, or processes, of exploring such a world being driven by an observer's proactive interpreting efforts and his/her internal mental models. Checkland has characterized such a process by introducing a *human activity system* model as an internal mental model of the interpreter. This is just a temporal, subjective image of the actual reality, not equal to the reality, but the process of how this model evolves through interacting with the reality may contain a systematicity.

Related with the above SSM's ideas, it is well-recognized that the efficiency and the robustness of human information processing is due to the acquisition of "schema", which comprise memory units each of which frames the decision context with various grain sizes [1]. Neisser has stressed a role of cognitive schema played in human learning. A perceptual cyclic loop proposed by Neisser that evolves via cognitive schema is illustrated in Fig.1. Here it is stressed that

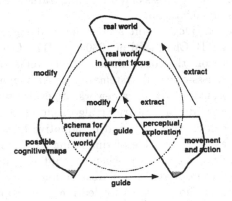

Figure 1: Neisser's perceptual cycle.

perception is strongly biased by the mental organization of the perceiver (i.e., schema) and this affects upon how the perceiver behaves in the real world. This change of behavior causes the alternation of the actor's experiences, which then affects upon the current organization of the perceiver's mental models. What is important here is not what will be acquired finally, but this cyclic process per se is important. By iterating this cycles, the actor, which is equivalent to the perceiver and the observer, comes to be embedded within the real world, and what are acquired within the actor becomes grounded to the world. This is a general learning model of observing systems, rather than observed systems, and have a continuous self-production process enabled by evolutional development through its internally-inspired activities.

In the following of this paper, we propose a new algorithm for mining data which may contain noisy and redundant information. The conventional data mining techniques were development of algorithms in which the raw data were input to the algorithm and some objectively true knowledge was the final product. Any human activity system models emphasized in SSM were not allowed to participate in the process, nor any bidirectional interactions between the data and the algorithm were not possible. Moreover, the data representation was assumed to be given and fixated, and reconstruction of the data representation was never attempted. Our proposing reproductive process-oriented data mining methodology can be illustrated in Fig.2 as an analogical framework of SSM.

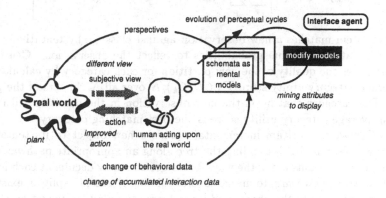

Figure 2: Reproductive process-oriented data mining.

3 Evolutional Concept Formation for Personal Learning Apprentice

Attempts to implement human information processing in forms of schemata have been attempted for a long time in the field of artificial intelligence. Especially, modeling of human categorization has also been approached in the research field of machine learning, especially in its subfield of unsupervised learning which forms a number of categories from a set of observations (*i.e.*, *conceptual clustering*) such as CLUSTER/2 [11] and COBWEB [5]. Conceptual clustering involves learning conceptually similar items while keeping dissimilar ones apart. The clustering is a hierarchy with more general classes near the top, with more specific classes grouped toward the leaf nodes, which are instances of their respective classes. The inputs to this learning module are instances represented by a set of features in the form of [attribute = value] or $[A_i = V_{ij}]$.

COBWEB clusters observations incrementally over a stream of observations, thereby assimilating new observations into existing hierarchical clustering. This process is guided by the following *category utility*.

$$CU(C_k) \equiv \sum_i \sum_j P(A_i = V_{ij})P(C_k \mid A_i = V_{ij})P(A_i = V_{ij} \mid C_k) \qquad (1)$$

Using the following Bayes theorem, equation (1) can be transformed into the following equation:

$$CU(C_k) = P(C_k) \left[\sum_i \sum_j P(A_i = V_{ij} \mid C_k)^2 - P(A_i = V_{ij})^2 \right] \qquad (2)$$

This system matches a new observation against class C_k by tentatively updating C_k's attribute value probabilities to reflect the observation. COBWEB then computes the quality of the new partition for each category by calculating the average category utility score $\sum_k CU(C_k)/N$ over all N clusters of the partition. The category that hosts the new observation in the partition with the greatest average category utility score is the best-matching category.

The COBWEB algorithm incrementally adds a new object to its tentative conceptual hierarchy by descending the tree along an appropriate pathway and updating feature counts along the way. The algorithm may decide, at each level, either to create a new class, to merge several existing classes, to split an existing class, or simply to add the object and its outcome to an already existing class.

The primary goal of a personal learning apprentice is to predict users' actions based on the available situational features inferring the internal concepts. This is based on the capability to reconstruct internal concepts as behavior-shaping constraints by observing operations as well as the information presented by the system. For this purpose, we adopted the concept formation method mentioned in the previous section. The features defining individual observation consist of actions a user takes and information that may be available to the user. Once the system can form the concepts by accumulating the observation, it should be possible to predict a user's action based on the currently available information and associations learned from prior behavior. Accordingly, the problem of how to determine an appropriate set of features that can make predictive reasoning based on the formed concepts as accurate as possible has to be solved. In the following, we attempt to model such an interactive process between stimulus categorization and dimensional learning; the former being left to the original COBWEB's ability, while the latter being realized by the mechanisms of mining feature sets.

Our proposing algorithm comprises two processes; adaptive feature selection and GA-based feature discovery. The former selects the essential attributes out of a provided set of attributes that may initially be either relevant or irrelevant, and the latter constructs new attributes using genetic algorithms applied to a set of elementary features logically represented in a disjunctive normal form. Due to the space limitation, in the following of this paper we concentrate on the latter GA-based feature discovery. The details of the former were published elsewhere [15].

4 GA-Based Feature Discovery

4.1 Finding Constructive Features through GA

Here, we introduce a method of genetic algorithm to determine a new feature constructed from the pre-existing elementary features, called *constructive* feature hereafter [3], [18].

The reasons why we adopted a technique of a GA as a feature discovering method are as follows. First, it is because a GA is well-recognized as a method for adaptive search for large, complex spaces. Since finding a new feature constructed from existing elementary features is a combinatorial problem, we introduced a GA for this purpose. This is the same motivation as DeJong and Janikow proposed; namely the use of a GA for genetic concept learning [3], [7]. Secondly, there was a necessity to combine concept formation and a GA. In contrast to those conventional genetic concept learning approaches whose final products are concept descriptions that cover only target concepts and uncover non-target concepts, our aim of introducing a GA was to reconstruct the features, the justification of which is left to the consequent process of concept formation using those reconstructed features. Moreover, the quality of the resulting concept formation was not determined solely by the existence of a single individual feature, but was dependent on the coexistence of useful features, that is, on how they revealed the richer correlations among the features. This means that the desirable feature set cannot be obtained by simply gathering some superior features solely based on their individual evaluation isolated from others, but it needs to be found through some combinatorial search among the available features. In this sense, a GA's way of search preserving good characters of individual groups is well-fitted for finding an appropriate set of mutually correlating features by considering a set of features such as the population of individuals and by taking the feedback of its fitness concerning the richness of appropriate correlations.

4.2 Representation of New Features and Their Coding

We generally define a constructive feature in a *disjunctive normal form* (*DNF*). A feature is represented by a disjunction of a number of *complexes*, each of which denotes a conjunction of the elementary features represented in the form of $[A_i = V_{ij} \lor V_{ij'}]$. We restrict a constructive feature to take a binary truth value, *i.e.*, true or false. For instance, assume a new constructive feature denoted by C from three elementary features $\{X, Y, Z\}$ each of which may take a value either of $\{1, 2, 3\}$ as follows;

$$[X = 3][Y = 2] \vee [Z = 1] \triangleright [C = 1], \tag{3}$$

which means that new attribute C takes a value of 1 or true when the left-hand side of the above is true and takes a value of 0 or false, otherwise. The purpose of our algorithm here is to construct new features (*i.e.*, to find appropriate logical combinations of features appearing in the left-hand side of the above) that may improve the accuracy of prediction when the concepts are formed by a new feature in addition to pre-existing elementary features.

After the method of coding constructive features proposed in [3], we transform an expression appearing in the left-hand side of the definition of a constructive feature into a bit string comprising a number of chromosomes, each of which corresponds to the individual disjunct (*i.e.*, complexes) such as $[X = 3][Y = 2]$ and $[Z = 1]$. Each chromosome has a substring whose length equals the sum of the domain sizes of the elementary attributes. In the above example, the length of each chromosome equals nine (*i.e.*, 3 ×3), and each disjunct can be coded as follows;

attributes	X	Y	Z
domain	1 2 3	1 2 3	1 2 3
complex $[X = 3][Y = 2]$	0 0 1	0 1 0	1 1 1
complex $[Z = 1]$	1 1 1	1 1 1	1 0 0

Then, an entire individual of a new constructive feature defined by Eq.(6) can be represented as

$$0\,0\,1\,0\,1\,0\,1\,1\,1 + 1\,1\,1\,1\,1\,1\,1\,0\,0 + 1,$$

where the last one bit denotes a value of the constructive feature[1].

4.3 Genetic Operations

The initial population of individuals is constructed at random as a population size P_{init}. Genetic operators are then applied at two different levels by performing crossovers with the boundaries of complexes and elementary features. These operations are called *disjunct-level* genetic operations and *conjunct-level* genetic operations, respectively [7]. The former explores the combination of disjuncts (*i.e.*, complexes) and the latter determines the combination of conjuncts making up the former. The population at the conjunct-level consists of different complexes, in which individuals (i.e., complexes) are ordered according to dependence on the attribute-for-prediction that can be calculated using the equation defined later (c.f., the definition of fitness). Individuals dealt with in

---

[1] This last bit is not used and is extracted from the coding in the following GA.

the disjunct-level genetic operations correspond to individual candidates of *constructive features* as coded in the previous subsection, while individuals dealt with in the conjunct-level genetic operations correspond to individual candidates of *complexes* making up one constructive feature. The algorithm iterates a fixed number of generations (*i.e.*, G_{max}) at the disjunct-level, during which the genetic operations at the conjunct-level are performed every N-times generations of the disjunct-level evolution, where G_{max} and N are parameters specified by the user. Regarding generic operations, *one point crossover* operations are applied at both levels as illustrated in Fig.3, and *mutation* is performed only at the conjunct-level by bit-wise reversal with a fixed probability. *Selection* is performed by preserving M elites out of the mixture of parents and children at the disjunct-level, while at the conjunct level selection is not performed so that the updated generation can preserve the elites as well as the diversity of populations.

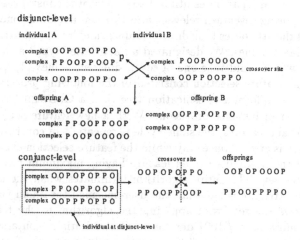

Figure 3: Crossover operations at a disjunct-level and a conjunct level.

4.4 Fitness

Fitness of an individual (*i.e.*, a feature A_N) at both levels can be defined as degree of dependence on the attribute-for-prediction (A_M), which is calculated by the following equation that is modified from Fisher's original definition of dependence.

$$R(A_N) \equiv \sum_{j_N} P(A_N = V_{Nj_N}) \sum_{j_M} [P(A_M = V_{Mj_M} | A_N = V_{Nj_N})^2 - P(A_M = V_{Mj_M})^2]$$

$$(4)$$

At the disjunct-level generic operations, an individual constructive feature is evaluated using the above equation, and at the conjunct-level generic operation, an individual complex is evaluated assuming that a new feature consists only of that single complex. In this way, new constructive features that reveal high dependence on the attribute-for-prediction A_N are preserved during evolution.

5 Schema Construction Using Mined Features

We develop an integrated algorithm of the above two capabilities of the personal learning apprentice of adaptive feature selection and GA-based feature discovery. To verify the usefulness of our method, we carried out the following experiments by applying our method to the popular data set of the "zoo" database. These data are available from the machine learning data base of University of California Irvine and are used by many machine learning researchers as a bench-mark testbed. Attributes utilized to represent the instances were thirty attributes comprising seventeen relevant and thirteen irrelevant ones generated at random. All the attributes took discrete values, and irrelevant attributes were restricted to binary values. We designated an attribute "type" as an attribute-for-prediction, which could take one of seven different values $\{1, 2, 3, 4, 5, 6, 7\}$. One cycle of the feature-selection consisted of the following processes. The algorithm attempts to form a classification tree (i.e., a COBWEB tree) 10 times, varying the order of instance-provision. With a new feature set obtained by excluding irrelevant features, the same cycle is repeated. In contrast, GA-based feature discovery is applied once only while the feature-selection cycle is iterated five times, and the newly-discovered feature having maximum fitness is added to the attributes set. The entire algorithm terminates when the difference in weights of each attribute is less than the user-specified threshold value.

Table 1 shows the results of applying the algorithm to the test data set. Herein, labels more than #1001 denote attributes initially contained as being irrelevant, and labels from #61-#261 denote newly discovered features. Table 2 shows the details of the features utilized in the experiment and the newly discovered features. Note that the elementary attributes making up the newly discovered complex feature do not remain solely in the final attribute set. This means that such attributes individually make less contribution to the appropriate concept formation, however, by being integrated to define a new feature they contribute much to the concept formation (e.g., attributes of "egg" and "milk").

Using the derived attribute set mined from the original attribute set, we performed the concept formation to discover how the overall structure in a form of a hierarchy changes. Fig.4 (a), (b) and (c) show a comparison of the results of the concept formation using the original attribute set, the attribute set obtained when only feature selection was applied, and the attribute set obtained by the hybrid algorithm, respectively. Each circular and rectangular

no. of cycles	excluded attribute	prediction accuracy	diff. in counters	new attribute
1	domestic	85	23.5	!!
2	#1006	87.2	23.3	!!
3	retry	83.6	22.9	!!
4	#1008	87.6	23.6	!!
5	#1012	87	23.1	!!
6	#1005	87.6	24.3	#61
7	#1006	88.4	24	!!
8	#1003	88.6	21.9	!!
9	#1009	86.8	22.2	!!
10	#1007	88.4	21.7	!!
11	#1000	90	22.1	#111
12	#1011	89.2	20.1	!!
13	#1001	88	18.9	!!
14	predator	89.6	19.4	!!
15	catsize	90	18.4	!!
16	#1010	88.8	18	#161
17	#1004	89	19.2	!!
18	#1002	90.6	18.4	!!
19	milk	88.6	16.6	!!
20	tail	89.2	15.9	!!
21	#111	90.8	16.5	#211
22	#161	88.8	13.1	!!
23	#211	88.4	12.8	!!
24	venomous	88.6	14.9	!!
25	fins	87.4	17.7	!!
26	eggs	88.6	14.2	#261
27	toothed	90.4	12.4	!!
28	breathes	90.2	13.5	!!
29	feathers	89.2	9.6	finished

Table 1: Results of an experiment using a hybrid algorithm.

nodes represents schema. The figures in leaf nodes represent the value of the attribute-for-prediction (*i.e.*, "type") to be predicted at the corresponding leaf node.

In Fig.4(a) many classes predicting the same value are constructed in several different parts of the tree, meaning that multiple and dissimilar concepts of schemata are recalled at the same time when an interface agent attempts to apply reasoning to a particular value of the attribute-for-prediction. In Fig.4(c) this is greatly improved and concepts of schemata predicting the same value are organized in a segmented fashion within the overall tree. In other words, an interface agent succeeds in constructing a perceptual category of the observations customized for applying reasoning to a value of a particular attribute such as an action attribute. This capability of constructing an *action-centered* view of the perceptual external world is essential to biological learning, and is currently discussed as a design principle of human-machine interface systems and is called "affordance" or "ecological interface".

initial attribute set	type hair legs aquatic airborne
!!	backbone domestic feathers breathes
!!	toothed eggs fins venomous tail
!!	milk catsize predator #1001-#1013
!!	(30 features in total)
final attribute set	type hair legs aquatic airborne
!!	backbone #61 #261
!!	(eight attributes)
!!	!!
newly discovered features	definition
#61	[milk=0][eggs=1] ∨
!!	[milk=0][backbone=0]
#111	[milk=1][backbone=1]
#161	[milk=1][venomous=0]
#211	[eggs=1][#61=1] ∨
!!	[hair=0][toothed=1][breathes=0] ∨
!!	[legs=0,2,5,6,8][backbone=0]
#261	[#61=0][breathes=1]

Table 2: An initial attribute set and a final attribute set.

6 Application to the Data Set of Experimental Plant Operations

Finally, we attempted to apply our proposed apprentice learning method to a human-machine systems domain. That is, we accumulated a collection of human-machine interactions that were observed when a human operator operates a simulator of a generic dynamic production process called PLANT. PLANT was originally developed by Morris, N.M. for the purpose of investigating the effects of type of knowledge upon human problem solving in a process control task [12]. A graphic illustration displaying a sample PLANT problem is shown in Fig.5(a).

Referring to Fig.5(a), in this system there are nine tanks, some of which are currently connected by open valves (represented by lines between tanks). Fluid enters the PLANT system at the left and exits at the right as a finished product. Each pair of connected tanks is modeled as a second-order system with rate of flow and its derivative as state variables and transition matrix determined by pipe diameter, tank cross-sectional areas, pipe lengths, and fluid characteristics. Further details concerning with the PLANT are shown in [13]. In general, the PLANT operator's task is to supervise the flow of fluid through the series of tanks interconnected by pumps, valves, and pipes so as to produce a specified product. The operator may open and close valves, adjust system input and output, check the flow between tanks in order to achieve the primary goal of maximizing production.

A skillful plant operator who has understood the physical principles of the simulator systems serves in a number of sessions (i.e., production runs), with the average length of each session being approximately 200 updates of system

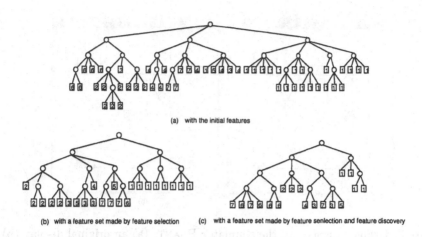

(a) with the initial features

(b) with a feature set made by feature selection   (c) with a feature set made by feature senlection and feature discovery

Figure 4: Comparison of concepts formed from three different attribute sets applied to a "zoo" data set.

states. 200 instances of human-machine interactions are gathered, each of which consists of thirty attributes and their values; nine attributes showing the states of levels (either of "high", "medium" or "low") of nine tanks, eighteen attributes representing the status of valves (either "open" or "closed") of eighteen connections among tanks, two attributes showing the current status of system input and output flows (either of 0, 100, 200, 300 or 400 units) and the attribute designating the operator's input command. The actions that the operator can take are; to open or close a particular valve between tanks, adjust system input and output flows, and to ignore some operations.

The algorithm mentioned in the previous section is applied to this data set, and we construct a schema hierarchy for predicting the values of a particular attribute of current status of the connection between TANK A and D. The newly discovered features are shown in Table 3, where the symbols [a b c d e f g h i] represent the attributes showing the current status of levels of nine tanks and the symbols [ad ae af bd be bf cd ce cf dg dh di eg eh ei fg fh fi] represent the attributes showing the current status of valves connecting the nine tanks.

To verify the appropriateness of the selected attributes for that human operator, we carried out an additional experiment by only presenting the information concerning those attributes derived by the the above experiment to the human operator requiring him to operate accordingly. The graphic display shown in Fig.5(b) illustrates only the information needed to judge the status of the valve connecting TANK A to D. During the experiment, the information on the current values of the discovered features were also presented with this display. The result was satisfactory and the operator could predict the status of the valve

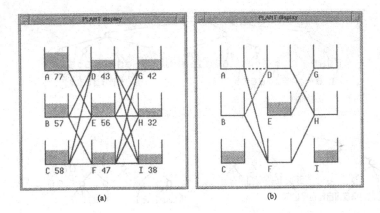

(a)   (b)

Figure 5: Graphic displays of the simulator PLANT. (a) an original display (b) a screened-out display

initial attribute set	ad ae af bd be bf cd ce cf
!!	dg dh di eg eh ei fg fh fi
!!	a b c d e f g h i
!!	commands pi po
!!	(30 features in total)
final attribute set	ad af bd bf dh eg fh c e i #111 #161
!!	(12 attributes)
newly discovered features	definition
#61	[cf=1][eh=0] ∨ [bd=1][fi=1] ∨ [fh=1]
#111	[#61=0] ∨ [cd=1][g=L]
#161	[111=1] ∨ [pi=300][po=0,200,300,400]

Table 3: An initial attribute set and newly discovered features in the experiment using PLANT.

correctly without any fruitless search for added information.

Finally, we consider how our method relates with the SSM discussed in section 2. Correspondences are overlaid in Fig.2. We can observe the following facts from the experiments done for plant operation mentioned in the previous section. The process of an initial attribute set's evolution corresponds to the evolution of the operator's *subjective* views on a particular plant status. This change of views forced him/her change the adopted operations, which results in the accumulation of instances of new human-system interactions. By applying our method to this new data set and by further mining the attributes from this data set, such a basic cycle of the process iterates recursively and promotes the evolution of the system's displays to the human operator as well as the evolution of the operator's internal grasping of the system status. We would like to stress that such reciprocity established during a continuous process is fundamentally important for designing a human-machine collaborative system. This is fundamentally different from the conventional typical human-machine system design principle to fix the individual roles such as a supervisor-supervisee roles among a human and a machine.

For instance, our system presents different displays to the operator according to whether he/she is a novice or a proficient expert. When the operator is still a novice, our system cannot construct satisfactory schema from their interaction accumulations, since they involve a lot of inconsistent operations (i.e., for the same system status, a novice operator may take different operations). As he/she becomes proficient and his/her operations come to be more consistent, the system succeeds in constructing such a coherent schema that can guide his/her correct operations, which does accelerate the operator's further and correct awareness of the plant status. This is exactly an ideal style of "human-in-the-loop system", and can be realized by the process-orientedness of our proposing method.

7   Conclusions

In this paper, to reconstruct the operator's conceptual structures behind the operations, we proposed a learning system that has the capability of eliminating features that do not contribute to the prediction of operator behavior and which finds new features that contribute to the improvement of prediction accuracy. Referring to the current popular SSM concepts, we put an emphasis on the systematicity in the process of human's proactive interactions with the artifacts, not solely in an accumulation of data isolated from the human intervention and from the human interpretation. We showed how such an aspect can be embedded within an interface agent, and discussed its potentials for designing a human-machine collaborative system.

References

[1] Bartlett, F.C., "Remembering: A Study in Experimental and Social Psychology", Cambridge Univ. Press, 1932.

[2] Checkland, P. and Scholes, J.: Soft Systems Methodology in Action, John Wiley & Sons, Ltd., 1990.

[3] De Jong, K.A., Spears, W.M. and Gordon, D.F., "Using Genetic Algorithms for Concept Learning", Machine Learning, 13, pp.161-188, 1993.

[4] Dent, L. et al., "A Personal Learning Apprentice", Proceedings of the Tenth National Conference on Artificial Intelligence, pp.96-103, 1992.

[5] Fisher, D. H., "Knowledge Acquisition via Incremental Conceptual Clustering", *Machine Learning*, 2, pp.139-172, 1987.

[6] Gluck, M. and Corter, J., "Information, Uncertainty and the Utility of Categories", *Proc. of the Seventh Annual Conf. on Cognitive Science Society*, pp.283-287, 1985.

[7] Janikow, C.Z., "A Knowledge-Intensive Genetic Algorithm for Supervised Learning", *Machine Learning*, 13, pp.189-228, 1993.

[8] Hermens, L.A. and Schlimmer, J.C., "A Machine-Learning Apprentice for the Completion of Repetitive Forms", *IEEE Expert*, 9-1, pp.28-33, 1994.

[9] Maes, P. and Kozierok, R., "Learning Interface Agents", *Proceedings of the Eleventh National Conference on Artificial Intelligence*, pp.459-465, 1993.

[10] Maes, P., "Agents That Reduce Work and Information Overload", *Communications of the ACM*, 37-7, pp.30-40, 1994.

[11] Michalski, R.S. and Stepp, R.E., "Learning from Observation: Conceptual Clustering", in Michalski, R.S. et al. (Eds.), *Machine Learning: An Artificial Intelligence Approach*, San Mateo, CA: Morgan Kaufmann, 1983.

[12] Morris, N. M. and Rouse, W. B., "The Effects of Type of Knowledge upon Human Problem Solving in a Process Control Task", *IEEE Trans. Syst. Man Cybern.*, SMC-15-6, pp.698-707, 1985.

[13] Morris, N. M., Rouse, W. B. and Fath, J. L., "PLANT: An Experimental Task for Study of the Human Problem Solving in Process Control", *IEEE Trans. Syst. Man Cybern.*, SMC-15-6, 1985.

[14] Neisser, U., "Cognition and Reality", San Francisco, W.H. Freeman and Company, 1976.

[15] Sawaragi, T., Tani, N. and Katai, O., "Evolutional Concept Learning from Observations through Adaptive Feature Selection and GA-Based Feature Discovery", to be appeared in *Journal of Intelligent and Fuzzy Systems*, 7-3, 1999.

[16] Smith, E.E. and Medin, D.L., "Categories and Concepts", Harvard University Press, Cambridge, MA, 1981.

[17] Wilson, B., "Systems: Concepts, Methodologies, and Applications", John Wiley & Sons, Ltd., 1990.

[18] Wnek, J. and Michalski, R.S., "Hypothesis-Driven Constructive Induction in AQ17-HCI:A Method and Experiments", *Machine Learning*, 14, pp.139-168, 1994.

Generalized Fuzzy Aggregation Operators

M Petrou and K R Sasikala

School of Electronic Engineering, Information Technology and Mathematics,
University of Surrey, Guildford, GU2 5XH, UK

Abstract. Fuzzy logic offers the option to try to model the non-linearity of the functioning of the human brain when several pieces of evidence are combined to make an inference. In the proposed scheme a Fuzzy reasoning system includes a training stage during which the most appropriate aggregation operators are selected. To allow for different importance to be given to different pieces of evidence, the Fuzzy membership functions used are allowed to take values in a range $[0, w]$, with $w \neq 1$. Then the need arises for the generalization of the aggregetion operators to cope with such membership functions. In this paper we examine the properties of such generalised operators, that make them appropriate for use in Fuzzy reasoning.

1 Introduction

One of the aspects of Machine Learning is related to trying to imitate the human expert who uses various sources of input information to draw a conclusion. The human expert "weighs" the evidence for its reliability and significance in an instinctive way, and draws conclusions. Many methods have been used in Artificial Intelligence and related fields to imitate this process. Apart from the rule-based schemes which are the most straight forward ones, several more sophisticated schemes try to operate taking into consideration the uncertainty in the sources of information, and their relevance to the problem. For example, Bayesian reasoning tries to capture the knowledge of the expert in the form of prior and conditional probabilities. Then the thought process that combines this information is modelled along the lines of probability theory.

Alternatively, people use Fuzzy Logic. If Fuzzy Logic is thought of as an extension of the rule-based approach, once the rules have been set up, there is almost no learning involved: there are straight-forward Fuzzy rules with which uncertain pieces of information are combined to yield the uncertainty in the conclusion. However, the strict application of Fuzzy Logic in the form of the so called "min-max" rules (ie rules effectively saying that "a chain is as strong as its weakest link" and "a connection between two points is as strong as the strongest link between them") has proven to be totally non-robust and unable to model properly the human process of reasoning with uncertainty. Alternative approaches of combining the uncertainty of predicates have been proposed, in the form of aggregation operators. This led to a considerable degree of arbitrariness in the way Fuzzy Logic has been applied to solve real problems. Opponents of the approach say that it is effectively an ad-hock method with no sound Mathematical basis. We believe that this arbitrariness of Fuzzy Logic makes it into an excellent tool for modelling in a flexible way the non-linearity of the reasoning process that takes place in the brain of the human expert. As problems vary and approaches to solutions differ from expert to expert, there seems to be a necessary front-end of such an approach where any automatic system that has to replace a human expert has to learn first the way the brain of that expert works with respect to the particular problem. Thus, the brain of the human expert is treated as a black box where we input uncertain data and we obtain decisions with various degrees of confidence. The problem is to use a process that will learn the non-linear behaviour of this box.

In [8] we followed this approach in solving the problem of ranking burned forests according to the risk they run to become arid and eventually desert. The factors that influence the competing processes of erosion and regeneration had to be derived from different maps, each with its own degree of uncertainty. In addition, some factors were more important than others in the process of erosion or regeneration. The problem was analysed in two stages: Conditions that combine in a conjunctive way to create a situation, and different combinations of conditions that in a disjunctive way lead to the same situation. So, it is necessary to choose operators that will combine the uncertainty in the fulfilment of conditions that lead to a certain conclusion, and operators that combine the uncertainty in different paths that lead to the same conclusion. In addition, one has to incorporate the relative importance of the various conditions to the final conclusion.

The first problem implies that we need a training phase during which we try various combinations of aggregation operators that have been proposed in the literature, using data for which we know what the expert had concluded. In effect at this stage we try to model the non-linear way of thinking of the expert. In order to incorporate the relative importance of the various factors, we proposed something very radical: we suggested the use of membership functions that take values greater than 1. A membership function in the crisp set theory takes only values 1 or 0, according to whether an object belongs to a set or not. In Fuzzy set theory a membership function is allowed to take values between 0 and 1 to express the partial fulfilment of a condition, ie the partial membership of an object to a set defined by that condition. By allowing the membership functions to take values between 0 and w where $w \neq 1$, we allow the user to quantify the relative importance of the various conditions: If a condition is less important than another, then even if it is completely fulfilled, the corresponding membership function should not be more than $w < 1$ to reflect the lesser importance of that condition. Similarly, if a condition is very important, when it is completely fulfilled, the corresponding membership function should be $w > 1$ to reflect the great importance of this condition relative to some reference condition which has maximum possible value of its membership function $w = 1$.

During the training phase then, the system does not only have to learn which operators model best the way of thinking of the expert, but also which are the maximum values of the membership functions that best describe the relative importance the expert places to the various contributing items of evidence.

At first sight, the idea of membership functions taking values in a range other than [0, 1], may seem to be nothing else than using weights with which we multiply the membership functions. However, this is not the case, as many of the possible aggregation operators are non-linear, and if we are to use non-conventional membership functions, we must generalise the aggregators too. In this paper we present these generalised aggregation operators, and examine whether they fulfil some of the fundamental properties such operators have to obey in order to be usable in Fuzzy reasoning.

There are quite a few publications that discuss the properties of many of these fuzzy aggregation operators to enable a good choice of an aggregation connective in any specific problem domain. Dubois and Prade in [5] provide an extensive survey on fuzzy set-theoretic operations, mainly concentrating on the properties of these operations. Yager in [13] discusses some of the issues involved in the selection of appropriate operators mainly for implementing the union and intersection of fuzzy subsets, based on the properties satisfied by these operators. There are many more publications available on the various fuzzy aggregation operators, of which a few notable ones are [6] [1] [5] [13] [9] [4] [2] [3] [14]. All these publications theoretically discuss the various classes of fuzzy aggregation operators like t-norms, t-conorms etc and the properties that each of these operators follows.

There have been a few publications that say how relative importances of combined factors could be incorporated in fuzzy reasoning. Of these, the most notable ones are by Yager [9] [10] [11] [12]. Yager has studied the issue of inclusion of relative importance in a great detail and has suggested various ways of incorporating it in a multi-criteria decision making problem. Inclusion of relative importances is normally achieved by retaining the aggregation operators as they are defined and then associating the weights with the membership functions as product, power or a max/min or a T-conorm/T-norm.

In section 2 of this paper, we present the proposed modification of the aggregation operators to handle non-conventional membership functions. In section 3, we shall discuss the effect of these modifications on the properties of the operators and we shall conclude in section 4.

2   Generalization of Fuzzy Aggregation Operators

Aggregation operations on fuzzy sets are operations by which several fuzzy sets are combined in a desirable way to produce a single fuzzy set. An aggregation operation on n fuzzy sets where $n \geq 2$ is formally defined by a function
$$f : [0, 1]^n \longrightarrow [0, 1]$$
When applied to fuzzy sets, this function produces an aggregate fuzzy set by operating on the membership grades of these sets [6]. This definition of an aggregation operation will hold only as long as the membership functions of say x and y vary between 0 and 1. If the fuzzy membership grades are not constrained

to ≤ 1, then the above given definition is not valid anymore. Hence, we extend the definition of an aggregation operation on n fuzzy sets to

$f : [0, w_1][0, w_2] \ldots [0, w_n] \longrightarrow [0, max(w_1, w_2, \ldots w_n)]$,

where w_i is the maximum possible membership value of the ith aggregate to any of its possible classes.

The nature of aggregation of two variables say x and y, could be any of the following [2].

1. Aggregation is conjunctive if
   $f(x, y) \leq min(x, y)$
   which states that a conjunctive operator has confidence at most as high as the smallest membership value and looks for the simultaneous satisfaction of all criteria that are being combined.
2. Aggregation is disjunctive if
   $f(x, y) \geq max(x, y)$
   which states that a disjunctive operator has confidence at least as small as the greatest membership value and looks for a redundancy between the criteria that are being combined.
3. Aggregation is a compromise if
   $min(x, y) \leq f(x, y) \leq max(x, y)$
   which is a cautious behaviour.

The aggregation operators themselves fall under 4 classes, namely

- T-norms
- T-conorms
- Symmetric Sums
- Means

where T-norms are conjunctive in nature, T-conorms are disjunctive in nature, Symmetric sums could be conjunctive or disjunctive depending on the values of the variables involved and Means are compromise operators. Each of these classes of operators are discussed below. The most common operators of each class, with their standard and generalised definitions are given.

2.1 T-Norms and T-Conorms

Table 1 presents the standard and modified definitions of the most commonly used T-norms and T-conorms. The generalised definitions of min, max and $algebraic\ product$ remain the same. The probabilistic sum operator, however, may yield negative values if x and y are allowed to take values greater than 1. In order to avoid this, the generalised definition of this operator is $\frac{w_2 x + w_1 y - xy}{max(w_1, w_2)}$.

2.2 Symmetric Sums

Symmetric Sums take the general form

OPERATOR	DEFINITION	
	ORIGINAL $0 \le x \le 1$ $0 \le y \le 1$	GENERALISED $0 \le x \le w_1$ $0 \le y \le w_2$
Intersection (min_1)	$minimum(x,y)$	$minimum(x,y)$
Union (max_1)	$maximum(x,y)$	$maximum(x,y)$
Probabilistic sum (sum)	$x + y - xy$	$\frac{w_2 x + w_1 y - xy}{max(w_1, w_2)}$
Algebraic product ($prod$)	xy	xy
Bounded sum (min_2)	$min(1, x+y)$	$min[min(w_1, w_2), x+y]$
Bounded difference (max_2)	$max(0, x+y-1)$	$max[0, x+y-max(w_1, w_2)]$

Table 1. Definition of T-norm and T-conorm operators used

$$f(x,y) = \frac{g(x,y)}{g(x,y)+g(1-x,1-y)}$$

and their behaviour as to whether they are conjunctive or disjunctive depends on the values of x and y. The symmetric sums considered here are

$\sigma_0 \equiv \frac{xy}{1-x-y+2xy}$ corresponding to $g(x,y) = xy$

$\sigma_+ \equiv \frac{x+y-xy}{1+x+y-2xy}$ corresponding to $g(x,y) = x + y - xy$

$min_3 \equiv \frac{min(x,y)}{1-|x-y|}$ corresponding to $g(x,y) = min(x,y)$

$max_3 \equiv \frac{max(x,y)}{1+|x-y|}$ corresponding to $g(x,y) = max(x,y)$

The nature of σ_0 and σ_+ depends on the values of x and y while min_3 and max_3 are compromise operators. All these operations involve complementation and hence have to be modified. We define complementation as $c(x) = w - x$, where w is the maximum value of x, in contrast to the standard definition $c(x) = 1 - x$. Then, the modified symmetrical sums take the form

$$f(x,y) = \frac{g(x,y)}{g(x,y)+g(w_1-x,w_2-y)}$$

In the modified σ_+ operator, $g(x,y)$ will be the generalised version of the probabilistic sum. The standard and the generalised symmetric sums are given in Table 2. All generalised symmetric sums take values in the range [0,1].

2.3 Means

The most commonly used mean operators are the arithmetic, harmonic and geometric mean. All mean operators yield a value in between the max and min and hence have a compromise behaviour. The mean operators are shown in Table 3. It can be seen that these operators can be used as they are in the generalised case.

OPERATOR	DEFINITION	
	ORIGINAL	GENERALISED
	$0 \leq x \leq 1$ $0 \leq y \leq 1$	$0 \leq x \leq w_1$ $0 \leq y \leq w_2$
max_3	$\frac{max(x,y)}{1+\|x-y\|}$	$\frac{max(x,y)}{max(x,y)+max(w_1-x,w_2-y)}$
min_3	$\frac{min(x,y)}{1-\|x-y\|}$	$\frac{min(x,y)}{min(x,y)+min(w_1-x,w_2-y)}$
σ_0	$\frac{xy}{1-x-y+2xy}$	$\frac{xy}{(w_1-x)(w_2-y)+xy}$
σ_+	$\frac{x+y-xy}{1+x+y-2xy}$	$\frac{w_2x+w_1y-xy}{w_1w_2+w_2x+w_1y-2xy}$

Table 2. Definition of symmetric sums used

OPERATOR	DEFINITION	
	ORIGINAL	GENERALISED
	$0 \leq x \leq 1$ $0 \leq y \leq 1$	$0 \leq x \leq w_1$ $0 \leq y \leq w_2$
Arithmetic mean (am)	$\frac{x+y}{2}$	$\frac{x+y}{2}$
Geometric mean (gm)	$\sqrt{xy}$	$\sqrt{xy}$
Harmonic mean (hm)	$\frac{2xy}{x+y}$	$\frac{2xy}{x+y}$

Table 3. Definition of mean operators used

All the above given operators have also been extended to more than 2 fuzzy sets and Table 4 shows the generalised version for 4 fuzzy sets. These can be extended in a similar way to any number of fuzzy sets.

3 Properties of the Generalized Aggregation Operators

Klir and Yuan state in [6] that for f to be an intuitively meaningful aggregation function, it must satisfy the following 3 axiomatic requirements.

1. $f(0,0,\ldots,0) = 0$ and $f(1,1,\ldots,1) = 1$.
2. f is monotonically increasing in all its arguments. From [6], f is said to be monotonically increasing in all its arguments if for any pair $(a_1, a_2, ...a_n)$ and $(b_1, b_2, ...b_n)$ where $a_i, b_i \in [0,1]$ for all i, if $a_i \leq b_i$ for every i, then $f(a_1, a_2, ..., a_n) \leq f(b_1, b_2, ...b_n)$.
3. f is a continuous function.

These three properties are generalised as follows.

1. $f(0,0,\ldots,0) = 0$ and $f(w_1, w_2, \ldots, w_n) \in [min(w_1, w_2, ...w_n), max(w_1, w_2, ...w_n)]$

2. f is monotonically increasing in all its arguments. We say that f is monotonically increasing if for any pair $(a_1, a_2, ...a_n)$ and $(b_1, b_2, ...b_n)$ with $a_i, b_i \in [0, w_i]$ for all i, if $a_i \le b_i$ for every i, then $f(a_1, a_2, ..., a_n) \le f(b_1, b_2, ...b_n)$.
3. f is a continuous function.

All the aggregation functions defined earlier satisfy the three properties stated above. Figures 1, 2 and 3 demonstrate the fulfilment of these properties for the special case of these functions: $f(y; w_1, w_2, x)$ with $w_1 = 1$, $w_2 = 2$ and $x \in \{0, 0.2, 0.6, 1\}$ while $y \in [0, 2]$. It can be seen from these figures that all the above properties are satisfied by all these generalised aggregation functions with the exception of the class of symmetric sums and the *prod* operator.

For the symmetric sums, always $f(w_1, w_2, ...w_n) = 1$. However, as parameters $w_1, w_2, ...w_n$ are chosen to reflect the *relative* importance of the aggregated factors, one of them is bound to be 1, so the first generalised property holds for the symmetric sums as well.

For the generalised product operator,
$f(w_1, w_2, \ldots, w_n) \in [min(w_1, w_2, ...w_n), max(w_1, w_2, ...w_n)]$ is valid only if one of the membership values is ≥ 1.

We discuss below the major properties of each class of operators as originally defined and the properties of the modified operators. For all the properties mentioned above and all those discussed below, formal proofs can be found in [7].

3.1 T-Norms and T-Conorms

Functions like T-norms and T-conorms have been extensively studied in the literature [2] [1] [6] and have been observed to have a number of properties of fuzzy intersection and union respectively.

A fuzzy *intersection* is formally defined as an operation on the unit interval that satisfies the following properties:

1. Monotonicity
2. Commutativity
3. Associativity
4. Boundary condition $i(x, 1) = x$

where $x \in [0, 1]$ and i here stands for an intersection operator.

When the operators are generalised to take values ≥ 1, the boundary condition is redefined as $i(x, w) = x$, where w is the maximum value that y could take. This condition means that the identity element is now not 1, but the maximum membership value that a fuzzy set that is aggregated with x could take. The three generalised T-norms are shown in figures 1(a) (intersection), 1(d) (algebraic product) and 1(f) (bounded difference).

From these figures, we can see that all these generalised operators satisfy the property of monotonicity. They are all commutative and associative but the generalised boundary condition is not satisfied by any of them. A boundary

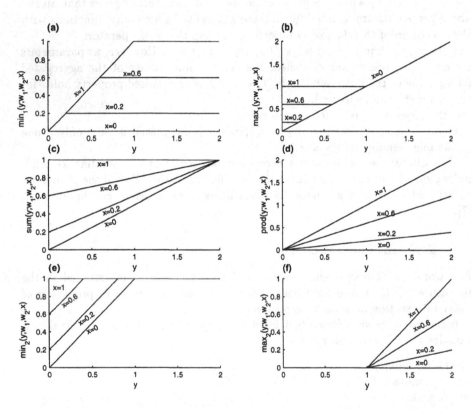

Fig. 1. T-norm and T-conorm Aggregation Functions with $w1 = 1$, $w2 = 2$, $x \in \{0, 0.2, 0.6, 1\}$ and $y \in [0, 2]$

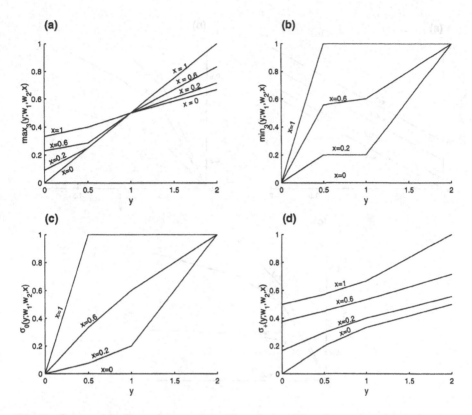

Fig. 2. Symmetric Sum Aggregation Functions with $w1 = 1$, $w2 = 2$, $x \in \{0, 0.2, 0.6, 1\}$ and $y \in [0, 2]$

condition implies that aggregating a fuzzy set x with the maximum confidence that any fuzzy set could take, results in the confidence placed on x. However, in our generalised definition of the boundary condition, viz, $i(x, w) = x$, w, which is the maximum membership value that the fuzzy set y could take, need not be greater than the maximum membership value that x can take. If the maximum membership value of y is greater than that of x, or if the maximum membership values of x and y are equal, then the generalised boundary condition will be valid for all operators other than the algebraic product operator. The boundary condition is satisfied by the algebraic product operator only when the maximum membership value of y is 1.

A fuzzy *union* is an operation on the unit interval that satisfies the properties

of

1. Monotonicity
2. Commutativity
3. Associativity
4. Boundary condition $u(x, 0) = x$

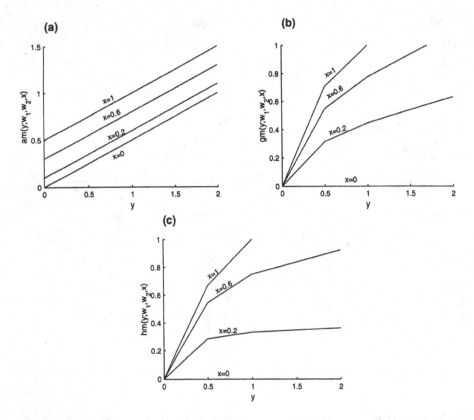

Fig. 3. Mean Aggregation Functions with $w1 = 1$, $w2 = 2$, $x \in \{0, 0.2, 0.6, 1\}$ and $y \in [0, 2]$

where $a \in [0, 1]$ and u stands for a union operator. All the properties of a union operator hold for the generalised definitions of T-Conorms shown in figure 1(b) (union), 1(c) (probabilistic sum) and 1(e) (bounded sum) with the exception of the boundary condition which is not satisfied by the generalised probabilistic sum and the bounded sum operators. The figures demonstrate that these generalised operators are all monotonic. The boundary condition of T-conorms means that aggregating a fuzzy set x with the least confidence that any fuzzy set could have, produces a result with confidence equal to x. The generalised boundary condition is satisfied by the probabilistic sum and the bounded sum operators as long as the maximum membership value of x is less than or equal to that of y.

The algebraic product and the probabilistic operator satisfy the conditions of conjunction and disjunction respectively, i.e.,

$prod(x, y) \leq min(x, y)$ and

$sum(x, y) \geq max(x, y)$.

However, the generalised *prod* and *sum* operators do not satisfy the same conditions. While the nature of the generalised algebraic product depends on the values of x and y, the probabilistic sum behaves like a compromise operator yielding a value in between $min(x, y)$ and $max(x, y)$.

In addition to the above general properties, some of the T-norms and T-conorms have some extra properties. We discuss below these special properties.

Idempotency:

The simplest of the T-conorms and the T-norms, namely max_1 and min_1 operators are the only idempotent operators i.e., they satisfy

$max_1(x, x) = x$ and

$min_1(x, x) = x$

This property means that aggregating a fuzzy set with an identical one, does not alter the degree of certainty. This property of idempotency is still satisfied by the generalised max_1 and min_1 operators.

Strict Monotonicity:

The standard algebraic product and the probabilistic sum satisfy strict monotonicity i.e.,

If $x_1 < x_2$ & $y_1 < y_2$ then

$prod(x_1, y_1) < prod(x_2, y_2)$

$sum(x_1, y_1) < sum(x_2, y_2)$

The strict monotonicity property is still followed by the generalised probabilistic sum and the algebraic product operators, examples of which are shown in figures 1(c) and 1(d) respectively.

Archimedian Property:

The standard algebraic product and probabilistic sum also satisfy the so called *Archimedian property* i.e., $\forall x \in (0, 1)$,

$prod(x, x) < x$ and $sum(x, x) > x$

These properties are also called as *subidempotency* and *superidempotency* respectively. The generalised algebraic product (figure 1(d)) does not follow the Archimedian property as the membership grades could take values greater than 1, but the generalised probabilistic sum satisfies it.

Hence the operator *sum* is an *Archimedian* T-conorm, while *prod* is not an Archimedian T-norm. The operator *sum* could also be termed a *Strict Archimedian* operator as it follows *Strict Monotonicity*.

Nilpotency:

The standard bounded difference and sum operators are nilpotent i.e., they satisfy the following:

For any sequence of fuzzy sets x_n, with $0 < x_n < 1$,

$\exists n < \infty$ such that $max_2(x_1, x_2, ...x_n) = 0$

$\exists m < \infty$ such that $min_2(x_1, x_2, ...x_m) = 1$

This property means that the aggregation of a finite number of fuzzy sets may lead to the identity element. For a T-conorm, total certainty may be attained when, say, m fuzzy sets have been aggregated. Similarly, for a T-norm, total uncertainty may be attained when, say, n number of fuzzy sets have been aggregated. Aggregation with anymore fuzzy sets will not alter the certainty or uncertainty already reached. In our generalised aggregation, the bounded differ-

ence max_2 shown in figure 1(f), satisfies the following:
$\exists n$ such that $max_2(x_1, x_2, ...x_n) = 0$
The bounded sum min_2 shown in figure 1(e) satisfies the following property.
$\exists m$ such that $min_2(x_1, x_2, ...x_m) = min[w_1, w_2, ...w_m]$

3.2 Symmetric Sums

The symmetric sums that are normally defined as operators from $f : [0, 1]^n \longrightarrow [0, 1]$ satisfy the following properties.

1. $\sigma(0, 0, ...0) = 0$, $\sigma(1, 1, ...1) = 1$
2. Commutativity
3. Monotonicity
4. Autoduality i.e., $1 - \sigma(x_1, x_2, ...x_n) = \sigma(1 - x_1, 1 - x_2, ...1 - x_n)$

where σ here stands for a symmetric sum operator. The generalised symmetric sums shown in figure 2(a) (max_3), 2(b) (min_3), 2(c) (σ_0) and 2(d) (σ_+) satisfy all these properties, with the first property modified as $\sigma(0, 0, ...0) = 0$, $\sigma(w_1, w_2, ...w_n) = 1$ and the last one modified as
$1 - \sigma(x_1, x_2, ...x_n) = \sigma(w_1 - x_1, w_2 - x_2, ...w_n - x_n)$

3.3 Means

The mean of n fuzzy sets is an operation that satisfies

1. $min(x_1, x_2, ...x_n) \leq m(x_1, x_2, ...x_n) \leq max(x_1, x_2, ...x_n)$
2. Commutativity
3. Monotonicity

where m stands for a mean operator and $m \notin \{max, min\}$. The definition of mean operations remain unaltered after generalisation. Hence, the mean operators shown in figures 3(a) (arithmetic mean), 3(b) (geometric mean) and 3(c) (harmonic mean) satisfy all the above properties just as the standard mean operators. They also follow the idempotency property that is followed by the standard mean operators i.e., they follow $m(x, x, ..., x) = x$.

4 Conclusion

We propose that Fuzzy Logic can be generalised to allow the modelling of the thought process by which a human expert makes certain decisions using incomplete or uncertain information. In our approach, Fuzzy systems can be generalised to include a learning stage during which the system learns the way the expert draws his/her conclusions and the relative importance he/she gives to the various factors. Once this has been learned, and the appropriate operators with which evidence can be combined have been identified, the system can be used to replace or imitate the expert in making decisions (with respect always to the same problem), using data that have not been seen before by either the system or the expert.

In this paper, we reviewed the properties of the generalised aggregation operators that have to be used by such a system.

References

1. Bandemer, H. and Gottwald, S., *Fuzzy Sets, Fuzzy Logic and Fuzzy Methods with Applications*, Wiley, 1995.
2. Bloch, I., "Information Combination Operators for Data Fusion: A comparative review with classification," *IEEE transactions on System, Man and Cybernetics*, **26**(1), January 1996, pp. 52–67.
3. Combettes, P. L., "The foundations of set theoretic estimation," *Proceedings of the IEEE*, **81**(2), 1993, pp. 182–208.
4. Czogala, E. and Drewniak, J., "Associative monotic operations in fuzzy set theory," *Fuzzy sets and systems*, **12**, 1984, pp. 249–269.
5. Dubois, D. and Prade, H., "A review of Fuzzy Set Aggregation Connectives," *Information Sciences*, **36**, 1985, pp. 85–121.
6. Klir, G. J. and Yuan, B., *Fuzzy Sets and Fuzzy Logic, Theory and Applications*, Prentice Hall, 1995.
7. Sasikala, K. R., *Fuzzy Reasoning with Geographic Information System - An aid to decision-making*, PhD thesis, School of Elec Eng, IT & Maths, University of Surrey,, Guildford GU2 5XH, U.K., September 1997.
8. Sasikala, K. R. and Petrou, M., "Generalised Fuzzy Aggregation in Estimating the Risk of Desertification of a burned forest", *Fuzzy Sets and Systems*, to appear, 1999.
9. Yager, R. R., "Multiple objective decision making using fuzzy sets," *International Journal of Man-Machine Studies*, **9**, 1977, pp. 375–382.
10. Yager, R. R., "Concepts, Theory and Techniques, A new methodology for ordinal multi-objective decision based on fuzzy sets," *Decision Science*, **12**, 1981, pp. 589–600.
11. Yager, R. R., "A note on weighted queries in Information Retrieval Systems," *Journal of the American Society for Information Science*, **38**(1), 1987, pp. 23–24.
12. Yager, R. R., "On ordered weighted averaging aggregation operators in multicriteria decision making," *IEEE transactions on Systems, Man and Cybernetics*, **18**(1), 1988, pp. 183–190.
13. Yager, R. R., "Connectives and Quantifiers in fuzzy sets," *Fuzzy sets and systems*, **40**, 1991, pp. 39–75.
14. Yager, R. R. and Kelman, A., "Fusion of Fuzzy Information with Considerations for Compatibility, Partial Aggregation, and Reinforcement," *International Journal of Approximate Reasoning*, **15**(2), 1996, pp. 93–122.

OPERATOR	GENERALISED DEFINITION(for 4 variables) $0 \leq x_i \leq w_i, \quad i = 1 \; to \; 4$
max_1	$maximum(x_1, x_2, x_3, x_4)$
sum	$\displaystyle\sum_{\substack{i=1}}^{4}(\prod_{\substack{l=1 \\ l\neq i}}^{4} w_l)x_i - \sum_{\substack{i=1}}^{4}\sum_{\substack{j=1 \\ j\neq i}}^{4}(\prod_{\substack{l=1 \\ l\neq i \\ l\neq j}}^{4} w_l)x_i x_j + \sum_{\substack{i=1}}^{4}\sum_{\substack{j=1 \\ j\neq i}}^{4}\sum_{\substack{k=1 \\ k\neq i \\ k\neq j}}^{4}\sum_{\substack{l=1 \\ l\neq i \\ l\neq j \\ l\neq k}}^{4} w_l x_i x_j x_k - \prod_{i=1}^{4} x_i$ $\displaystyle\prod_{i=1}^{4} w_i / min(w_1, w_2, w_3, w_4)$
min_2	$min_2[min_2\{min_2(x_1, x_2), x_3\}, x_4]$
min_1	$minimum(x_1, x_2, x_3, x_4)$
$prod$	$\displaystyle\prod_{i=1}^{4} x_i$
max_2	$max_2[max_2\{max_2(x_1, x_2), x_3\}, x_4]$
am	$\displaystyle\frac{1}{4}\sum_{i=1}^{4} x_i$
gm	$\sqrt[4]{(\displaystyle\prod_{i=1}^{4} x_i)}$
hm	$\displaystyle\frac{4\displaystyle\prod_{i=1}^{4} x_i}{\displaystyle\sum_{i=1}^{4}\sum_{\substack{j=1 \\ j\neq i}}^{4}\sum_{\substack{k=1 \\ k\neq i \\ k\neq j}}^{4} x_i x_j x_k}$
min_3	$\displaystyle\frac{min(x_1, x_2, x_3, x_4)}{min(x_1, x_2, x_3, x_4) + min(w_1 - x_1, w_2 - x_2, w_3 - x_3, w_4 - x_4)}$
max_3	$\displaystyle\frac{max(x_1, x_2, x_3, x_4)}{max(x_1, x_2, x_3, x_4) + max(w_1 - x_1, w_2 - x_2, w_3 - x_3, w_4 - x_4)}$
σ_0	$\displaystyle\frac{\displaystyle\prod_{i=1}^{4} x_i}{\displaystyle\prod_{i=1}^{4}(w_i - x_i) + \displaystyle\prod_{i=1}^{4} x_i}$
σ_+	$\displaystyle\frac{sum(x_1, x_2, x_3, x_4)}{sum(x_1, x_2, x_3, x_4) + sum(w_1 - x_1, w_2 - x_2, w_3 - x_3, w_4 - x_4)}$

Table 4. Generalised Definition of operators

A Data Mining Application for Monitoring Environmental Risks

Angela Scaringella[1, 2]

[1] Presidenza del Consiglio dei Ministri,
DSTN, Servizio Idrografico e Mareografico Nazionale
Via Curtatone 3 I-00185 Roma, Italy
scaringella@simn.dstn.pcm.it
[2] CATTID, Università di Roma "La Sapienza"

Abstract. We describe the guidelines of a system for monitoring environmental risk situations. The system is based on data mining techniques and in particular classification trees working on the data base collected by the Italian National Hydro-geological Net. The goal of our application is to achieve a better discrimination among cases then that obtained by the system which is presently in use. The decision trees are evaluated and selected via a metric that takes a weighted account of the errors of different kinds.

1. Introduction

Italy is a country with high hydro-geological risk. It is therefore of crucial importance the availability of an efficient monitoring system capable of detecting the occurrence of dangerous situations. The necessity of improving methods for prediction and prevention of risk situations has become apparent after recent catastrophic events such as that of Sarno in May of 1998.

The National Net of the "Servizio Idrografico e Mareografico del Dipartimento dei Servizi Tecnici Nazionali della Presidenza del Consiglio dei Ministri" collects data relative to rain-gauging, hydrometry, weather and climate. The data are collected in each Department and from there to the central servers where they are inserted in a data base so that they are accessible and can be elaborated and interpreted.

The existence of a data base with millions of data from the whole national territory suggests the use of data mining techniques for the construction of a risk prevention system. Data mining is a set of techniques for estrange valuable information (knowledge discovery) and prediction methods from large volumes of data ([6]). This paper presents an attempt in this direction.

Many software packages are presently on the market for data analysis and construction of applications for specific goals. They usual contain moduli for statistical analysis and visualization of global characteristics of large sets of data. The user can choose methods for discretization and reduction of features, choose the most relevant features and study their statistical distribution.

Various techniques are applied for classification and prediction. Some of the packages, as for example "Decision Master" of Ibai Solution ([4]), are based on induction rules and classification trees ([1], [6]). We have chosen this approach for our application.

Classification trees are used to subdivide cases into classes. Starting from the root of the tree one proceeds in the classification going through a sequence of node where the next node is chosen according to the values of the features of the cases. Classification trees are constructed using a set of cases (learning set) and a metric appropriate for the problem in hand; the performance of a selected tree is tested on another set of cases (test set) disjoint from the first. The approach based on classification trees has the advantage that the user has access to the decision procedure; this is not the case for other methods based on neural nets or genetic algorithms.

2. Description of the System Presently in Use

Let us first briefly describe the way how data are collected and the risk monitoring system that is presently in use. Italian territory is subdivided into departments: each department collects data about rain-gauging and water level in rivers from different locations. Data are organized, stored and become available through a net that connects all departments to the Central Direction of "Direzione Generale del Servizio Idrografico Mareografico Nazionale". Rain fall is measured in square millimeters per square meter, hydrometric level in rivers, temperature and atmospheric pressure are also measured. Data are collected at fixed intervals of time and are coded in digital form. Data relative to departments are inserted in ASCII files. Machines located at the center of the net periodically gets these ASCII files and convert them into a relational data base. The general Italian Hydrological situation, and the working situation of local sensors can be obtained from the data base. Vector maps can also be produced that allow to monitor in real time the Italian situation through geographical maps where the locations of sensors are indicated with the corresponding measurements. An automatic risk monitoring system is also in function, based on thresholds for rain ganging and hydrometric levels of rivers. When one of levels is above the corresponding threshold an risk situation is automatically signaled. It is natural to think of more general risk monitoring system and that data mining techniques could be used to build them. Indeed a Risk situations could be related to the association of several measurements such as the hydrometric at different locations or of different rivers, or the persistence of moderate rains for a long period of time. Even if other features such as weather situation, weather forecasts and data from different locations could be considered at the same time, an improvement with respect to the system presently in use is obtained by allowing a more general dependence from the data of a single location relative to rain-gauging level and hydrometric level.

We observe that the system in use can be represented in terms of a decision rule or classification tree ([1], [6]) whit a set of numeric features and some classes corresponding to the probability of occurrence of floods , landslides and so on. The rule can be formally described in the following way: if ..., A_{m-1}, A_m, A_{m+1}, ... is the sequence of rain gauging levels at a given location for consecutive intervals of one hour, one defines:

$$B_m^{(1)} = A_m$$
$$B_m^{(2)} = A_m + A_{m-1} + A_{m-2}$$
$$B_m^{(3)} = A_m + A_{m-1} + A_{m-2} + A_{m-3} + A_{m-4} + A_{m-5}$$
$$B_m^{(4)} = A_m + A_{m-1} + \ldots\ldots + A_{m-11}$$
$$B_m^{(5)} = A_m + A_{m-1} + \ldots\ldots + A_{m-23}$$
$$B_m^{(6)} = A_m + A_{m-1} + \ldots\ldots + A_{m-47}$$
$$B_m^{(7)} = A_m + A_{m-1} + \ldots\ldots + A_{m-71}$$
$$B_m^{(8)} = A_m + A_{m-1} + \ldots\ldots + A_{m-95}$$
$$B_m^{(9)} = A_m + A_{m-1} + \ldots\ldots + A_{m-191}$$

these quantities represent rain fall levels for intervals 1, 3, ..., 192 hours preceding time m. Starting from these quantities one determines risk level that can take four values: absence of risk, attention, alert, alarm. The classification is based, as we said, on thresholds that are of course higher for higher levels of risk.

The graphical display relative to a particular location and time as it can be obtained from the data base is shown in Fig. 1.

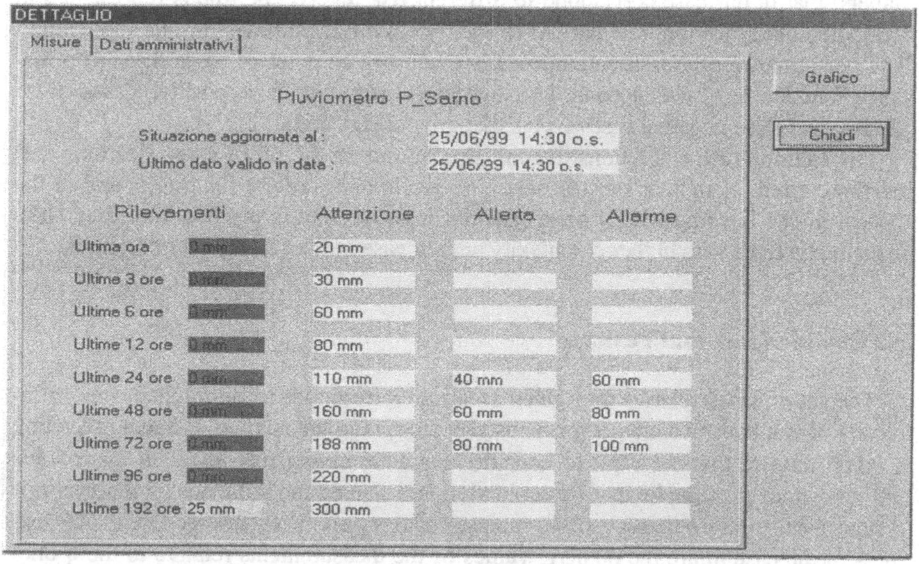

DETTAGLIO

| Misure | Dati amministrativi |

Pluviometro P_Sarno

Situazione aggiornata al : 25/06/99 14:30 o.s.
Ultimo dato valido in data : 25/06/99 14:30 o.s.

Grafico
Chiudi

Rilevamenti		Attenzione	Allerta	Allarme
Ultima ora	0 mm	20 mm		
Ultime 3 ore	0 mm	30 mm		
Ultime 6 ore	0 mm	60 mm		
Ultime 12 ore	0 mm	80 mm		
Ultime 24 ore	0 mm	110 mm	40 mm	60 mm
Ultime 48 ore	0 mm	160 mm	60 mm	80 mm
Ultime 72 ore	0 mm	188 mm	80 mm	100 mm
Ultime 96 ore	0 mm	220 mm		
Ultime 192 ore	25 mm	300 mm		

Fig. 1. Graphical display of relevant measurements at a given location and time

3. Description of the Application

Our application is based on the data-mining techniques for the construction of a classification tree.

3.1 Basic Criteria

The construction of an the decision rule proceeds through a sequence of steps that are implemented in numerous available programs such as the previously quoted "Decision Master" ([4]). The first phase consists in data preparation. In our case files in XLS format are available containing the data to be used. Starting from XLS files, the set of cases with the corresponding features. A case in our example corresponds to a time and the features are the measurement results is some preceding time interval.

A statistical analysis is then performed to determine the most relevant features for the application: The analysis can lead to a suitable discretization and reduction of features. Statistical methods are used at this stage such as principal components and cluster analysis.

The next step is the research of the rule for attributing a case to one of the classes (labels) that in our case correspond to different risk levels. The rule is represented in terms of a classification tree that has to satisfy natural hypotheses for our application. The performance of classification trees is evaluated on a set of cases through a distance function that takes account in a weighted manner of false positive cases (false alarms) and false negative case (events that are not signaled).

The solution or the solutions that are singled out on the set of cases (learning set) are then tested on another set (test set). The performance of the solution(s) and of the system in use is compared. If no substantial improvement is reached, the research is resumed on trees with higher complexity and on cases with a larger set of features.

3.2 Choice of Relevant Features

The set of cases relative to a given location corresponds to discretized time in intervals of one hour. An integer q is chosen representing the number of hours preceding a given time m that we want to consider for determining risk level. In this choice limitations on the complexity of computation and also on the influence of observations distant from m more than a certain number of days are taken into account. The features of the case m are the numeric values of the measurements relative to the q one-hour intervals preceding m. As stated before, some discretization and reduction of data is performed at this stage with statistical methods.

3.3 Definition of the Metric

The choice of the risk level for a given case is implemented by a classification tree. An example is represented in Fig. 2 where C_1 and C_2 indicate two different risk levels and C_0 denotes absence of risk. Note that typical classification trees have a much higher complexity.

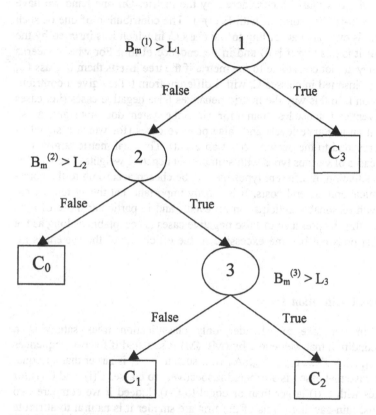

Fig. 2. Example of a binary classification tree

Each leaf of the tree is associated to one of the classes C_0, C_1 and C_2. The nodes 1, 2 and 3 represent points of decision, each one with a Boolean condition. Following a sequence of nodes each case is directed to one of the leaves and associated to the corresponding class. Our problem is to determine a classification tree that uses the features, $A_{m-1},\ldots\ldots, A_{m-q}$ and possibly one more efficient than that presently in use. In our case the classification is of the "low prevalence" type ([6]), as the majority of cases is in class C_0 and only few in the other classes. The relevant characteristics of the latter cases must be studied for determining risk situations. Events such as floods, landslides and so on are classified into p groups according to their gravity. A variable

$E_j(m)$, $j=1,...,$ p is put equal to 1 if during the interval following time m an event of gravity j starts to occur and equal to 0 otherwise.

We define $E(m)= E_1(m)+...+ E_p(m)$; $E(m)$ is equal to one if an event starts to occur in the interval following time m and equal to 0 otherwise. Cases following for a certain period of time an m with $E(m)=1$ are not considered as they cannot be relevant for prediction.

The predictive capacity of a tree can be evaluated by introducing a suitable metric ([6]). Two types of cases must be considered by the metric. On one hand we have cases j such that $0<m-j\leq q$ for some m with $E(m)=1$. The contribution of one of such cases to the metric is evaluated according to the class C_i in which it is inserted by the tree (in particular it is positive if $i=0$) and in dependence of m-j. For what concerns the other cases, they do not contribute to the metric if the tree inserts them in class C_o, whereas if they are inserted in classes C_i with i different from 0 they give a contribution that depends on i. In this way the metric penalizes false negative cases (i.e. cases that precede an event at distance less than q for which the system does not signal a risk situation or not at an adequate level) and false positive cases (for which a signal of risk does not correspond to the occurrence of an event). The total metric is given by the sum over all cases of various types with suitable nonnegative weights. The weights corresponding to situation of different types have to be chosen according to the corresponding economical and general costs. It is mostly important that the system be capable to detect with reasonable anticipation all events and in particular those of high gravity; in view of this the presence of false negative cases is acceptable as long as the corresponding cost does not became excessive or the efficiency of the system is affected.

3.4 Choice of the Classification Tree

It is natural in our case to consider only classification trees satisfying a "monotonicity" condition that we denote by (M): (M) is satisfied if for two sequences ......A_{m-1}, A_m, A_{m+1}, ... and ....A'_{m-1}, A'_m, A'_{m+1}.... such that A'_i is larger than or equal to A_i for all i we have that case i is attributed respectively to classes C(i), and C'(i) for the two sequences with C'(i) larger than or equal to C(i). Indeed if we compare two situations such that rain-gauging levels of the first are smaller it is natural to attribute the first to a lesser risk level. In the set of trees satisfying (M) one can consider the subset for which the conditions on the nodes are of the type $B'_{m,i} > L_i$, where $B'_{m,i}$ are linear combinations with nonnegative weights of A_m, A_{m-1},....A_{m-q}. It is easy to see that trees satisfying (M) can be approximated arbitrarily well with trees satisfying (M'). The complexity can however become quite larger. We restrict ourselves to consider trees satisfying (M'). The procedure for the choice of the classification tree is then the following: using a set of cases (training set) one tries to optimize the choice of the weights that determine the $B'_{m,i}$'s and of the corresponding threshold values L_i's with respect to the chosen metric with respect to the chosen metric. The solutions found are then compared between themselves and with the system in use. The procedure stops if one of the solutions is found to be satisfactory, otherwise the research is resumed among trees with higher complexity and increasing the number of features.

4. Possible Developments

Other features could be added such as weather data provided by Meteosat and weather forecasts. Data corresponding to a whole region or hydrological basin could be grouped together. It would be desirable to compare the performance of the system with what could be obtained with other methods such as neural nets and genetic algorithms ([2], [3], [5]).

Acknowledgements.

I would like to thank Dr. Giuseppe Batini Chairman of "Dipartimento dei Servizi Tecnici Nazionali della Presidenza del Consiglio dei Ministri" for giving the possibility to perform this work and Dr. Attilio Colagrossi for his help in the access to data and for useful discussions.

References

1. Breiman, L., Friedman, J., Olshen, R., Stone, A.: Classification and Regression Trees. Wadsworth (1994).
2. Masters, M., Chang, C.-C.K., Gravano, L., Paepcke, A.: Neural, Novel and Hybrid Algorithms for Time-Series Prediction. Wiley, New York (1995).
3. Miller, G., Todd, G., Hedge, S.: Designing neural networks using genetic algorithms . In Proceedings of the third Int'l Conference on Genetic Algorithms. Morgan Kaufmann, san Francisco, (1989).
4. Perner, P.: Decision Master. http://www.ibai-solutions.de/
5. Ripley, B.: Neural networks and related methods for classification. Journal of The Royal Statistical Society, Series B, (1994).
6. Weiss, S. M., Indurkhya, N.: Predictive Data Mining : A Practical Guide. Morgan Kaufmann Pub., San Francisco CA (1998).

Author Index

Lecture Notes in Artificial Intelligence (LNAI)

Lecture Notes in Computer Science